Temples of Gopakṣetra

TEMPLES OF GOPAKṢETRA

A Regional History of Architecture and Sculpture in Central India AD 600–900

MICHAEL D. WILLIS

PUBLISHED FOR THE TRUSTEES OF
THE BRITISH MUSEUM BY
BRITISH MUSEUM PRESS

Published by British Museum Press
A division of The British Museum Company Ltd
46 Bloomsbury Street, London WC1B 3QQ

A catalogue record for this book is available from the British Library

ISBN 0 7141 1477 4

Designed by Andrew Shoolbred
Jaipur-Hindustan font by Ken Bryant

Printed in Great Britain by Henry Ling Ltd, The Dorset Press,
Dorchester

Contents

List of Illustrations 6
Foreword 10
Acknowledgements 11
Preface 12
Abbreviations 15

1. Geographical, Historical and Historiographical Setting 16
    Geography 16
    History 18
    Historiography 27
    Summary 31
    Notes 32

2. Beginning of a Regional Tradition 36
    Seventh Century: Early Phase (c. AD *600–650)* 36
    Seventh Century: Late Phase (c. AD *650–700)* 39
    Summary 42
    Notes 43

3. Regional Architecture in Maturity 44
    Eighth Century: Early Phase (c. AD *700–735)* 44
    Eighth Century: Middle Phase (c. AD *735–65)* 47
    Eighth Century: Late Phase (c. AD *765–800)* 54
    Summary 62
    Notes 63

4. The Gurjara-Pratīhāra Age 65
    Ninth Century: Early Phase (c. AD *800–825)* 65
    Ninth Century: Middle Phase (c. AD *825–75)* 70
    Ninth Century: Late Phase (c. AD *875–900)* 76
    Early Tenth Century 79
    Mid-Tenth Century 80
    Summary 81
    Notes 83

5. Religious and Royal Patronage in Northern India 85
    Inscriptions and the Nature of Religious Gifts 85
    Religious Giving and Temple Patronage 87
    Royal Patronage in the Age of Pratīhāra Supremacy 92
    Dynastic Temples after the Disintegration of Pratīhāra Hegemony 96
    Notes 99

Select Bibliography 102

Maps 103

Index 108

Plates following p. 112

Illustrations

FIGURES

1 Main architectural parts of the north Indian temple (drawing courtesy of and copyright Michael W. Meister) 13
2 Mahuā (Shivpuri), *maṇḍapikā*-shrine dedicated to Śiva, first half of the seventh century 36
3 Selected *vedībandha* mouldings from across northern India: 1. Rāmgarh (Shāhbād), Muṇḍeśvarī temple; 2. Mahuā (Shivpuri), *maṇḍapikā*-shrine dedicated to Śiva; 3. Mahuā, Śiva temple; 4. Chandravati (Jhālāwār), Śitaleśvar Mahādev temple; 5. Kanswa (Kota), Śiva temple; 6. Gyāraspur (Vidisha), ruined temple near Mānasarovar tank; 7. Gwalior (Gwalior), Telī kā Mandir; 8. Deogarh (Lalitpur), Jaina temple 12; 9. Naresar (Morena), Durgā temple; 10. Naresar, Mātā kā Mandir; 11. Pāroli (Morena), Batesar Mahādev temple; 12. Amrol (Gwalior), Rāmeśvar Mahādev temple; 13. Terāhī (Shivpuri), Śiva temple; 14. Indor (Shivpuri), Gargaj Mahādev temple; 15. Kuchdon (Lalitpur), Maṛhiā Dhār 37
4 Mahuā, Śiva temple, late seventh century 39
5 Dāng (Bhind), Śiva temple, early eighth century 45
6 Naresar (Morena), site map showing location of temples 48
7 Naresar, temple dedicated to Śiva as 'Śrī Bhītupreneśvara-deva', mid-eighth century 48
8 Naresar, temple dedicated to Śiva as 'Śrī Krakoṭakeśva[ra]-deva', mid-eighth century 49
9 Naresar, Śiva temple, mid-eighth century 49
10 Naresar, Durgā temple, mid-eighth century 49
11 Naresar, Mātā kā Mandir, mid-eighth century 50
12 Amrol (Gwalior), Rāmeśvar Mahādev temple, mid-eighth century 51
13 Pāroli (Morena), Batesar Mahādev temple, late eighth century 54
14 Amrol (Gwalior), Dhane Bābā temple, late eighth century 55
15 Indor (Guna), Gargaj Mahādev temple, late eighth century 60
16 Terāhī (Shivpuri), Śiva temple, early ninth century 68
17 Kheldhar (Guna), Śiva temple, early ninth century 69
18 Gwalior (Gwalior), Caturbhuj temple, dated VS 932/AD 875–6 70
19 Sesai Buzurg (Shivpuri), Sūrya temple, late ninth century 76

MAPS

1 Ancient centres and regions in central India (*c.* AD 400-1100) 103
2 Archaeological and historical sites in the Gwalior region 104
3 Detail of the Gwalior region 105
4 Detail of the Mahuā region 105
5 Inscription sites of the Vardhanas and their contemporaries 106
6 Inscription sites of the Gurjara Pratīhāras and their contemporaries 107

PLATES following p. 112

1 Mahuā (Shivpuri) *maṇḍapikā*-shrine dedicated to Śiva, south side, first half of the seventh century
2 Mahuā, *maṇḍapikā*-shrine, over-door (*uttarāṅga*)
3 Mahuā, *maṇḍapikā*-shrine, south side, niche (*rathikā*) with image of Gaṇeśa
4 Mahua, *maṇḍapikā*-shrine, west side, niche (*rathikā*) with image of Māhiṣāuramardinī
5 Mahuā, *maṇḍapikā*-shrine, door-jambs (*śākhā*) with pilaster flanking the door
6 Pāroli (Morena), hero-stones, first half of the seventh century (left) and late eighth century (right) (Archaeological Museum, Gwalior; photo courtesy of James Harle)
7 Rājāpur (Shivpuri), stone *stūpa*, c. sixth or seventh century
8 Mahuā (Shivpuri), Śiva temple, north side, late seventh century
9 Mahuā, Śiva temple, south-west corner (*karṇa*), showing podium mouldings (*vedībandha*) and wall (*jaṅghā*)
10 Mahuā, Śiva temple, west side, subsidiary offset (*pratiratha*) and dentils (*nīvrapaṭṭikā*) in podium mouldings (*vedībandha*)

11 Mahuā, Śiva temple, east side, entrance door (photo courtesy of the AIIS Centre for Art and Archaeology, Vārāṇasī)
12 Mahuā, Śiva temple, east side, entrance door, river goddess and attendants
13 Deogarh Fort (Lalitpur), Varāha temple, main image of Vāraha, late seventh century
14 Gyāraspur (Vidisha), Ambikā, late seventh century (Archaeological Museum, Gwalior)
15 Indragarh (Mandasaur), seated Gajalakṣmī, datable vs 767/ AD 710–11 (Central Museum, Indore)
16 Kota (Shivpuri), standing goddess, early eighth century (Archaeological Museum, Gwalior)
17 Gwalior Fort (Gwalior), seated Gaṇeśa, early eighth century (Archaeological Museum, Gwalior)
18 Bārāhet (Bhind), Gaṇeśa image on a linga, early eighth century
19 Bārāhet, Viṣṇu image on a linga
20 Bārāhet, architectural fragment, early eighth century
21 Gwalior Fort (Gwalior), fragment of a niche (*rathikā*), early eighth century
22 Gwalior (Gwalior), pillar, early eighth century (Archaeological Museum, Gwalior)
23 Dāng (Bhind), Śiva temple, north-west side, early eighth century
24 Dāng, Śiva temple, south side, wall of porch (*prāggrīva*)
25 Dāng, Śiva temple, east side, door
26 Dāng, Śiva temple, south side, central niche (*rathikā*) with image of Gaṇeśa
27 Dāng, Śiva temple, east side, base of superstructure, niches (*rathikā*) containing images of Kṛṣṇalīlā and Kārttikeya
28 Naresar (Morena), general view of temples in the lower section of the complex
29 Naresar, temple dedicated to Śiva as 'Śrī Bhītupreneśvaradeva', north-east side, mid-eighth century
30 Naresar, Bhītupreneśvara temple, north-west side
31 Naresar, Bhītupreneśvara temple, entrance door
32 Naresar, temple dedicated to Śiva as 'Śrī Krakoṭakeśvaradeva', east side, mid-eighth century
33 Naresar, Krakoṭakeśvara temple, entrance door
34 Naresar, Śiva temple, west side, mid-eighth century
35 Naresar, Sitaleśvaradevī temple, entrance door, mid-eighth century
36 Naresar, Sitaleśvaradevī temple, inscription recording a land grant, *c.* ninth century
37 Naresar, Durgā temple, south-west side, mid-eighth century
38 Naresar, Durgā temple, entrance door
39 Naresar, Durgā temple, entrance door, damaged river goddess and attendant figures
40 Naresar, Durgā temple, dancing figure in corner niche
41 Naresar, Durgā temple, east side, central spire offset (*madhyalatā*)
42 Naresar, screens and seat adjacent to Durgā temple, mid-eighth century
43 Naresar, Mātā kā Mandir, south-west side, mid-eighth century
44 Naresar, Mātā kā Mandir, entrance door
45 Naresar, Mātā kā Mandir, entrance door, damaged river goddess and attendant figures
46 Amrol (Gwalior), Rāmeśvar Mahādev temple, south side, mid-eighth century
47 Amrol, Rāmeśvar Mahādev temple, south side, central offset with image of Gaṇeśa
48 Amrol, Rāmeśvar Mahādev temple, east side, entrance door
49 Amrol, Rāmeśvar Mahādev temple, north side, dancing figure in corner niche
50 Amrol, Rāmeśvar Mahādev temple, north side, Īśāna figure in porch (*prāggrīva*) niche
51 Gwalior Fort (Gwalior), miniature dormer (*candraśālā*) with head of Śiva (Scindia School, Gwalior)
52 Gwalior Fort, part of a shrine wall, mid-eighth century (Scindia School, Gwalior)
53 Kota (Shivpuri), Indrāṇī, mid-eighth century (Archaeological Museum, Gwalior)
54 Kota, Kaumārī, mid-eighth century (Archaeological Museum, Gwalior)
55 Kota, Śiva, mid-eighth century (Archaeological Museum, Gwalior)
56 Kota, Gajāntaka, mid-eighth century (Archaeological Museum, Gwalior)
57 Kota?, Śiva, mid-eighth century (Archaeological Museum, Gwalior)
58 Tumain (Guna), Mātṛkā fragment, mid-eighth century (Collection of Sāgar University, Sāgar; photo courtesy of the AIIS Centre for Art and Archaeology, Vārāṇasī)
59 Deogarh Fort (Lalitpur), Jaina goddess built into wall surrounding temple 12, mid-eighth century
60 Batesar (Morena), general view of main temple complex from the west
61 Batesar Mahādev temple, east side, detail of arched antefix (*śukanāsā*), late eighth century
62 Batesar Mahādev temple, north side, superstructure
63 Batesar Mahādev temple, north side, mouldings and niches of porch (*prāggrīva*) and corner section (*karṇa*), late eighth century
64 Batesar Mahādev temple, east side, detail of door jambs
65 Batesar, Śiva temple immediately west of the Batesar Mahādev temple, east side, superstructure, early ninth century
66 Batesar, Śiva temple immediately east of the Batesar Mahādev temple, south side, early ninth century
67 Batesar, Śiva temple immediately north of the Batesar Mahādev temple, east side, early ninth century
68 Batesar, Śiva temple immediately north of the Batesar Mahādev temple, west side
69 Batesar, superstructure of a shrine buried in rubble beside the Batesar Mahādev temple, early ninth century

70 Batesar, row of three Śaiva shrines to the north of the Batesar Mahādev temple, early ninth century

71 Batesar, Śaiva shrine to the north of the Batesar Mahādev temple, north-west side, early ninth century

72 Batesar, Vaiṣṇava shrine to the north of the Batesar Mahādev temple, east side, mid-ninth century

73 Batesar, Vaiṣṇava shrine, entrance door

74 Batesar, *maṇḍapikā*-shrine to the north-east of the Batesar Mahādev temple, west side, early ninth century

75 Batesar, *maṇḍapikā*-shrine, entrance door

76 Batesar, ruined shrine to the south-east of the Batesar Mahādev temple, open porch (*mukhacatuṣkī*), early ninth century

77 Batesar, ruined shrine to the south-east of the Batesar Mahādev temple, ceiling panel

78 Batesar, partially ruined and rebuilt shrine beside tank, entrance door, early ninth century

79 Batesar, ruined temple to the south-east of the Batesar Mahādev temple, detail of south side showing central offset (*bhadra*), subsidiary offset (*pratiratha*) and corner section (*karṇa*), early ninth century

80 Batesar, ruined temple to the south-east of the Batesar Mahādev temple, entrance door

81 Batesar, carved panel in rebuilt shrine beside tank, Kalyāṇasundara, late eighth century

82 Batesar, fragmentary set of Mātṛkā figures, early ninth century

83 Amrol (Gwalior), Dhane Bābā temple, east side, late eighth century

84 Gwalior Fort (Gwalior), Telī kā Mandir, west side, long back wall (*pṛṣṭhabhadra*), mid- to late eighth century

85 Gwalior Fort, Telī kā Mandir, north side, depressed barrel vault (*skandhavedī*) and barrel-vaulted crown (*valabhī*)

86 Gwalior Fort, Telī kā Mandir, west side, long back wall (*pṛṣṭhabhadra*), central niche in the form of a door

87 Gwalior Fort, Telī kā Mandir, west side, long back wall (*pṛṣṭhabhadra*), subsidiary offset (*pratiratha*) and corner section (*karṇa*)

88 Gwalior Fort, Telī kā Mandir, south side, wall of porch (prāggrīva) with niche in the form of a temple

89 Gwalior Fort, Telī kā Mandir, east side, entrance door with later infill

90 Gwalior Fort, Telī kā Mandir, east side, river goddess on entrance door

91 Gwalior Fort, Telī kā Mandir, north side, river goddess on niche of porch (*prāggrīva*)

92 Gwalior Fort, Telī kā Mandir, south-east corner section (*karṇa*), detail of recess (*antarapatra*) in *vedībandha*

93 Indor (Guna), Gargaj Mahādev temple, south side, late eighth century

94 Indor, Gargaj Mahādev temple, entrance door

95 Indor, Gargaj Mahādev temple, south side, wall of porch (*prāggrīva*)

96 Indor, Gargaj Mahādev temple, north side, wall of porch (*prāggrīva*), image of Īśāna

97 Gwalior Fort (Gwalior), bust of Parśvanātha (Scindia School, Gwalior), late eighth century

98 Pāroli (Morena), Kubera and Ṛddhi, early ninth century (Archaeological Museum, Gwalior)

99 Gwalior (Gwalior), Jaina stele, early ninth century (Archaeological Museum, Gwalior)

100 Terāhī (Shivpuri), Śiva temple, south-west side, early ninth century

101 Terāhī, Śiva temple, south wall (*jaṅghā*)

102 Terāhī, Śiva temple, entrance door

103 Terāhī, Śiva temple, pilaster in open porch (*mukhacatuṣkī*)

104 Gwalior Fort (Gwalior), miniature temple, early ninth century (Archaeological Museum, Gwalior; photo courtesy of the AIIS Centre for Art and Archaeology, Vārāṇasī)

105 Gwalior Fort, temple model, possibly a miniature spire (*kūṭa*) from a temple hall (*maṇḍapa*), early ninth century (Private Collection)

106 Sihoniyā (Morena), ruined hall of the closed type (*gūḍhamaṇḍapa*), early ninth century

107 Gwalior Fort (Gwalior), Caturbhuj temple, south-east side, dated by inscription vs 932/AD 875–6

108 Gwalior Fort, Caturbhuj temple, south side, mouldings, wall and entablature (*maṇḍovara*)

109 Gwalior Fort, Caturbhuj temple, north side of superstructure

110 Gwalior Fort, Caturbhuj temple, north side, Viṣṇu Trivikrama in central niche (*rathikā*)

111 Gwalior Fort, Caturbhuj temple, entrance door

112 Khiaoda (Shivpuri), Sūrya temple, east side, mid-ninth century (photo courtesy of Klaus Bruhn)

113 Khiaoda, Sūrya temple, south side (photo courtesy of Klaus Bruhn)

114 Gwalior (Gwalior), seated Jina, mid-ninth century (Archaeological Museum, Gwalior)

115 Gwalior Fort (Gwalior), standing Tīrthaṁkara in cave near Urwāhī Gate, mid-ninth century

116 Gwalior Fort, strut from a temple hall, mid-ninth century (Private Collection)

117 Sihoniyā (Morena), Viṣṇu Viśvarūpa, mid-ninth century (Archaeological Museum, Gwalior)

118 Sakarra (Guna), Śiva temple 1, north side, mid-ninth century

119 Sakarra, Śiva temple 2, east side, Ardhanarīśvara in central niche, mid-ninth century

120 Deogarh Fort (Lalitpur), Jaina temple 12, west side, screen wall with niche flanking entrance, datable before ad 862

121 Badoh (Vidisha), monumental pillar (*dhvajastambha*) known as Bhīmgaja, detail of platform mouldings, dated vs 917/AD 861 (photo courtesy of the AIIS Centre for Art and Archaeology, Vārāṇasī)

122 Gyāraspur (Vidisha), Cār Khambā, fragment of a temple spire (*kūṭa*), datable MS 936/AD 879–80

123 Gyāraspur , Cār Khambā, detail of pillar, datable MS 936/AD 879–80

124 Gyāraspur , Hindola Toran, datable MS 936/AD 879–80

125 Gwalior (Gwalior), fragmentary female figure, probably a Jaina goddess, late ninth century (National Museum of India, New Delhi)

126 Gwalior Fort (Gwalior), cave near Urwāhī Gate with Jaina divinities, late ninth century

127 Gwalior Fort, cave near Urwāhī Gate with Tīrthaṁkara, late ninth century

128 Amrol (Gwalior), Kumāra, late ninth century (Private Collection)

129 Hathlau (Datia), Varāha temple, main image, late ninth century

130 Terāhī (Shivpuri), hero-stone, detail showing battle scene, dated by inscription VS 960/AD 904

131 Pāroli (Morena), open hall (*raṅgamaṇḍapa*), interior, early tenth century

132 Pāroli, open hall (*raṅgamaṇḍapa*), interior, early tenth century

133 Bhainsora (Morena), Śiva temple, central offset (*bhadra*) with opening for spout (*praṇāla*), early tenth century (photo courtesy of Donald M. Stadtner)

134 Bārāhet (Bhind), ruin of an open hall (*raṅgamaṇḍapa*) with fragment of fence-like parapet (*vedikā*), early tenth century

135 Sihoniyā (Morena), Dubalia, ruined shrine, south-east side, early tenth century

136 Chhimkā (Bhind), Śiva temple, east side, early tenth century

137 Kadwāhā (Guna), temple in the Morāyat group, early tenth century

138 Khajurāho (Chhatarpur), Lakṣmaṇa temple, south-east subsidiary shrine (devakulikā), datable after AD 955

139 Khajurāho, Lakṣmaṇa temple, detail of sculpture on the wall section (*jaṅghā*), dated VS 1011/AD 954–5 (photo courtesy of the AIIS Centre for Art and Archaeology, Vārāṇasī)

140 Surwāyā (Shivpuri), Śiva temple 1, entrance door, mid-tenth century

141 Terāhī (Shivpuri), Mohañjmātā temple, south-east side, mid-tenth century

142 Terāhī, Mohañjmātā temple, freestanding gate, mid-tenth century (photo courtesy of the AIIS Centre for Art and Archaeology, Vārāṇasī)

Foreword

The British Museum was established by an Act of Parliament in 1753 and the first piece of Indian sculpture to enter the collections, an alabaster Śiva linga from northern India, was presented by Charles Bathurst in 1786. In the two centuries since, a wide range of gifts and careful purchases has made the Indian collections what they are today: an encyclopaedic holding of archaeological finds, sculpture, inscriptions, coins, seals, terracottas, bronzes and ritual objects. Although the maintenance of this great cultural legacy is one of the British Museum's key duties and concerns, the Department of Oriental Antiquities is not simply a repository. Over its history, the Museum has fostered a programme of historical research and publication that has transformed a 'cabinet of Asiatic curiosities' into a pre-eminent centre for the study of Indian civilisation.

In the pages that follow, Dr Willis has made a significant contribution to this scholarly tradition. This book is the first account of early temple architecture and sculpture in central India. The seventh, eighth and ninth centuries AD were a time of extraordinary building activity, as a perusal of the illustrations in this book will readily show. Fragments from this period are found almost everywhere, but the Gwalior region (or Gopakṣetra as it was then known) is unique by reason of its many well-preserved temples, images and inscriptions. Gwalior is thus a critical reference point for the history of temple art throughout northern India. Of special interest in this study is Dr Willis' lucid analysis of how prevailing styles coexisted with humbler or 'sub-regional' idioms. The plurality of styles in any given period has been one of the long-standing problems in the study of Indian art and I am delighted to see this issue examined in a detailed and convincing manner. Dr Willis' survey of temple patronage is also the first of its kind and should stimulate much-needed debate about the role of temples in Indian society. That such problems are addressed is a matter of continuing concern to the British Museum for it is only when the material culture of ancient India is reassessed in challenging ways that the collections gain renewed meaning for the scholarly community and for our ever-growing public audience.

J. R. Knox
Keeper, Department of Oriental Antiquities
The British Museum, London

Acknowledgements

Over the last century the monuments of the Gwalior region have been rediscovered and brought under repair, their inscriptions have been located, copied and edited, and sundry stray images and other antiquities have been deposited in museums established for the purpose. The achievements have been considerable and without them this book could not have been written. By expressing my thanks, therefore, to the Archaeological Survey of India I hope that the substantial contribution of the Survey and its scholarly tradition will be recognised. Sister organisations have also played a significant role, particularly the Department of Archaeology and Museums, Madhya Pradesh, and its forerunner the Department of Archaeology, Gwalior State. The American Institute of Indian Studies Centre for Art and Archaeology in Vārāṇasī was a great source of personal and immediate help; I am not the first visitor who has benefited from the Centre's library and extensive picture archive. The advice of M. A. Dhaky and Krishna Deva at the Centre also proved indispensable as this project went forward. I am equally appreciative of the interest which Pramod Chandra and Robert Skelton have expressed in this work.

My research in India was funded by fellowships from the Shastri Indo-Canadian Institute and the Social Sciences and Humanities Research Council of Canada; the Shastri Institute is to be especially praised for the gracious handling of my affairs. During my stays in Gwalior, a city that figures prominently in this study, I enjoyed the learned company of Harihar Nivās Dvivedī and R. N. Misra. Both helped in so many ways it would be impossible to recount them all. Dvivedī once said he would curse me if I did not finish this work and that, if necessary, he would curse me from heaven after his death. The threat of a Brāhmaṇa curse, even from heaven, is not taken lightly by any student of ancient India and it has kept my attention fixed on bringing this project to conclusion.

I could not close without thanking my friends and colleagues at the British Museum. Without support on this front I would have never written this book; I am equally grateful to the Trustees of the British Museum for undertaking the publication. At the British Museum Press I must thank Colin Grant for his patience and effort. The maps, a crucial part of the work, were prepared by Ann Searight, the temple plans by S. Jaleen Grove. On the personal side, I am indebted to Arthur Hughes and Jagdish Mishra for encouragement and much practical help. My parents were the most faithful supporters of my research efforts in India and it is to their memory that I dedicate this monograph.

Michael D. Willis
April 1997, London

Preface

From a civilisation that has been pre-eminent in most serious matters for twenty centuries we can rightly expect an architecture that is complex, varied and profound. General surveys of this architecture can do it little justice, and detailed studies, still relatively scarce, must acknowledge a host of practical limitations. In accepting the necessary limitations, I have focused on a specific period, region and theme. The period is the three centuries between AD 600 and 900, the region is that of Gwalior in Madhya Pradesh and the theme is chronology.

I have taken this focus because the centuries in question were marked by crucial developments in architecture and sculpture. The geographical horizon is set by the numerous temples preserved in the Gwalior region, unlike other areas of northern India. The theme of chronology springs from the paucity of dated buildings; with less than ten securely dated monuments in north India between 600 and 900, architectural developments have tended to resist chronological definition. By way of conclusion, my closing chapter introduces the supplementary theme of religious and royal patronage.

The temples of the Gwalior region have been presented in a somewhat novel way in the following pages. In the first place, Sanskrit terminology is used to describe architectural features. Culled from technical manuals on building and image-making (*śilpa-śāstra*), these terms lend considerable precision to the description and analysis of architecture. The old *śilpa* treatises give the names of general elements like the plinth (*pīṭha*), wall (*jaṅghā*) and superstructure (*śikhara*), and provide terms for almost every moulding and motif in the temple ensemble (fig. 1). A disadvantage with this descriptive vocabulary is that it makes heavy reading for the uninitiated. This problem is hopefully mollified by the use of Sanskrit and English side by side.

Another novel aspect of this study is the integrated presentation of architecture, sculpture and ornament. That architectural form and sculptural decoration are closely allied is evident from temples throughout the subcontinent; those built in the Gwalior region AD 600 and 900 are no exception. The sculptures that decorate these buildings were not seen as ornamental appendages but as essential ingredients to a complete and fitting whole.[1] The *śilpa* texts indicate that the temple was, among other things, the body of god. As a concrete manifestation of divinity, the building achieved through architectural means what the sculptures achieved through anthropomorphic representation. This vision of the temple has prompted me to

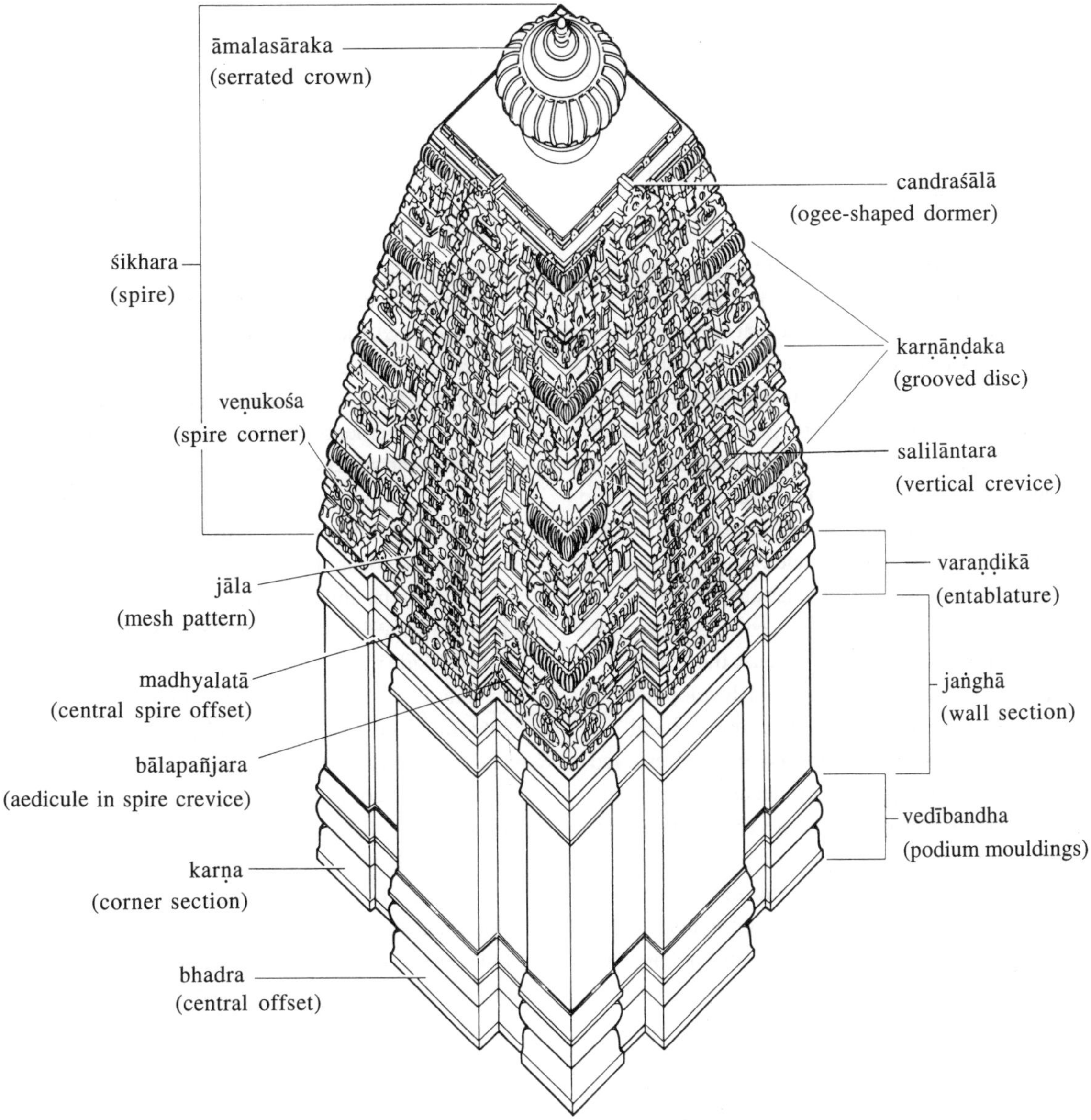

1 Main architectural parts of the north Indian temple (drawing courtesy of and copyright Michael W. Meister)

provide an integrated analysis of architectural form, sculpture and ornament. The results of this approach will be evident in the descriptions that follow.

The last novel aspect of this study is the avoidance of dynastic names for period and styles of architecture. For reasons fully detailed in Chapter 1, dynastic nomenclature has been replaced by a system mentioning the century and region in which the temple or sculpture was made. This scheme begins with the seventh century AD, our point of departure in Chapter 2. A vital new approach to temple building emerged in the seventh century, the most salient feature being the curvilinear superstructure with serrated crown, a hallmark of north Indian architecture. Many iconographic forms and schemes for the placement of images were also established at this time. These conventions were elaborated during the eighth century, a period of strong regionalism. These developments are charted in Chapter 3. During the seventh and eighth centuries there are long periods when little is known about the rulers of Gwalior. With history uncertain and the monuments ignored by comparison to the fifth and sixth centuries, the omission of 'post-Gupta' as a period designation is both appropriate and uncontroversial.[2] The centuries after AD 600 have often been called 'medieval', but this word (derived from *medium aevum* and other seventeenth-century terms) is unsuited to the architecture and history of India. Its consistent omission hardly needs mention.[3]

In the ninth century regionalism waned and a unity of style began to emerge across northern India. These developments are explored in Chapter 4. Regional variation was not eradicated, but a growing homogeneity, especially in sculpture, extended across large areas of the country. Many temples have survived from the ninth century, and those built between AD 825 and 875 are notable for their uniform elegance and decorative richness. These years mark a pinnacle of accomplishment, but the standard was not long sustained. By the mid-tenth century the style had congealed into an exact and sterile mould that only the invasions of Maḥmūd of Ghazna and his successors were to break. With the appearance of this rigid idiom there are, ironically, a substantial number of dated monuments, and developments can be charted with relatively few problems. The tenth century thus forms a convenient and logical point to end the chronological portion of this study. In the concluding chapter I move into an exploration of temple patronage in an effort to reconstruct the religious and social environment in which the buildings were constructed.

Notes

1 Ananda Coomaraswamy, 'Ornament', *Art Bulletin* 21 (1939): 375–82. Compare the approaches found in Philippe Stern, *Colonnes indiennes d' Ajanta et d' Ellora* (Paris: Universitaires de France, 1972), and Rāmāśraya Avasthī, *Khajurāho kī deva-pratimāyeṁ* (Agra: Oriental Publishing House, 1967). The same fragmented approach is implicit in any sculpture catalogue.

2 See J. C. Harle, 'The Post-Gupta Style in Indian Temple Architecture and Sculpture', *Journal of the Royal Society of Arts* 125 (1977): 570–89 for a summary of the ad-hoc labels that have been applied to the period.

3 On the origin of the term 'medieval' and the question of periodisation in general, see William A. Green, 'Periodization in European and World History', *Journal of World History* 3 (1991): 13–53.

Abbreviations

AA	*Artibus Asiae*
AAA	*Archives of Asian Art*
ABORI	*Annals of the Bhandarkar Oriental Institute*
AI	*Ancient India*
AO	*Ars Orientalis*
ARE	*Annual Report on Indian Epigraphy*
ASIAR	*Archaeological Survey of India, Annual Report*
ASIR	*Archaeological Survey of India, Report*
BAIHA	*Bulletin of Ancient Indian History and Archaeology*
BDCRI	*Bulletin of the Deccan College Research Institute*
BSOAS	*Bulletin of the School of Oriental and African Studies*
CII	Corpus Inscriptionum Indicarum
EI	*Epigraphia Indica*
GAR	Archaeological Department, Gwalior State, *Annual Report*
IA	*Indian Antiquary*
IHQ	*Indian Historical Quarterly*
JAOS	*Journal of the American Oriental Society*
JAS	*Journal of the Asiatic Society*
JBBRAS	*Journal of the Bombay Branch of the Royal Asiatic Society*
JBOAS	*Journal of the Bihar and Orissa Research Society*
JISOA	*Journal of the Indian Society of Oriental Art*
JMPIP	*Journal of the Madhya Pradesh Itihas Parishad*
JOI	*Journal of the Oriental Institute*
JRAS	*Journal of the Royal Asiatic Society*
JRASB	*Journal of the Royal Asiatic Society of Bengal*
JUPHS	*Journal of the United Provinces Historical Society*, later *Journal of the Uttar Pradesh Historical Society*
KS	Kalacuri *saṁvat*
MASB	*Memoirs of the Asiatic Society of Bengal*
MS	Mālava *saṁvat*
OA	*Oriental Art*
PRASIWC	*Progress Report of the Archaeological Survey of India, Western Circle*
PRASINC	*Progress Report of the Archaeological Survey of India, Northern Circle*
VS	Vikrama *saṁvat*

Chapter 1

Geographical, Historical and Historiographical Setting

Emphasising the importance of balanced geographical and historical knowledge in the late sixteenth century, Richard Hakluyt remarked: 'Geographie and Chronologie are the sune and moone, the right eye and left eye of all history.' In the study of temple architecture this emphasis remains apt, for a history of temples must set the buildings both geographically in space and chronologically in time. Equally crucial is historiography; as a third eye to Hakluyt's metaphor, it permits an understanding of how we have come to perceive temple architecture through study and publication. The setting for the temples examined in this monograph thus requires a consideration of geography, history and historiography.

Geography

In the three centuries between AD 600 and 900 many temples were built in the region once known as Gopakṣetra (map 1). This region is now part of the modern state of Madhya Pradesh, specifically the districts of Gwalior, Bhind, Morena and Shivpuri. Portions of Guna and Jhānsī district (the latter in Uttar Pradesh) also fall within Gopakṣetra.[1] For the most part these state and district divisions are a legacy of the colonial era and are not indicative of the entrenched linguistic and cultural geography of this part of India. We must, therefore, lift the current boundaries and begin with a survey of Gopakṣetra and the surrounding country as it stood in ancient days.

The most striking natural feature that marks off Gopakṣetra from neighbouring regions is the River Chambal (ancient Carmaṇvatī). With its winding tributaries and maze-like ravines, this great river is a formidable buffer that has effectively discouraged the movement of travellers and invading armies. For those approaching from the north or west the Chambal is an immediate barrier; for those coming from the south the Chambal turns Gopakṣetra into a cul-de-sac. This geographical configuration has been an important factor in preserving monuments and in fostering a distinct regional identity.

The leading city of Gopakṣetra is Gwalior, known in ancient times as Gopagiri and Gopādri. The rock of Gopādri, described in a tenth-century inscription as 'the unique abode of marvel', rises with abrupt magnificence from the plain with sheer cliffs up to one hundred metres.[2] Cave paintings in the vicinity suggest that Gopādri was inhabited by prehistoric man, but it is from the sixth century AD that the rock came to be embellished with an increasing number of temples, palaces and rock-cut images. Gwalior was one of the strongest forts in

India, and all the major historical powers of the north have attempted to control it.

Gopādri was not the only important settlement in Gopakṣetra. To the north, near the banks of the Āsan, was Siṁhapānīya (modern Sihoniyā), an important centre for the Kacchapaghāta dynasty and the site of a large Śiva temple built by the kings of that house.[3] Nearby were Naleśvara (modern Naresar) and Paḍhāvali (modern Pāroli), towns that preserve over fifty temples between them.[4] To the south of Gwalior, at the confluence of the Sindhu and Pārvatī rivers, stood Padmāvatī, one of the capitals of the Nāga kings of the first three centuries AD. Padmāvatī (modern Pawāyā) was a flourishing city in the eighth century AD to judge from the description of the poet Bhavabhūti, but by the eleventh century it had been eclipsed by the more strategically sited Nalapura.[5] Nalapura (modern Narwar), the city associated by tradition with the epic hero Nala, became a capital of the Yajvapāla kings in the thirteenth century.[6] Little is left of Padmāvatī and Nalapura, their temples having been subject to the iconoclastic zeal of Sikandar Lodī in the fifteenth century.

Not far from Narwar is Shivpuri or Sipri. Though known mainly as a nineteenth-century Mahratta town, sculpture fragments attest that temple building took place at Shivpuri in the eighth and ninth centuries. Even earlier is the brief mention of the city under the name Maheśvarapura by the Chinese pilgrim Xuan Zang.[7] To the south-east of Shivpuri is Rannod, the ancient Araṇipadra. This site is notable for an eleventh-century monastic building associated with Śaiva Siddhānta ascetics.[8] Affiliated monasteries with their accompanying temples are found nearby at Surwāyā (ancient Sarasvatīpaṭṭana), Terāhī (ancient Terambi) and Kadwāhā (ancient Kadambaguhā).[9] The oldest remains near Rannod are at Mahuā, the village near the source of the Māhuar river (maps 2 and 4). The ancient name for the river is provided by a tenth-century hero-stone that records a warrior's death 'on the banks of the Madhu' (*madhuveṇiyām*). Bhavabhūti's play *Mālatīmādhava* (Act IX) confirms this name by mentioning the confluence of the Rivers Sindhu and Madhumatī.[10] Mahuā itself also appears to have been called Madhumatī, for a dedicatory inscription from distant Bilheri records that a Śaiva *ācārya* from the place bore the epithet *madhumateya*.[11] The district around the source of the river marks the southern fringe of Gopakṣetra; the Jaina text *Pariśiṣṭaparvan* (12: 2–3) states that neighbouring Tumbavana lay in Mālwa (map 1). Even today the land between Mahuā and Tumain is the rough dividing line between where Gvāliyarī Hindi and the dialect known as Mālavī are spoken.

To the south of Gopakṣetra is the Mālwa plateau. Before the tenth century this area was divided into two regions, Daśārṇa and Avanti. Unlike Gopakṣetra, these regions are often mentioned in Sanskrit records and their geographical parameters are more easily defined.[12] The area covered by the two provinces is shown in map 1. Daśārṇa is so named because the River Daśārṇā (modern Dhasān) has its source there. Most of the river, however, lies in neighbouring Bundelkhand. This region was known as Vatsa before the ninth century, but later records make common use of the terms Jejākadeśa, Jejākabhukti and Jejākamaṇḍala.[13] Home of the Bundelkhaṇḍī dialect, the area is bounded by three rivers: the Yamunā in the north, the Ken in the east and the Betwā in the west. It is the Betwā (ancient Vetravatī) that divides Gopakṣetra and Jejākadeśa (map 1).

The rivers of Gopakṣetra and Jejākadeśa flow north-eastward to meet the Yamunā. The Yamunā and its sister Gaṅgā are, as is well known, the two most sacred rivers in India, and the lands adjacent to them were traditionally known as the 'middle region', or Madhyadeśa. As the heartland of India from Vedic times, Madhyadeśa was the hub of Indian civilisation and the geographical centre of the Indian universe. On the River Gaṅgā stood Kānyakubja, now the town of Kannauj. Once a great metropolitan centre, Kānyakubja was the capital of the major dynasties of north India from the sixth to the eleventh centuries.

Routes of travel in ancient India tell us how Gopakṣetra was connected to the surrounding country. Road-building was never a major interest in India and our knowledge of routes is sketchy. Nevertheless, we can be certain that one of the major lines of communication was through Madhyadeśa, affording movement between Mathurā, Kānyakubja, Prayāga (modern Allahābād) and Vārāṇasī. Outside Madhyadeśa travel towards the south was through Kālpī (ancient Kālapriyanātha) and thence to Vidiśā.[14] This route probably lay between the Betwā and Māhuar rivers as this afforded a link to Tumbavana and Vidiśā with few river crossings (map 1). The Aśokan inscription at Gujarrā on the River Pahūj (map 2) suggests movement up and down this corridor from earliest historical times.[15] From Vidiśā the route bifurcated westward to Avanti and Gujarāt, and southward to the Ḍāhala country and south Kosala. The complexity of the Chambal river system shows why this route bypassed the northern part of Gopakṣetra. With bridge-building little cultivated by Indian architects, Gwalior was isolated from the north and west, and was chiefly approached from the south.[16] Even today the Chambal is spanned in only two places and travel north of Gwalior is difficult. The usual path was thus through Virāṭa and Uparamāla, or down the Yamunā to Kālpī and from there to Vidiśā. In this general scheme Gopakṣetra was skirted. This configuration encouraged the development of regional customs, dialects of language and, as we shall see in the following chapters, a local architectural style.

This geographical survey of Gopakṣetra and the neighbouring provinces demonstrates that modern administrative units are of little use in the study of temple architecture. Some attempt at furnishing a more satisfactory designation has been made by inventing 'Central India', a term now common due to its use in a number of books and articles.[17] Unfortunately 'Central India' is so vague that it has been variously used to mean Bundelkhand and Mālwa, Ḍāhaladeśa, south Kosala and even parts of Mahārāṣṭra and Karṇāṭaka. The Central India Agency of British India is the origin of the term, but such an entity no longer exists. With the Sanskrit inscriptions and other sources in hand, we can reinstate the ancient names and give our endeavours a historically accurate frame of reference.

History

The historical geography just given forms the basis for a précis of historical events in Gopakṣetra and neighbouring territories between the seventh and tenth centuries AD. Such a history is necessary for a variety of reasons. First, a survey of political developments provides an approximate chronological horizon for those temples that have been found in association with inscriptions that mention undated rulers and events. Second, there is an established practice of describing the architecture and sculpture of Gopakṣetra during this period as 'post-Gupta' and 'Pratīhāra'. While these terms have served as convenient labels in the past, a consideration of the territorial holdings and chronology of the Gurjara-Pratīhāra rulers and their forerunners should elicit appropriate scepticism about their use. Our history does not aim to be encyclopaedic but rather focuses on main events and the general order of government that prevailed in north India from the time of king Harṣa Vardhana (AD 606–47).

Maukharis and Vardhanas

A regional history has inevitable gaps, but we have a reasonably secure starting point with the collapse of the Hūṇa kingdom in the third decade of the sixth century. This led to the emergence of new powers, the most important being the Maukhari house. The Maukharis seem to have begun as minor local chiefs, much like their contemporaries the later

Guptas, Aulikaras, Parivrājakas and Uccakalpas. Two inscriptions giving the Maukhari lineage provide the names Harivarman, Ādityavarman, Īśvaravarman and Īśānavarman.[18] The latter was ruling in *c.* AD 550 and seems to have been bettered in battle by one Kumāragupta. If the usual estimate of twenty-six years for each generation is taken, the genealogy of Īśānavarman suggests his family attained station in *c.* AD 475, just when the Gupta dynasty was in decay.[19] Īśānavarman was followed by Sarvavarman, Avantivarman and Grahavarman. According to the *Harṣacarita*, Grahavarman formed an alliance through marriage with Prabhākara Vardhana of Thanesar but was suddenly killed in *c.* AD 605 by the king of Mālava. This king of Mālava is not named in the *Harṣacarita*, but he has been identified by historians with the Devagupta mentioned in the copper-plate inscriptions from Madhuban and Banskhera.[20]

The distribution of epigraphs containing information about the Maukharis gives some idea of their origins and the extent of their kingdom in the sixth century. With the exception of the Asīrgarh seal, which is out of geographical context, the findspots of the inscriptions and coins suggest that the Maukharis ruled most of Madhyadeśa.[21] The oldest records – seals with the names of Maukhari lords – were found in Magadha, indicating that this was their original home. The political upheavals of the sixth century allowed them to extend their power westward.[22] Although they were a considerable power, there is no evidence that the Maukharis ruled south of the Yamunā River. In Gopakṣetra a stone inscription from Gwalior Fort mentioning Mihirakula and datable to *c.* AD 525 indicates that the region was under the Hūṇas in the first quarter of the sixth century.[23] The next inscription belongs to Nāgavarman, who seems to have been an independent ruler in the mid-sixth century.[24] There are no records after this until the seventh-century temple inscription from Mahuā (discussed below, p. 20). In neighbouring Daśārṇa the Bhānugupta *satī* memorial of AD 510–11 is the last evidence until the Kalacuri plate of Buddharāja, dated AD 609–10.[25] In Jejākadeśa, where no earlier records of historical importance have been found, the rock inscription of Svāmibhaṭṭa at Deogarh is symptomatic. This inscription can be placed palaeographically in the late sixth century, but no king or era is mentioned.[26] Thus the evidence, and in some places the lack of it, indicates that the Maukharis did not rule south of the Yamunā.

The emergence of the Vardhanas (also called Puṣyamitras) in the Gangetic plain during the seventh century helps but little in clarifying the local history of Gopakṣetra and neighbouring provinces. Like the Maukharis, the Vardhanas of Thanesar (ancient Sthāneśvara) seem to have been a regional house that successfully established itself in the late fifth or early sixth century. As mentioned above, the Vardhanas were allied by marriage to the Maukhari king Grahavarman. With Grahavarman's unexpected death without issue, the Vardhanas assumed control of his domain. This coincided with the accession of Harṣa, the most well-known king of the Vardhana line. Harṣa (AD 606–47) ruled from Kānyakubja, and some events in his early life are recorded in Bāṇa Bhaṭṭa's contemporary eulogy, the *Harṣacarita*. Extensive details about Harṣa, albeit with a Buddhist bias, are also furnished by accounts of the Chinese pilgrim Xuan Zang.[27] These writings tend by their simple existence to exaggerate the importance of Harṣa in relation to other rulers of the period. This is readily seen by looking at the archaeological records, which in both distribution and number give perspective to Harṣa's historical significance. A seal of Harṣa was found at Nālanda (map 5, site 1) and copper plates and seals at Banskherā (map 5, site 3), Madhuban (map 5, site 2) and Sonepat (map 5, site 6).[28] Coins identified as Harṣa's were found at sites in Uttar Pradesh and Bihar, as were a number of later stone inscriptions that use the Harṣa era.[29] In addition, the Aihole inscription of Pulakeśin, dated

AD 634, mentions Harṣa as defeated by that southern monarch.[30] These records show Harṣa's kingdom embraced Madhyadeśa and Magadha, as well as his ancestral home in Thanesar.

Independent princes

The fringes of the Vardhana domain are indicated by a number of inscriptions such as the Nermand plate (map 5, site 7), a land grant issued by one mahārāja Samudrasena in anno 6.[31] The plate belongs to Harṣa's time palaeographically but mentions no overlord; the year is probably a regnal one of Samudrasena. This indicates Samudrasena was an independent ruler who was under no obligation to recognise Harṣa by mentioning his name or using his era.

In Gopakṣetra the Mahuā inscription of Vatsarāja (map 5, site 5) tells the same story. This eulogy is datable to the time of Harṣa on palaeographical grounds and on the basis of the architectural style of the temple on which it is cut. The epigraph provides the genealogy of Vatsarāja going back five generations, but no overlord or date is given.[32] This becomes an important point when we realise that the poet who composed Vatsarāja's inscription came from Kānyakubja, Harṣa's capital city. Furthermore, Mahuā was no provincial backwater but, as shown in our section on historical geography, on the main line of communication between Kānyakubja and Vidiśā. The collective implication of these facts is that Vatsarāja was independent of the Vardhanas and that even at the height of their power the Vardhanas did not control Gopakṣetra or the lands further south.[33] The fact that the Madhuban plate states Harṣa defeated Devagupta, who is thought on the basis of the *Harṣacarita* to have been a king in the Mālava region, does not show the Vardhanas established rule south of the Yamunā. This is born out by the testimony of the Chinese pilgrim Xuan Zang who describes Mathurā, Ujjayinī and Citrakūṭa as independent kingdoms.[34]

Xuan Zang's kingdom of Mathurā can be connected with the seventh- to eighth-century stone inscription of Karka Diṇḍirāja. This inscription, found at Mathurā, traces Karka's lineage back to one Śrī Kṛṣṇarāja who was probably ruling in the first half of the seventh century.[35] The kingdom of Ujjayinī mentioned by Xuan Zang changed hands several times during the course of the late sixth and early seventh centuries. The old Aulikara house of Yaśodharman was apparently displaced by the Kalacuris who moved north from the Narmadā basin under pressure from the Cāḷukyas of Vātāpi. This is documented by the Abhona plates of Śaṅkaragaṇa, dated KS 347/AD 596–7, which were issued from Śaṅkaragaṇa's victorious camp at Ujjayinī. The Kalacuris soon extended their power over Daśārṇa as evidenced by the Vadner plates of Śaṅkaragaṇa's son Buddharāja. These plates were issued from Vidiśā in KS 360/AD 609–10.[36] The rising power of the Maitrakas under Śīlāditya Dharmāditya I and his successor Kharagraha I forced the Kalacuris out of Avanti; Kharagraha issued the Virdi plates from Ujjayinī in AD 616–17.[37]

The kingdom of Citrakūṭa, which Xuan Zang also describes as independent, appears to have no epigraphic evidence associated with it. The facts, however, point in only one direction: Mathurā, Vidiśā, Ujjayinī and Mahuā were all ruled by independent minor princes, making it improbable that Citrakūṭa and other parts of Rājasthān were under direct Vardhana control. We may conclude, therefore, that the general pattern during the first half of the seventh century was analogous to the sixth century when local mahārājas were clustered around the central power of the Maukharis.

Regional chiefs after Harṣa

History becomes difficult to chart with the death of Harṣa in AD 647 and termination of the Vardhana house. With little evidence about the rulers of Gopakṣetra after Harṣa, a survey of the parochial powers of northern India provides the necessary framework for carrying forward this local history.[38]

Beginning in Magadha, surviving epigraphs show that Ādityasena and his son Devagupta were ruling in the second half of the seventh century. Though Gupta in name, none of the genealogies of these Gupta kings trace their ancestry to the imperial Guptas of the fifth century. The later-Gupta domain seems to have been restricted to Bihar. Further east in Gauḍa and Vaṅga, there is little evidence about rulers after the erroneously maligned Śaśāṅka. The Khaḍga dynasty appears to have established itself in the second half of the seventh century, but the house was not long-lived. The Kalipur grant of Dharmapāla describes things as dog-eat-dog (*matsyanyāya*) until the accession of Gopāla (*c.* AD 750), founder of the Pāla dynasty.[39]

In the eastern Doab an epigraph with the name Manorathavarman was found in Kāśī district.[40] A number of theories have been proposed to explain this king's ancestry and significance but, as the record is undated and provides no genealogy, the most that can be said is that Manorathavarman was a local ruler sometime in the seventh century.[41]

To the west there are records that show Rājasthān was divided into a variety of small principalities. In Marudeśa the Pratīhāras of Mandor (ancient Māṇḍavyapura, Maḍḍodara) were founded by Hariścandra in the mid-sixth century. The names of a number of his successors are preserved, but nothing substantial is known about them. In the early eighth century the ruler Śiluka faced the Arab raids, which began in AH 93/AD 711–12 with Muḥammad ibn al-Qāsim's conquest of Sind. In Medapāṭa, Uparamāla and the northern edge of Avanti clans of later Mauryas ruled from a number of centres. The most important may be briefly mentioned. The Dabok inscription of VS 701/AD 644–5 mentions a king named Dhavalappa. He may have been the scion of the Maurya house in Rājasthān.[42] Both he and the Maitraka Dharasena IV seem to have assumed imperial titles at this time.[43] The Maurya Dhavalātman (Kannada: Dhavalappa) mentioned in the Kanswa inscription of MS 795/AD 738–9 was probably a descendant of the Dhavalappa of the Dabok record.[44] The Jhālarāpātan inscription of VS 746/AD 689–90 mentions the building of a temple by the official Voppaka in the time of the Maurya king (*narendra*) Durggagaṇa.[45] Two inscriptions, now lost, record the Maurya Māna and Mānabhaṅga (probably the same king) as ruling Chittaur in the late seventh or early eighth century.[46] Some of these Maurya kings had tributaries and one named Ṇaṇṇappa is testified by an inscription from Indragarh dated VS 767/AD 710–11.[47] The Guhilas were important followers of the Maurya kings and sometime after the first Arab incursions they assumed control at Chittaur.

A Maurya family also seems to have controlled parts of western Madhyadeśa in the second half of the seventh century. A stone inscription from Mathurā (dated palaeographically to the seventh or eighth century) records the names Śrī Kṛṣṇarāja, Candragupta, Āryarāja and Karka Diṇḍirāja of Maurya lineage; the latter is mentioned as having led a successful expedition against Kannauj.[48] As noted above, this Maurya line probably represents the independent kingdom of Mathurā mentioned by Xuan Zang. Of more immediate interest is the Jaina tradition in the *Prabhāvakacarita* which records that Yaśovarman of Kannauj was descended from the Maurya Candragupta.[49] If we choose to equate the Candragupta of the Jaina texts with the Candragupta of the Mathurā inscription, then because Yaśovarman's date of accession has been fixed to *c.* AD 720, Śrī Kṛṣṇarāja, Candragupta, Āryarāja and Karka Diṇḍirāja can be placed in the seventh and early eighth centuries.[50]

The synopsis of developments just given sheds little direct light on the history of Gopakṣetra. All the same, it shows that there were no first-rate powers that could have dominated the area in the second half of the seventh century. The later Guptas were confined to Bihar, and the Mauryas of

Mathurā to western Madhyadeśa. When the Arabs appeared in Sind they were unable to do more than raid the minor princely states of Rājasthān. Gopakṣetra and neighbouring areas were apparently divided into a number of small principalities which were, in all probability, less stable than the entities that existed in these lands during the time of Harṣa. While this conclusion is necessarily provisional, its seems to be born out by a memorial pillar from Sesai (District Shivpuri) that records the death of one Durgarāja in a struggle with cattle-lifters and the subsequent self-immolation of his mother.[51] For Gopakṣetra and the neighbouring lands south of the Yamunā, Tāranātha's description of eastern India in these unsettled times seems the best summary: 'Every Kṣatriya, Brāhmaṇa and merchant was a king in his own area, but there was no king ruling over the country.'[52]

Yaśovarman and Āma

As we move into the eighth century, the political conditions of northern India become more stable with the rise of the monarch Yaśovarman of Kannauj. The earliest rulers of Yaśovarman's family, as already noted, were possibly the Mauryas from Mathurā who captured Kannauj in the early eighth century. Yaśovarman (*c.* AD 720–50) can be considered the most important of the line and some facts about his reign are preserved in Sanskrit, Prakrit and Chinese sources.[53] Little archaeological material can be connected with the king, but one stone inscription was found at Nālanda (map 5, site 1). While praising Yaśovarman in general terms without providing much historical information, the inscription at least suggests the extent of his dominion in eastern India. Vākpati's *Gauḍavaho*, which recounts the *digvijaya* (world conquest) of his patron, gives information on the regions incorporated into Yaśovarman's kingdom. While we need not accept the statements that Yaśovarman overran the far south and west (which are described in vague terms), there is little reason to doubt the substantial truth of those specific areas in the north that are described as his conquests. S. M. Mishra's appraisal of the *Gauḍavaho* matched against the known facts yields the conclusion that Yaśovarman's territory was essentially equal to that of Harṣa Vardhana.[54]

Some specifics may be added about Gopakṣetra. On the testimony of Rājaśekharasūri it is evident that Yaśovarman held sway over Gwalior.[55] The *Bappabhaṭṭisūricarita* states that Yaśovarman's successor Āma held court at Gopagiri. Late in his reign, Āma was intimately associated with the place and built a temple to Mahāvīra there; eventually he abdicated and became a monk.[56]

Gurjara Pratīhāras

Sometime during Yaśovarman's reign, the Gurjara-Pratīhāra king Nāgabhaṭṭa I established himself at Ujjayinī.[57] He is represented in an inscription of *c.* AD 875 as having 'crushed the large armies of the powerful *mleccha* king', which evidently refers to his successful repulsion of an Arab attack on Ujjayinī.[58] In the course of these engagements Nāgabhaṭṭa extended his influence westward to Broach (ancient Bhṛgukaccha) where his tributary Bhartṛvaḍḍha II issued a grant in VS 813/AD 756–7.[59] The degree to which Nāgabhaṭṭa also pushed north-west into Gopakṣetra cannot be determined, but given what we know about Yaśovarman, it seems unlikely that he attempted any significant expansion into the region.

Little is known about Nāgabhaṭṭa's immediate descendants Kakustha and Devarāja, who ruled shortly after the middle of the eighth century. The same holds true for Yaśovarman's descendants Āma, Dunduka and Bhoja who were in power at the same time. The Bhāgalpur plate of Nārāyaṇapāla describes how Dharmapāla installed Cakrāyudha on the throne of Kannauj, indicating Āma and his successors no longer held Madhyadeśa.[60] Jaina historical traditions inform us that Āma (*c.* AD 750–75) held court at Gopagiri; Dunduka and

Bhoja no doubt did the same.[61] This allows us to infer that the Pratīhāras Kakustha and Devarāja were controlling Avanti and parts of Rājasthān. The Kalipur grant records that the king of Avanti, among others, gave his ascent to Cakrāyudha's installation at Kannauj under Dharmapāla's sponsorship.[62]

Vatsarāja and Nāgabhaṭṭa II

The Pratīhāra and Maurya kings did not long enjoy their patrimony. Rāṣṭrakūṭa raids north of the Narmadā river led to a full-scale invasion under Govinda III (*c.* AD 794–814) and the humiliation of Cakrāyudha of Kannauj and his patron Dharmapāla.[63] The Rāṣṭrakūṭas further succeeded in defeating Vatsarāja (*c.* AD 777–808), the next Pratīhāra after Devarāja. The Sanjān, Rādhanpura and Waṇi plates all record the abasement of the Gurjara at Ujjayinī and his flight to Marudeśa.[64] These events are corroborated by the findspots of inscriptions mentioning Vatsarāja (map 6, sites 17, 19).[65] The strength of the Rāṣṭrakūṭas forced Vatsarāja and his successor Nāgabhaṭṭa II (*c.* AD 810–33) to set aside territorial ambitions toward the south and to look eastward. Gopakṣetra was probably conquered in the late eighth or early ninth century. Whether the Maurya's final disappearance was due to Rāṣṭrakūṭa raids or Pratīhāra expansion is difficult to determine.[66] The growth of Pratīhāra power ultimately led to Nāgabhaṭṭa's conquest of Kannauj which, as we have seen, was under Cakrāyudha. This event, an important step in the development of the Pratīhāra kingdom, is recorded in the Gwalior inscription of *c.* AD 875 that states Nāgabhaṭṭa 'became eminent' after 'defeating Cakrāyudha, whose lowly demeanour was manifested by his dependence on others [i.e. Dharmapāla]'.[67]

On the basis of the records just mentioned historians often speak of the 'Gurjara-Pratīhāra empire' and maps are used to show the geographical extent of this political entity. Such schemes are based on the assumption that major dynasties were responsible for organising a powerful and centralised administration. According to this interpretive model, princes and nobles functioned as feudatories and their main significance was that they either supported or opposed the dominant power. Scholars using this approach have produced a number of notable books, some of them now classics of Indian historical writing.[68] These works, indispensable as they are, do not always provide a satisfactory account of events in relation to internal political arrangements and the constitution of power. This has prompted a number of scholars to examine the structure of Indian kingdoms. Burton Stein, using the Cōḷas of Tamilnadu as his example, has proposed that the kingdom was a decentralised 'segmental state' and that the king was an almost entirely symbolic figure.[69] Power rested not in the hands of a centralised government, but in what Stein calls 'ethno-agrarian micro-regions'. Ronald Inden, using the Rāṣṭrakūṭa dynasty of the Deccan as his starting point, has argued that the king was important but that his power was continually being constituted, contested and re-made.[70] The business of 'imperial formation' took place, according to Inden, in an environment of shifting human agencies. Finally, Nicholas Dirks, working mainly with much later dynasties in south India, has described how 'large kingdoms' and 'little kingdoms' coexisted and were interdependent. Authority was shared and could fluctuate, transforming a small kingdom into a large one.[71]

None of these models are directly applicable to northern India during the Pratīhāra period. They alert us, however, to the potential complexity of the situation. While a reassessment of political arrangements under the Pratīhāras is beyond the scope of this essay, it will not be out of place to examine a number of inscriptions that articulate the distribution of power in the Pratīhāra realm. Nāgabhaṭṭa's encroachments into eastern India, for example, are not documented by imperial records but by inscriptions of tributary princes in Rājasthān (map 6, sites 16, 18).[72] These inscriptions, and those of other nobles, suggest that Rājasthān was the seat of Nāgabhaṭṭa's staunchest allies.[73] Even so, events and personalities in these records are seen from a local point of view with the Pratīhāra monarch featuring as a relatively incidental figure. One way of interpreting this would be to say that the inscriptions were concerned with the establishment of particular temples and as such have a strictly parochial focus; for this reason they only hint at the real nature of events and political relationships. A more convincing explanation, however, is that the epigraphic texts were composed by educated poets and accurately represent their patrons' point of view. From this perspective the submission of clans and princes to the monarch appears to have been a compromise between equals. Pratīhāra hegemony was not an autocratic exercise but rather a delicate balance between powerful tributary princes and the imperial centre.

This interpretation is supported by a number of records, but one of the most illuminating is the inscription of Bāuka dated VS 894/AD 837–8.[74] This epigraph gives a long account of Bāuka's family and culminates with a ghoulish description of his victory in a battle. Bāuka was a Pratīhāra prince who ruled from Mandor but did not belong to the imperial line. After the death of Nāgabhaṭṭa II Bāuka asserted independence and laid claim to the full range of royal titles. That was during the unstable period of king Rāmabhadra (*c.* AD 833–6). Though Bāuka's political ambitions were suppressed by Mihira Bhoja (*c.* AD 836–85), his inscription is imperial in aspiration and character.[75] From this we can assume that in times of wavering leadership Pratīhāra princes felt it appropriate to make a bid for power and supreme dominion.

However we choose to construe events, it is difficult to avoid the conclusion that the system encouraged fragmentation and violent competition. This is confirmed by many records, a useful example being the pillar inscription of Parabala at Badoh (map 6, site 9).[76] In the past, Parabala has been described as an ally of the Rāṣṭrakūṭas of Malkhed (ancient Mānyakheṭa) because the inscription states he belonged to a Rāṣṭrakūṭa lineage. Consequently his title *kṣmāpāla* ('protector of the earth', i.e. king) has been translated 'governor'. This ignores some key facts. The first is that the inscription describes how one of Parabala's forbears gained control of Lāṭa (coastal Gujarāt) after defeating the Kārṇāṭas (a common name for the Rāṣṭrakūṭas in northern epigraphs). This makes it difficult to see Parabala as an ally of the Rāṣṭrakūṭas in the Deccan. The second fact is that princes claiming a Rāṣṭrakūṭa clan affiliation or lineage are occasionally found in northern India, but these princes have no connection with their more famous namesakes.[77] Nor was Parabala an ally of the Pratīhāras. On this front, the Badoh inscription states that Parabala's father Karkarāja put Nāgāvaloka (i.e. Nāgabhaṭṭa II) to flight and invaded his home. These points show that Parabala's clan either shifted their allegiance or were altogether independent; whatever the case, the record highlights the inadequacy of the centralised model and demonstrates that Pratīhāra India was more of a political mosaic than previously admitted.

From the foregoing inscriptions we must not assume that Nāgabhaṭṭa and his successors were symbolic figureheads with no substantial power. Even though the capital of Kannauj was sacked in later times and imperial records are few, village grants make clear that many areas were controlled directly by the king. A key element in the maintenance of this imperial authority was the control of strategically important forts. The Gwalior inscription of *c.* AD 875 speaks of Nāgabhaṭṭa's seizure of hill-forts in Ānarta, Mālava, Kirāta, Turuṣka, Matsya and Vatsa.[78] These areas can be identified: Ānarta was northern Gujarāt, Mālava was the Mahī river valley, Kirāta was probably the area around Kiradu, Turuṣka was probably Multān, Matsya was the same area as Virāṭa, and Vatsa was the territory immediately south of the Yamunā.[79] The inscription does not mention areas in Rājasthān where Nāgabhaṭṭa's tributaries were ruling, indicating that the crown did not claim to control these areas directly. When the Pratīhāra house went into decline in the tenth century, inscriptions of their adversaries, as we shall see, clearly name the important forts they were able to capture or threaten. This confirms that the successful control of forts helped define the relationship between major and minor powers. The location of Gwalior was especially critical for the Pratīhāras because it guarded the southern flank of Madhyadeśa against the Rāṣṭrakūṭas. That this was a real and constant threat is evidenced by Nāgabhaṭṭa's defeat at the hands of Govinda III (*c.* AD 794–814).[80]

Mihira Bhoja

The circumstances that prevailed in the time of Nāgabhaṭṭa II continued under his celebrated successor Mihira Bhoja (*c.* AD 836–85). That the Rāṣṭrakūṭas continued to be a threat is shown by the Bagumra plates (dated Śaka 789/AD 867) which record the defeat of Gurjara Mihira (i.e. Mihira Bhoja) at the hands of Dhruva II.[81] In western India, however, Mihira Bhoja seems to have enjoyed some success against the Rāṣṭrakūṭas. The Partābgarh inscription of AD 946–7 refers back to a tributary who was a 'source of great pleasure to king Bhojadeva',[82] and further west the Bhāvanagar inscription (map 6, site 27) records the Pratīhāra defeat of Kṛṣṇa II (*c.* AD 875–911). These facts no doubt help corroborate the tradition in the *Skanda Purāṇa* that Bhoja sent an army to Saurāṣṭra.[83]

Inscriptions from Gopakṣetra show that the area remained firmly in Pratīhāra hands. Two records from Gwalior indicate that it was a Pratīhāra seat of importance and that the royal court was occasionally in residence there.[84] In neighbouring Jejākadeśa the Barah inscription recounts Bhoja's renewal of a land grant originally sanctioned by Nāgabhaṭṭa II 'in the Udambara *viṣaya* of the Kāliñjara *maṇḍala*', showing the area had long been in Pratīhāra hands.[85]

The extent of the Pratīhāra kingdom in other areas during Bhoja's time is outside the scope of this local history, but it can be briefly mentioned that Pratīhāra rule continued to be recognised in Rājasthān. The Siwāh plate of AD 843–4 records the renewal of a grant first made in Vatsarāja's time. The Chātsu inscription refers to the feudatory Harṣarāja Guhila who conquered kings in the north and presented horses to Bhoja, events confirmed by an inscription from Pehoa (ancient Pṛthūdaka) dated AD 882–3 in the reign of Bhojadeva.[86] In the east the frontier between the Pratīhāras and the powerful Pāla kingdom is unclear.[87]

Pratīhāras after Mihira Bhoja

Mihira Bhoja's successor Mahendrapāla I (*c.* AD 885–910) pushed the Pālas to near extinction with his aggressive campaigns in eastern India. The Pāhārpur pillar inscription dated in the fifth year of Mahendrapāla is indicative of the remarkable expansion of Pratīhāra power during his reign (map 6, site 1).[88] Records from other parts of India show the kingdom was maintained, but some hero-stones from Terāhī (dated VS 960/AD 903) are symptomatic of disturbances in imperial territory.[89] These disturbances escalated after Mahendrapāla's death with the rivalry between his competing successors Bhoja II and Mahīpāla. Just as Mahīpāla (*c.* AD 912–45) was establishing his power, the Rāṣṭrakūṭas under Indra III (*c.* AD 915–28) launched an ambitious raid against the north, advancing to Kālpī and then to Kannauj.[90] During the rule of Indra II's inept successor Govinda IV, Mahīpāla recouped Pratīhāra losses through a series of campaigns toward the south. The records indicate that these operations focused on Avanti and extended as far south as Māndū (ancient Maṇḍapadurga).[91] This did not stop the Rāṣṭrakūṭas from taking further initiatives. The Deoli and Karād plates show that some time before AD 940 the Rāṣṭrakūṭa Kṛṣṇa III (*c.* AD 939–67), while still crown prince, threatened the great forts of Kāliñjara and Citrakūṭa.[92] The Kannada inscription at Jura (map 6, site 5) demonstrates that a substantial portion of the Ḍāhala country was in Rāṣṭrakūṭa hands during the mid-tenth century.[93] The same pattern of events was seen much earlier when a Vakāṭaka tributary occupied parts of Ḍāhala during the decline of the Guptas.[94]

In this debacle Gopakṣetra continued to be held by the Pratīhāras. This is shown by the Rakhetra inscription of VS 999 and 1000/AD 942–3 and 943–4.[95] This records the construction of some irrigation works in the time of Mahīpāla. The epigraph mentions the area as being under the 'lord of Gwalior' (*gopagirīndra*). Princes in Rājasthān also continued to support Pratīhāra authority, as records of Mahīpāla's tributaries indicate that they served as allies in his military operations against the Rāṣṭrakūṭas.[96]

Regional dynasties

The subsequent Pratīhāra kings Mahendrapāla II (*c.* AD 944–6) and Devapāla (*c.* AD 948–59) maintained the Pratīhāras in Madhyadeśa, but the disturbances created by succession problems and Rāṣṭrakūṭa incursions fostered the development of strong regional dynasties.[97] The Candellas of Jejākadeśa are the most well known of these regional houses. They first appeared as a power of note when Harṣadeva Candella supported Mahīpāla in his successful bid for the Pratīhāra throne.[98] Yaśovarman (*c.* AD 925–54) raised the prestige and power of the Candellas by taking the fortress of Kāliñjara and forcing the Pratīhāra Devapāla to surrender a celebrated metal image of Vaikuṇṭha, which was subsequently set up in a temple built by Yaśovarman.[99]

In the Mālwa region the Paramāra Vairisiṁha seems to have ruled Dhārā as a tributary of the Rāṣṭrakūṭas.[100] Vairisiṁha's son Harṣa Sīyaka, who was ruling in AD 948–9, rebelled and defeated the Rāṣṭrakūṭa Khoṭṭiga (AD 967–72), devastating Mānyakheṭa in the process.[101] Vākpati Muñja, son of Harṣa Sīyaka, issued a charter from Ujjayinī in AD 974–5, and subsequent Paramāras ruled over Mālwa for several centuries.[102]

In Gopakṣetra these events were paralleled by the appearance of the Kacchapaghāta Lakṣmaṇa (*c.* AD 950–75). According to the Sās Bahu temple inscription, Lakṣmaṇa's successor Vajradāman (*c.* AD 975–1000) 'put down the rising power of the ruler of Gādhinagara [Kannauj] and his proclamation drum . . . resounded on the fort of Gopādri'.[103] Thus ended two centuries of Pratīhāra dominion over Gopakṣetra and the fortress of Gwalior. In Rājasthān the Pratīhāras were able to maintain some tributaries, but their relative decline is documented by inscriptions from Rajor, Bayānā, Harasnāth and Garh.[104] The Candellas, Paramāras and Kacchapaghātas shared a common origin as tributaries of the leading powers; when their overlords faltered in the mid-tenth century, they assumed increasing power and independence.

Summary

Some conclusions about the history of Gopakṣetra can be drawn from the foregoing narrative of events. First and foremost, beyond the generalities of pan-Indian history there is little exact evidence who was ruling when and where. In Gopakṣetra there is a major historical gap after the Hūṇas until the time of Harṣa and his contemporaries. After this there is another hiatus until Yaśovarman and the Pratīhāras. History then becomes reasonably firm, but, even with dated events and ruler's names, fixing the exact territory of each house or the dates when a dynasty moved into a particular area remains ill-informed guesswork. Analogous and equally dramatic gaps exist in the history of the provinces neighbouring Gopakṣetra, as close attention to the inscriptional evidence detailed above will readily show.

The implication of this observation for architectural history is that the undated and anonymously erected temples of the seventh, eighth and ninth centuries cannot be classified by dynasty. If we have no evidence which dynasty was in power, then a dynastic designation is not apt. This is simple logic. We must also take into account the complex political arrangements that prevailed during the centuries under consideration. Kannauj was the capital and Madhyadeśa the heartland, but other areas were usually under regional princes and their subordinates. These rulers were frequently kings in their own right and often bore such titles as *kṣitipati*, *nṛpa* and *śrīmahārāja*. Temples can hardly bear the designation of a distant royal family when regional rulers were the major force in day-to-day affairs. Furthermore, an analysis of temple inscriptions, taken up in the closing chapter, shows that the local authorities and their subjects were the principal patrons of temple construction and endowment. These points together demonstrate that dynastic classifications of architectural styles are not historically accurate. As a consequence dynastic nomenclature has been discarded here in favour of chronological and geographical labels. In the light of historical facts and their reasonable interpretation there is no other acceptable possibility.

Historiography

The genres of scholarship that have been applied to Indian architecture and sculpture originated in the nineteenth century and since that time have been slowly modified by changing approaches and concerns. A study of these genres and their development is essential for revealing the special contribution of this work and the place it holds in the discipline.[105]

Archaeology

The earliest (and first officially sanctioned) study of Indian art had a decidedly archaeological and antiquarian tone. Alexander Cunningham (1814–93) set this tone in his twenty-three-volume *Archaeological Survey of India Reports* which he began writing in 1861 upon his retirement from the army. Cunningham was assigned to Gwalior during his military career (1844–5 and 1849–53), and the great fortress appears to have been an important stimulus to his archaeological interests. This accounts for the valuable details found in his description of Gwalior and nearby sites.[106] At heart, Cunningham was a numismatist and field archaeologist, and his studies almost always focused on coins, inscriptions and history at the expense of architecture and sculpture.[107]

The Archaeological Survey of India, which Cunningham founded and which continues to this day, maintained his approach and fostered the development of sister organisations in the princely states before Indian independence. One of the most important of these organisations was the Archaeological Department of Gwalior State, headed by M. B. Garde. Charged with the care and study of antiquities throughout the Scindia dominion, Garde devoted almost half a century to maintaining buildings of importance and writing annual reports that recorded the progress being made in epigraphy, numismatics and the inventory of ancient sites.[108] Garde's most enduring contribution was the Archaeological Museum in Gwalior which houses one of the most comprehensive collections of sculpture in India.[109]

Since the Second World War the Archaeological Survey has focused its investigative resources on prehistoric archaeology and excavation. To foster work on standing monuments, the Archaeological Survey of Temples was set up in 1955 with Krishna Deva (b. 1914) in charge of the northern sector. Under his direction, the Temple Survey brought to light many important buildings in northern India.[110] For Gopakṣetra the most important contribution of the Temple Survey has been *Temples of the Pratīhāra Period in Central India*.[111]

Textual studies

Coeval with the archaeological study of ancient India was an approach initiated by Ram Raz (1790?–1833) with his book *Essay on the Architecture of the Hindus.*[112] This method involved a study of temple buildings and ancient architectural texts with the aid of craftsmen trained in the time-honoured manner. The texts, like any technical literature, contain ordinary words that have assumed specialised meanings. The traditional architects preserve knowledge of this technical language, at least for the building types they continue to use. Their knowledge is essential in rendering the texts meaningful, and once this is done the results can be checked against the temples themselves.

Ram Raz's approach is sound and sensible, but it was not taken up at the time. While archaeology enjoyed systematic growth, Ram Raz's method lay at a complete standstill for a century. It was not until the 1920s that the task of coordinating texts and buildings was again addressed, this time by Ananda Coomaraswamy in several articles on the architecture of the first two centuries BC.[113] For later temples the method was carried forward by N. K. Bose in his study of Orissan architectural *śāstra.*[114] The architecture of Orissa after the sixth century AD is a vigorous one, but somewhat different from the rest of northern India in its style and descriptive terminology. It was not until M. A. Dhaky and Krishna Deva began a study of *śilpa-śāstra* from Gujarāt and Mālwa that northern texts were understood in a comprehensive way. Pramod Chandra has detailed the growth of this scholarship and it would serve no useful purpose to restate his observations.[115] We only need note that the old building traditions of Gopakṣetra and many other parts of northern India have been displaced by the late Mughal manner; the *śilpa* texts of these regions seem to have disappeared when craftsmen started to take up more innovative styles in the late fifteenth century. This obliged Krishna Deva to use the terminology of Gujarāt and Mālwa in his seminal article 'The Temples of Khajurāho', published in 1959.[116] A work of primary methodological importance, this article brings the technical Sanskrit vocabulary to the first analytical description of the Khajurāho temples.

The work of M. A. Dhaky, Krishna Deva and their followers is more, however, than a simple continuation of the methods first propounded by Ram Raz. One innovation has been the adoption of elements from the archaeological method. Inscriptions are called in to provide evidence, temples are carefully measured to furnish plans and moulding profiles are drawn and compared. The most notable innovation, however, has been the elaboration of a scheme of regional schools, each with a distinctive style. This has seen comprehensive formulation in the writing of M. A. Dhaky. His article 'Genesis and Development of Māru-Gurjara Temple Architecture' breaks new ground in many areas, the most important being the abandonment of sectarian and dynastic nomenclature (inherited from Cunningham and his contemporaries) in favour of ancient geographical names for architectural periods and styles.[117] In this light Trivedi's *Temples of the Pratīhāra Period in Central India*, while providing documentation of unprecedented accuracy, marks a regression to arbitrary geographical terminology and a dynastic conception of style.

Formalism

The question of style brings us to writers who have employed formalist theories in their analysis of Indian art. Formalism and its specialised language have evolved slowly over the last two centuries as art historians have become more sophisticated in their description and analysis of art. Heinrich Wölfflin (1864–1945) gave this approach comprehensive formulation and his writing had an immediate and widespread impact.[118]

Though Wölfflin's periodisation of European art has been largely overtaken, many art historians continue to use and refine Wölfflin's terminology and comparative approach. Ludwig Bachhofer (1894–1976), a student of Wölfflin, brought the method to Chinese and Indian art, opening up new areas of investigation in these fields. Bachhofer's *Early Indian Sculpture* displays a sophisticated methodology, already powerful and fully formed.[119] Here is no slow forging of a method like those we have just discussed, but one that appears completely developed in the first instance. Bachhofer's strength lay in his perception of the aesthetic dignity of Indian sculptural forms; yet because no other scholars of Indian art participated in the development of this method, it did not find wide application. Indeed Ananda Coomaraswamy's review of *Early Indian Sculpture* went so far as to criticise the approach by stating that the inner spiritual meaning of Indian art must always hold primacy over an appreciation of its formal qualities.[120] This was Coomaraswamy's deeply held conviction and, as he had an acute (albeit idiosyncratic) sense of style, it was perfectly valid. Subsequent writers, however, lacked Coomaraswamy's sensibilities; the end result was that Indian sculptures came to be seen as 'documents' of culture. Under the weight of such a mood investigations into the formal qualities of Indian sculpture inevitably waned.

In architecture the same fate befell the pioneering efforts of James Fergusson (1808–86). Like Bachhofer, Fergusson had a keen eye for style and he applied it to telling effect in his *History of Indian and Eastern Architecture*, first published in 1876.[121] Given the state of architectural studies in India or Europe in 1876, we must concede that this book is remarkable for its scope, coverage of monuments and attention to theoretical problems. Unlike Bachhofer, who never visited India, Fergusson was deeply involved in field research. His diligent followers, James Burgess (1832–1916) and Henry Cousens (1854–1934), continued his work of documentation, but unanimated by Fergusson's lively investigation into the philosophy of architecture, theirs became a predominantly archaeological approach which paid little heed to Fergusson's subtle perception of style. One reason the work of Burgess and Cousens took this direction was Fergusson's cantankerous interaction with colleagues and the criticism his writings occasioned in the early twentieth century. As his work became unfashionable, inquiry into the formal qualities of Indian architecture subsided.

More recently, Fergusson has been rediscovered, chiefly because time has shown him to hold a place of significance in the history of architectural criticism.[122] With this has come, though perhaps coincidentally, a re-emergence of an appreciation of style. The contribution of Krishna Deva, M. A. Dhaky and others to the study of temples and *śilpa* texts has already occasioned remark; this work, however, cannot be classed simply as an exercise in textual exegesis. M. A. Dhaky in particular has carried the study of the texts to a deeper level. In a series of articles he distinguished the different temple traditions of Rājasthān and northern Gujarāt, a distinction based on the formal and morphological features of the buildings.[123] In sculpture a resuscitation of stylistic analysis appeared in the writing of Pramod Chandra (b. 1930). His *Stone Sculpture in the Allahabad Museum*, to select but one work, extended and amplified areas of investigation first suggested by Ludwig Bachhofer.[124] F. M. Asher's *Art of Eastern India* applied this approach to a study of sculpture in Bihar and Bengal, but in this work the emphasis on formalism was substantially tempered by archaeological and iconographic concerns.[125]

Typological studies

The work of French scholars, such as Jouveau-Dubreuil, Stern and Viennot, takes us to an approach that is related to formalism but attempts to be more systematic or 'scientific'. The method may be considered typological, since it relies on a comparison of architectural or sculptural motifs.[126] This work shows the impact of Darwinism in that motifs and designs are seen as developing gradually in a continuous linear sequence, beginning with the simplest and ending with the most complex. The artefact is dated by the motif's position in this temporal sequence. Typological studies of Indian art have made little use of plans and moulding profiles, or the auxiliary evidence of epigraphy and numismatics. French scholars have also been slow in taking up the descriptive vocabulary extracted from the *śilpa-śāstra*.

The typological method has been applied to a variety of periods in Indian art and has, in the field of north Indian temples, received its greatest elaboration at the hand of Odette Viennot. In *Les divinités fluviales* she traced the evolution of the Gaṅga and Yamunā images on temple doorways from the first to the tenth century.[127] Many sculptures were published in this book for the first time and, as some images have been subsequently vandalised, the work remains an indispensable reference tool. In a later book, *Temples de l'Inde centrale et occidentale*, Viennot applied the same method to the monumental task of surveying temple architecture across northern India from the sixth to the middle of the tenth century.[128] Like her earlier work on sculpture, this is a useful compilation, publishing many temples from Gopakṣetra for the first time. Valuable as the typological approach may be, we must be cautious in using it, for George Kubler has convincingly argued that artefacts do not evolve in the manner of biological organisms.[129]

Cultural history and iconology

Formalism also exerted considerable influence on Stella Kramrisch (1898–1993). In her book *Indian Sculpture*, as well as numerous articles, her insights were captured in a thought-provoking language that pulsates with the life of the art it describes.[130] Like Josef Strzygowski, with whom she studied, Kramrisch attempted to explain styles on the basis of *Weltanschauungen* that are born of the inherent psychological traits found in different races. This contrasts with scholars of the Wölfflin-Bachhofer tradition who generally refused to speculate on the cause of stylistic change. This deeper thrust, a move beyond formalism in its narrowest sense, led Kramrisch to search for the forces that shape the artistic process and ultimately to the spiritual profundities of Indian art. In the work of her mature scholarship, of which *The Hindu Temple* is the most well known, there was a continued sensitivity to formal beauty, but emphasis was given to the atemporal that the forms were meant to embody.[131] Kramrisch's work thus emerged as a forceful synthesis of visual sensibility and a search for deeper meaning. Here Kramrisch was in harmony with Ananda Coomaraswamy; both sought to understand the subject matter and its contents, the social and religious factors that lend shape to Indian art, and above all its conceptual and symbolic significance. Their approach transcended formalism without abandoning it and became a history of culture and civilisation. At its best, the writing of Kramrisch and Coomaraswamy was superlatively well judged and eloquent, sustaining a brilliant literary style, their words translated art into language and became works of art in themselves.

An integrated method

The preceding paragraphs have outlined the main genres of scholarship that have given shape to the study of Indian art. For brevity's sake only a few contributions could be mentioned. It should also be clear that no writer has worked in a vacuum or pursued a favoured methodology with unwavering rigidity. Each mind has been tinged by diverse considerations and each has worked with an eclectic method that defies ready definition. Yet the dominant hues of different methods emerge clearly enough, and from each this book draws appropriate elements for grappling with sculpture and architecture in Gopakṣetra.

From the archaeological method comes the drawing of temple plans and moulding profiles.

While these do not form a corner-stone in the present dating scheme, attention to them is necessary to show the scale of the buildings, their orientation and the arrangement of their parts. The archaeological approach also provides dates for monuments on the basis of history and epigraphy. In the absence of other evidence in Gopakṣetra, epigraphic style and historical data can help establish a chronology.

From the methodology that takes the *śilpa* as its starting point comes the Sanskrit terminology used to describe temples and their parts. This terminology brings to temple studies a precision that can only be described as scientific, and its use has gained such currency that European architectural terms can be dispensed with. The case for a descriptive vocabulary that is both indigenous and specialised hardly needs arguing. With it also comes a certain emphasis on regional art traditions, because the texts from which the terms are drawn are regional phenomena.

The emphasis on style and the morphology of temple architecture comes from an approach that may be broadly classed as formal. The use of this method, however, has been complicated by the destruction of numerous temples and the subsequent establishment of museums to house the remains. In art-historical and archaeological studies this has created a false division between sculpture and architecture. We must remember that most images in India were made for use in and on temple buildings. As a consequence the method applied here seeks to re-establish the formal link between sculpture and architecture.

Finally, the attempt to outline the social environment of temple building is derived from cultural studies and iconology. Patronage has received scant attention because epigraphic records have been used primarily as diagnostic tools for the writing of political history. Inscriptions contain much historical information, but their main purpose was to document religious giving. The approach followed here has been to take the inscriptions at face value and see what they say about temple building in ancient India.

Summary

In creating a setting for the study of temple architecture in the Gwalior region between AD 600 and 900, the first focus of the chapter was historical geography. A survey of that part of Madhya Pradesh where the temples in question are found demonstrated that the region is best described by its ancient name Gopakṣetra. Historically speaking, the temples also have a setting. A perusal of inscriptions showed, however, that so little is known about the territorial holdings of different royal houses that it is impossible to link the temples with the history of the main ruling houses of northern India. As a consequence, dynastic names for periods and styles of architecture are untenable. The final element of the setting, historiography, assessed the significance of this endeavour and its contribution to the discipline. The significance of this work is that it employs an integrated method that draws on the special strengths of archaeological, textual, formal and cultural studies. As for the contribution of this book, it is the first comprehensive treatment of the early temples in Gopakṣetra and, because this region is one of the few to preserve temples and sculpture intact, it lays a foundation for understanding these centuries in the rest of northern India.

Notes

1 For the term Gopakṣetra in epigraphs of the Kacchapaghāta dynasty, see V. K. Sinha, 'Kacchapaghāta rājavaṁśa kā navīna abhilekh', in *Gvāliyar darśan*, ed. Harihar Nivās Dvivedī (Gwalior: Gvāliyar Śodh Saṁsthān, 1980), pp. 217–19. Some material here has been presented in my 'Introduction to the Historical Geography of Gopakṣetra, Daśārṇa and Jejākadeśa', BSOAS 51 (1988): 273–8.

2 Gopagiri and Gopādri are mentioned in many inscriptions, for example IA 15 (1886): 36, 41; EI 1 (1889–92): 154, 134, the latter providing the description of Gopādri as the unique abode of marvel.

3 IA 15 (1886): 33–46 (verses 9–11); also my 'Architecture in Central India under the Kacchapaghāta Rulers'. In this monograph the spelling of place names follows the maps published by the Survey of India and *Corpus Topographicum Indiae Antiquae (Part I, Epigraphical Find Spots)* by R. Stroobandt (Gent: N.F.W.O., 1974).

4 The ancient name Paḍhāvali is provided by an inscription on a hero-stone (see pl. 6); see also Harihar Nivās Dvivedī, *Gvāliyar rājya ke abhilekh* (Banāras: Sulemānī Press, vs 2004): nos 121, 377, and my *Inscriptions of Gopakṣetra: Materials for the History of Central India* (London: British Museum Press, 1996), p. 118 (pl. 3). I am grateful to Dr Richard Salomon for providing a reading of the hero-stone inscription.

5 Vasudev Vishnu Mirashi, *Bhavabhūti* (Delhi: Motilal Banarasidass, 1974), pp. 77–8. Another description of Padmāvatī is found in the Vaidyanātha temple inscription at Khajurāho, EI 1 (1889–92): 147 (verses 6–7).

6 H. V. Trivedi, 'The Yajvapālas of Narwar', JMPIP 2 (1960): 22–32. The change from Nalapura to Narwar suggests the ancient name of Naresar was Naleśvara, not Nareśvara. For the Naleśvara inscription, see *Inscriptions of Gopakṣetra*, pp. 7, 13 (pls 14–15).

7 Thomas Watters, *On Yuan Chwang's Travels in India*, 2 vols (London: Royal Asiatic Society, 1904), 2: 251.

8 Richard Davis, *Ritual in an Oscillating Universe* (Princeton: University Press, 1991), pp. 14–15. V. V. Mirashi, 'Gwalior Museum Inscription of Pataṅga Śambhu', JMPIP 4 (1962): 6, has shown that the town was called Araṇipadra, not Raṇipadra.

9 In 'Gwalior Museum Inscription of Pataṅga Śambhu', p. 6, and *Inscriptions of the Kalachuri-Chedi Era*, CII vol. 4 (Ootacamund: Government Epigraphist for India, 1955), p. clii, Mirashi has argued that the original Terambi and Kadambaguhā were in the Ujjain region; according to this interpretation, the ascetics named places in Gopakṣetra after their former seats.

10 IA 17 (1888): 201–2; the hero-stone is illustrated in our pl. 130. Bhavabhūti, *Mālatī-Mādhava*, trans. Ramkrishna Gopal Bhandarkar, rev. with additional notes by V. V. Mirashi (Poona: Bhandarkar Oriental Institute, 1970), pp. 374, 571.

11 CII 4: 220–21. The Chandrehe inscription (ibid., pp. 198–204) also describes the *ācārya* Śikhāśiva as *madhumatīpati*. The Sānchī donative records mentioning Madhuvana would seem to be referring to the Mahuā area.

12 P. K. Bhattacharyya, *Historical Geography of Madhya Pradesh from Early Records* (Delhi: Motilal Banarsidass, 1977); reviewed by S. B. Chauduri in JAS 22 (1980): 57–61.

13 Hem Chandra Ray, *The Dynastic History of Northern India*, 2 vols (Calcutta: University of Calcutta, 1931–6), 2: 669–70; R. K. Dikshit, *The Candellas of Jejākabhukti* (Delhi: Motilal Banarsidass, 1977).

14 V. V. Mirashi, 'Three Ancient Famous Temples of the Sun', *Purāṇa* 8 (1966): 38–51.

15 For Gujarrā, see *Inscriptions of Gopakṣetra*, p.108. For Rāṣṭrakūṭa and later invasions along this route, see D. C. Sircar, *Studies in the Geography of Ancient and Medieval India* (Delhi: Motilal Banarsidass, 1971), p. 305.

16 As demonstrated by Sikandar Lodī's invasion of Gwalior from the south in the fifteenth century; the same route was followed by the British under Sir Hugh Rose. For bridges, see Jean Deloche, *Les ponts anciens de l'Inde* (Paris: L'école française d'Extrême-Orient, 1973).

17 Krishna Deva, *Temples of North India* (Delhi: National Book Trust, 1969), p. 49; O. Viennot, *Temples de l'Inde centrale et occidentale*, 2 vols (Paris: L'école française d'Extrême-Orient, 1976), *passim.*

18 D. C. Sircar, *Select Inscriptions Bearing on Indian History and Civilization*, 2 vols (Calcutta: University of Calcutta, and Delhi: Motilal Banarsidass, 1965–83), 1: 385; J. F. Fleet, *Inscriptions of the Gupta Kings and their Successors*, CII vol. 3 (Calcutta: Superintendent of Government Printing), p. 228.

19 For calculations regarding the length of generations, see IA 13 (1884): 417 and EI 18 (1925–6): 89, n. 3.

20 EI 1 (1889–92): 72; EI 7 (1902–3): 157; EI 4 (1896–7): 210; Bāṇa, *The Harṣacarita*, trans. E. B. Cowell and F. W. Thomas, p. 173.

21 Maukhari inscriptions have been found at Jaunpur (Inscription of Īśānavarman [CII 3: 228]) and Harāha (Inscription of Sūryavarman [EI 14 (1917–18): no. 5]); Maukhari coins have been recovered at Ayodhya and Rāmnagar Fort (ASIR 9: 27)

22 R. S. Tripathi, *History of Kanauj to the Moslem Conquest* (Benares: Indian Book Shop, 1937), pp. 30–32, discusses the origins of the Maukharis. For a useful synopsis of the dynasty, see R. C. Majumdar, ed., *The History and Culture of the Indian People: The Classical Age* (Bombay: Bhāratīya Vidyā Bhavan, 1954), pp. 67–71.

23 Sircar, *Select Inscriptions* I: 424–6.

24 *Inscriptions of Gopakṣetra*, p. 111 (pl. 2).

25 Sircar, *Select Inscriptions* I: 345; CII 4: 47.

26 EI 18 (1925–6): 126. Sircar, 'The Maukharis and Later Guptas', JRASB, Letters 11 (1945): 71, holds the Barah grant of Bhoja I (EI 19 [1927–8]:17) mentioning Sarvavarman shows Bundelkhand was under the Maukharis, but the identification of this Sarvavarman with the Maukhari of the same name is not certain.

27 *Si-yu-ki: Buddhist Records of the Western World*, 2 vols, trans. Samuel Beal (London: Kegan Paul, 1906); also *Hwui Li, The Life of Hiuen-Tsiang*, with an introduction by Samuel Beal (London: Kegan Paul, 1911) and Watters, *On Yuan Chwang's Travels in India.*

28 EI 21 (1931–2): 74; EI 4 (1896–7): 208; EI 7 (1902–3): 155; CII 3: 231.

29 EI 20 (1929–30): 189–94; Tripathi, *History of Kanauj*, p. 117.

30 IA 8 (1879): 244; EI 6 (1900–1901): 6.

31 CII 3: 288.

32 *Inscriptions of Gopakṣetra*, p. 114; also discussed in Chapter 2 below.

33 Tripathi, *History of Kanauj*, p. 114 arrives at the same conclusion on different evidence.

34 *Si-yu-ki*, trans. Samuel Beal, 1: 181 and 2: 270–71. Following Tripathi, *History of Kanauj*, corrigenda (no pagination), I take Zhi Ji Tou to equal Citrakūṭa. For further commentary, see Watters, *On Yuan Chwang's Travels in India*, 1: 301 and 2: 250–51.

35 EI 32 (1957–8): 207. As shown below, Yaśovarman may have been descended from Karka and, taking the usual rate of twenty-six years for each generation (IA 13 [1884]: 417; also EI 18 [1925–6]: 89, n. 3), we can work back four generations from Yaśovarman's accession (*c.* AD 720) to the first half of the seventh century.

36 EI 19–23 (1927–36): appendix, nos 1206, 1207; CII 4: 41, 49.

37 A. S. Gadre, *Important Inscriptions from the Baroda State* (Baroda: Baroda State Press, 1943): 7. An inscription of the Cālukya Maṅgaleśa (dated AD 601–2) also documents a victory over Buddharāja, IA 19 (1890): 7–20.

38 See Majumdar, *History and Culture of the Indian People: The Classical Age*, pp. 153–63, upon which our account is partially based.

39 EI 4 (1896–7): 248. These are usually called the Khalipur plates, but Survey of India map 78 D.5.2 spells the name Kalipur.

40 EI 34 (1961–2): 246.

41 For a synopsis of opinions, see S. M. Mishra, *Yaśovarman of Kanauj* (Delhi: Abhinav, 1977), pp. 37–8.

42 EI 35 (1963–4): 100–102. The inscription is not dated AD 726–7 as first thought.

43 EI 19–23 (1927–36), appendix, nos 1348–9.

44 IA 19 (1890): 57. Kanaswa or Kamsuvan = Kanswa, Survey of India map 45 D.16.5.

45 IA 5 (1876): 180; IA 56 (1927): 213.

46 For references, see C. G. Lin-Bodien, 'The Chronology of Chandravati, Kusuma, Chitorgarh: A Case Study in the Use of Epigraphic and Stylistic Evidence', AAA 33 (1980): 52.

47 EI 35 (1963–4): 101; EI 32 (1957–8): 112–17; IHQ 31 (1955): 99–104.

48 EI 32 (1957–8): 211.

49 Prabhācandrācārya, *Prabhāvakacarita*, ed. Jina Vijaya Muni (Ahmedabad: Sañcālaka-siṁghī Jaina Granthamālā, 1940), p. 81 (verses 46–7); see also JBBRAS 3 (1927): 314. Vākpati's *Gauḍavaho* (Shankar Pandurang Pandit and Narayan Bapuji Utgikar, eds, *The Gauḍavaho: A Prakrit Historical Poem* [Poona: Bhandarkar Oriental Resarch Institute, 1927], v. 1065) also describes Yaśovarman as of the family of *rajanīramaṇa*, i.e. *candra*. These statements, like those in epigraphs, follow established patterns of rhetoric and can only be accepted with considerable caution.

50 Chiefly working from palaeographic evidence, D. C. Sircar has also placed Karka at the end of the seventh century, EI 35 (1963–4):101.

51 *Inscriptions of Gopakṣetra*, pp. 119–20; D. R. Patil, *The Descriptive and Classified List of Archaeological Monuments in Madhya Bharat* (Gwalior: Department of Archaeology, Madhya Bharat Government, 1952), no. 1507.

52 IA 4 (1875): 366; R. C. Majumdar and Sir Jadu-Nath Sarkar, eds, *The History of Bengal*, 2 vols (Dacca: The University of Dacca, 1943–8), 1: 183.

53 See Mishra, *Yaśovarman of Kanauj*, pp. 21–35; also, preferring a slightly earlier date, Shoshin Kuwayama, 'Dating Yaśovarman of Kanauj on the Evidence of Huichao', *Zinbun: Annals of the Institute for Research in Humanities – Kyoto University* 29 (1994): 1–15.

54 Mishra, *Yaśovarman of Kanauj*, pp. 88–92.

55 '*Kānyakubjadeśe Gopālagiridurganagare Yaśovarmanṛpateḥ*'. Rājaśekharasūri, *Prabandhakośa*, ed. Jina Vijaya (Śāntiniketan: Adhiṣṭāta-siṁghī Jaina Jñānapīṭha, 1935), p. 27.

56 Ibid., pp. 28–9; *Prabhāvakacarita*, pp. 94 (verses 139–40) and 107; also JBBRAS 3 (1927): 323.

57 Tripathi, *History of Kanauj*, pp. 225–7

58 EI 18 (1925–6): 107.

59 EI 12 (1913–14): 202.

60 IA 15 (1886): 304.

61 See note 56 for references.

62 EI 4 (1896–97): 248. In the list of kings supporting Cakrāyudha the Mauryas of Gwalior are absent, which is not surprising considering they had just been forced out of Kannauj.

63 Rāṣṭrakūṭa raids, IA 12 (1883): 159; EI 18 (1925–6): 243–4. Govinda IV's defeat of Dharmapāla and Cakrāyudha, EI 18 (1925–6): 245 (verse 23).

64 EI 18 (1925–6): 243 (verse 9); EI 6 (1900–1901): 243 (verse 8); IA 11 (1882): 157.

65 EI 5 (1898–9): 208–13. Though called the Daulatpur copper plate, the inscription was actually found at Sewa (= Siwāh, Survey of

India map 45 I.11.7) and this is the site shown on our map 6. For the Osiān inscription mentioning Vatsarāja, see ASIAR (1908–9): 108; JRAS (1907): 1010. The inscription at Delhi dated Śaka 717 has no provenance, but the general area of its discovery in the north-west circle of the Archaeological Survey does not contradict our analysis of events; EI 41 (1975–6): 49–57.

66 The Sanjān plates (dated Śaka 793) credit Govinda III with 'carrying away in battles the fame of kings Nāgabhaṭṭa and Candragupta', (EI 18 [1925–6]: 245 [verse 22]).

67 EI 18 (1925–6): 108. Like most inscriptional records, the account is partisan; it gives no credit to Govinda III for his part in bringing down Cakrāyudha, the Rāṣṭrakūṭas being long-standing enemies of the Pratīhāras.

68 The most important for our concern and one we have already cited is Tripathi, *History of Kanauj*; in other parts of India see, for example, K. A. Nilakanta Sastri, *The Colas* (Madras: Madras University, 1955), and A. S. Altekar, *The Rāshtrakūtas and their Times* (Poona: Oriental Book Agency, 1934). My assessment of this material owes much to discussions with my colleague Prof. Andrew Cohen.

69 Burton Stein, *Peasant State and Society in Medieval South India* (Oxford: University Press, 1980).

70 Ronald Inden, *Imagining India* (Oxford: Blackwell, 1990).

71 Nicholas B. Dirks, *The Hollow Crown: Ethnohistory of an Indian Kingdom* (Cambridge: University Press, 1988).

72 EI 18 (1925–6): 87–99; EI 12 (1913–14): 10–17.

73 EI 2 (1892–94): 116–20. This inscription is later but refers back to tributaries during the time of Nāgabhaṭṭa.

74 EI 17 (1925–6): 87–99. The inscription was recovered from Jodhpur; though belonging to the ninth century, it refers to events and building activities from as early as *c.* AD 600.

75 The reassertion of imperial Pratīhāra power in the region is evidenced by the Siwāh plate (map 6, site 17), which records that Bhoja reinstated a grant of Vatsarāja that was in abeyance, EI 5 (1898–9): 208–13.

76 EI 9 (1907–8): 248–56; the inscription is dated VS 917/AD 861.

77 EI 32 (1957–58): 112–17. Cālukya princes are likewise found but they are unrelated to the Cālukyas of Vātāpi, see EI 9 (1907–8): 1–10.

78 EI 18 (1925–6): 108 (verse 11).

79 Sircar, *Studies in the Ancient and Medieval Geography of India*, pp. 205–10, has shown that Mālava denoted the Mahī river valley until the tenth century; note that the order of areas given by the inscription implies that Mālava lay next to Ānarta. An inscription on the Someśvara temple at Kiradu records the ancient name of the place was Kīrāṭakūpa, PRASIWC (1908), pp. 40–42.

80 EI 18 (1925–6): 245 (verse 22); IA 40 (1911): 239–40.

81 IA 12 (1883):184 (verse 40).

82 EI 14 (1917–18): 184.

83 Tripathi, *History of Kanauj*, p. 245.

84 EI 1 (1889–92): 154–62; EI 18 (1925–6): 89–114. The significance of Gwalior in this period is explored in Salomon and Willis, 'Three Inscribed Hero-stones from Terāhī', forthcoming.

85 EI 19 (1927–8): 18; as noted above, the forts of Vatsa were conquered by Nāgabhaṭṭa II, EI 17 (1925–6): 108 (verse 11).

86 EI 12 (1913–14): 15 (verse 19); EI 1 (1889–92): 186.

87 Tripathi, *History of Kanauj*, p. 240, and R. C. Majumdar, ed., *The History and Culture of the Indian People: The Age of Imperial Kanauj* (Bombay: Bhāratīya Vidyā Bhavan, 1955), pp. 30–31, overemphasise Bhoja's exploits in the east. This again results from a centralised model of state.

88 ASIAR (1925–6), p. 141. Inscriptions of Mahendrapāla were found in Bihar and Bengal, see Tripathi, *History of Kanauj*, p. 362, but more recently see Gouriswar Bhattacharya, 'A Puzzling Report on a British Museum Buddhist Pedestal Inscription', *South Asian Studies* 6 (1990): 39–42.

89 *Inscriptions of Gopakṣetra*, p. 2.

90 For destruction of temple of Kālapriyanātha and sack of Kannauj, see Cambay plates of Govinda IV, EI 7 (1902–3): 38.

91 The Partābgarh inscription of Mahendrapāla II suggests these operations took place in the time of Mahīpāla; EI 14 (1917–18): 176–88.

92 EI 4 (1896–7): 284; EI 5 (1898–9): 194.

93 EI 19 (1927–8): 287–90.

94 Sircar, *Select Inscriptions Bearing on Indian History*, p. 456.

95 *Inscriptions of Gopakṣetra*, p. 3.

96 EI 12 (1913–14): 10–17; see also Hadāla plates for recognition of Mahīpāla in Gujarāt, IA 12 (1883): 190–95.

97 See Majumdar, *History and Culture of the Indian People: The Age of Imperial Kanauj*, p. 37, for the complexities of the imperial succession after Mahendrapāla II.

98 EI 1 (1889–92): 122 (line 10). The inscription was found near the Vāmana temple, Khajurāho.

99 EI 1 (1889–92): 129 (verse 43). The inscription, dated VS 1011, was found 'amongst the ruins at the base of the temple known as Lakshmanjī' at Khajurāho. S. Huntington, *The Art of Ancient India* (New York: Weatherhill, 1985): 469, suggests that the main image in the Lakṣmaṇa temple is a tenth-century replacement for the metal Vaikuṇṭha; the current Lakṣmaṇa image, however, appears to date to the eleventh century (Richard Davis, 'Indian Art Objects as Loot', *Journal of Asian Studies* 52 [1993]: 22–48).

100 ARE (1957–8): 2.

101 For date of Harṣa Sīyaka, see EI 19–23 (1927–36), appendix, no. 64; EI 1 (1889–92): 137 (verse 12); for literary references to sack of Mānyakheṭa, see Ray, *Dynastic History of Northern India* 2: 850–51.

102 EI 19–23 (1927–36): appendix, no. 84.

103 IA 15 (1886): 36 (verse 6); Harihar Nivās Dvivedī, 'Gopakṣetra ke kacchapaghāta', in *Gvāliyar darśan*, pp. 186–216.

104 EI 3 (1894–95): 263–7; EI 22 (1933): 120–27; EI 2 (1892–4):

116–30; EI 39 (1972): 189–98, the latter giving a fresh summary of the problems of late Pratihāra history.

105 For this section I have drawn on Pramod Chandra, 'The Study of Indian Temple Architecture', in *Studies in Indian Temple Architecture* (Delhi: American Institute of Indian Studies, 1975), pp. 1–39, and Pramod Chandra, *On the Study of Indian Art* (New York: Asia Society, 1983).

106 ASIR 2 (1863–4): 330–401; ASIR 20 (1882–3): 105–12. See also *The Dictionary of Art* (London: Macmillan, 1996), s.v. 'Alexander Cunningham'.

107 Cunningham's priorities are revealed in ASIR 1 (1861–2): i–xlii.

108 Archaeological Department, Gwalior State, *Annual Report, Saṁvat 1980, Year 1925–26* to *Saṁvat 1997, Year 1940–41* (Gwalior, 1937–43); *Quinquennial Administration Report for Saṁvats 1998–2002 (Years 1942–46)* (Gwalior, 1949). As a general introduction, see M. B. Garde, *Archaeology in Gwalior*, 2nd edn (Gwalior: Alijah Darbar Press, 1934).

109 Department of Archaeology, Gwalior State, *A Guide to the Archaeological Museum at Gwalior* (Gwalior: [Alijah Darbar Press, 1930s?]); D. R. Patil, *A Guide to the Archaeological Museum, Gwalior* (Gwalior: Alijah Darbar Press, 1945); S. R. Thakore, *Catalogue of Sculptures in the Archaeological Museum, Gwalior, Madhya Bharat* (Lashkar: [Madhya Bharat Government], n.d.); S. K. Dikshit, *A Guide to the Central Archaeological Museum, Gwalior* (Bhopal: Department of Archaeology and Museums, Madhya Pradesh, 1962). A proper catalogue, threatened from various quarters over the years, remains to be written.

110 Some results of the Temple Survey appeared in A. Ghosh, ed., *Archaeological Remains: Monuments and Museums*, 2 vols (Delhi: Archaeological Survey of India, 1964).

111 R. D. Trivedi, *Temples of the Pratīhāra Period in Central India* (Delhi: Archaeological Survey of India, 1990).

112 Ram Raz, *Essay on the Architecture of the Hindus* (London: Oriental Translation Fund of Great Britain and Ireland, 1834).

113 Ananda Coomaraswamy, 'Indian Architectural Terms', JAOS 48 (1928): 250–75; 'Early Indian Architecture: I. Cities and City Gates, Etc.; II. Bodhigharas', *Eastern Art* 2 (1930): 209–35; 'Early Indian Architecture: III. Palaces', *Eastern Art* 3 (1931): 181–217.

114 N. K. Bose, *Canons of Orissan Architecture* (Calcutta: R. Chatterjee, 1932).

115 Pramod Chandra, 'Study of Indian Temple Architecture', pp. 1–39.

116 Krishna Deva, 'The Temples of Khajurāho', AI 15 (1959): 43–65.

117 M. A. Dhaky, 'Genesis and Development of Māru-Gurjara Temple Architecture', in *Studies in Indian Temple Architecture*, pp. 114–65.

118 W. Eugene Kleinbauer and Thomas P. Slavens, *Research Guide to the History of Western Art* (Chicago: American Library Association, 1982), p. 83.

119 Ludwig Bachhofer, *Early Indian Sculpture*, 2 vols (New York: Pegasus, 1929). For Bachhofer's general contribution, see Harrie Vanderstappen, 'Ludwig Bachhofer (1894–1976)', AAA 31 (1977–8): 110–111.

120 Ananda Coomaraswamy, 'Indian Sculpture: A Review', *Rūpam* 42–44 (1930): 2–11.

121 James Fergusson, *History of Indian and Eastern Architecture* (London: John Murray, 1876). The book was reprinted several times but was not changed until J. Burgess' edition of 1910.

122 Pramod Chandra, *On the Study of Indian Art*, p. 115, n. 6; Phoebe B. Stanton, 'The Rôle of the Critic in the Formation of Style, 1815–Present', paper read for the Robert B. Mayer Memorial Lecture Series, The University of Chicago, 24 November 1981.

123 M. A. Dhaky, 'Kiradu and the Māru-Gurjara Style of Temple Architecture', *Bulletin of the American Academy of Benares* 1 (1967): 35–45; Dhaky, 'Genesis and Development of Māru-Gurjara Temple Architecture', in *Studies in Indian Temple Architecture*, pp. 114–65.

124 Pramod Chandra, *Stone Sculpture in the Allahabad Museum* (Poona: American Institute of Indian Studies, 1970). Pramod Chandra followed Bachhofer at the University of Chicago which helps account for connections between their work. The Art Department at the University of Chicago was a bastion of traditional formalism until the late 1980s.

125 F. M. Asher, *The Art of Eastern India, 300–800* (Minneapolis: University of Minnesota Press, 1980). Other studies of regional traditions of sculpture include S. Huntington, *The 'Pāla-Sena' Schools of Sculpture* (Leiden: E. J. Brill, 1984), and S. Schastok, *The Śāmalājī Sculptures and Sixth Century Art in Western India* (Leiden: E. J. Brill, 1985).

126 G. Jouveau-Dubreuil, *Archéologie du sud de l'Inde*, 2 vols (Paris: Geuthner, 1914), and P. Stern and M. Benisti, *Evolution de style indien d'Amaravati* (Paris: Presses universitaires de France, 1961), are among the earliest works to employ this typological method.

127 Odette Viennot, *Les divinités fluviales Gaṅgā et Yamunā aux portes des sanctuaires de l'Inde* (Paris: Presses universitaires de France, 1964).

128 Viennot, *Temples de l'Inde centrale et occidentale.*

129 George Kubler, *The Shape of Time: Remarks on the History of Things* (New Haven: Yale University Press, 1962): 8–10. For other criticisms, see Heinrich von Stietencron, *Gaṅgā und Yamunā* (Wiesbaden: Otto Harrassowitz, 1972); James Harle in OA 11 (1965): 272–3; Pramod Chandra, 'Study of Indian Temple Architecture', p. 22.

130 Stella Kramrisch, *Indian Sculpture* (London: Oxford University Press, 1933), and Kramrisch, 'Candella Sculpture: Khajurāho', JISOA 1 (1933): 97–104.

131 Kramrisch, *The Hindu Temple*, 2 vols (Calcutta: University of Calcutta, 1946).

Chapter 2

Beginning of a Regional Tradition

The seventh century marks the beginning of sustained building activity in Gopakṣetra and the beginning of a regional tradition of temple architecture. Earlier remains are few and fragmentary, as in many parts of India. The fifth-century brick platform at Pawāyā, for example, has no parallel in the Gwalior region and few demonstrable links to coeval brick structures in the Gangetic plain. The same holds true for sculpture, there being less than twenty pieces from Gopakṣetra that can be placed to any period before the seventh century. A significant transformation takes place shortly after AD 600. Temples were constructed in considerable numbers and enough of these buildings have survived for us to construe a continuous architectural history. While none of the monuments are dated, historical data and comparative material in other parts of India allow for a chronology of some accuracy.

Seventh Century: Early Phase (*c.* AD 600–650)

On the southern fringe of Gopakṣetra, at the source of the River Māhuar, is the village of Mahuā. The ruined houses and temples around this village are all that is left of the ancient town of Madhumatī (map 1). One of the temples at this site is crucial for understanding the development of architecture and sculpture in the first half of the seventh century (pl. 1). Known as the smaller Śiva temple, the shrine is described as a *maṇḍapikā* in the inscription incised on the building.[1] This inscription informs us that one Vatsarāja commissioned the *maṇḍapikā* and that Īśāna Bhaṭṭa of Kānyakubja composed the verses of the eulogy (*praśasti*). While the rulers mentioned in the epigraph are otherwise unknown, Īśāna can be identified and the temple thus dated, a fact hitherto unrecognised. Īśāna of Kānyakubja seems to be the poet Īśāna described by Bāṇa Bhaṭṭa as his contemporary in the *Harṣacarita*.[2] This well-known panegyric recounts the events leading up to Harṣa's accession to the throne of Kannauj (ancient Kānyakubja) in AD 606.

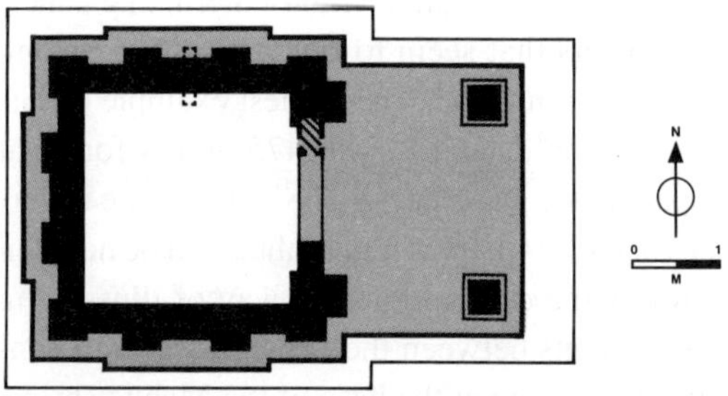

2 Mahuā (Shivpuri), *maṇḍapikā*-shrine dedicated to Śiva, first half of the seventh century

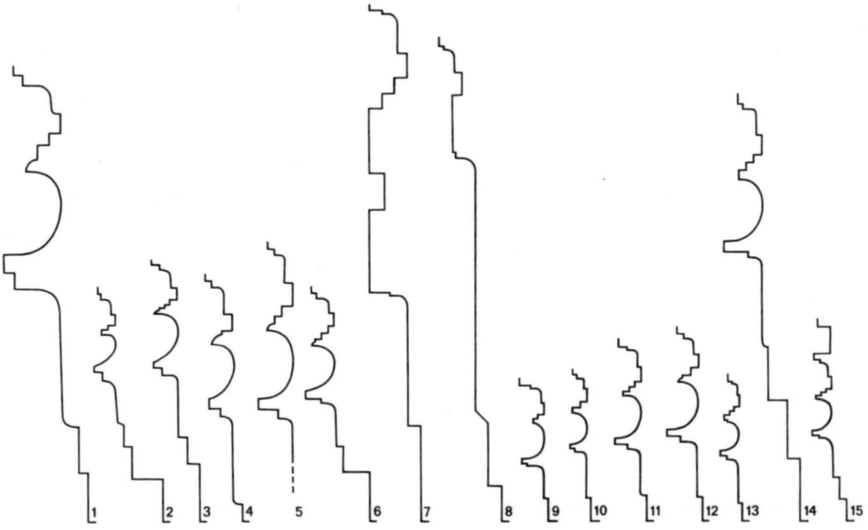

3 Selected *vedībandha* mouldings from across northern India: 1. Rāmgarh (Shāhbād), Muṇḍeśvarī temple; 2. Mahuā (Shivpuri), *maṇḍapikā*-shrine dedicated to Śiva; 3. Mahuā, Śiva temple; 4. Chandravati (Jhālāwār), Śitaleśvar Mahādev temple; 5. Kanswa (Kota), Śiva temple; 6. Gyāraspur (Vidisha), ruined temple near Mānasarovar tank; 7. Gwalior (Gwalior), Telī kā Mandir; 8. Deogarh (Lalitpur), Jaina temple 12; 9. Naresar (Morena), Durgā temple; 10. Naresar, Mātā kā Mandir; 11. Pāroli (Morena), Batesar Mahādev temple; 12. Amrol (Gwalior), Rāmeśvar Mahādev temple; 13. Terāhī (Shivpuri), Śiva temple; 14. Indor (Shivpuri), Gargaj Mahādev temple; 15. Kuchdon (Lalitpur), Maṛhiā Dhār

Giving the same chronological horizon to Īśāna and king Harṣa (r. AD 606–47) places the *maṇḍapikā* in the first half of the seventh century, an estimation that is not contradicted by the epigraphical style of the inscription or the date most commonly suggested for the building.[3]

As the earliest datable building in north India after the fifth century, the *maṇḍapikā* merits close examination. The shrine's most notable feature is the wall section (*jaṅghā*) with its alternating panels and pilasters that seem to imitate post and plank construction in wood. The earliest example of this configuration dates to *c.* AD 475 and is found at Chapāra in the Daśārṇa region.[4] Some of the differences between Chapāra and Mahuā will be noted in the following description as a way of illustrating developments between the fifth and seventh centuries. Beginning at the base of the Mahuā shrine, the podium (*vedībandha*) has the full complement of mouldings (*khura, kumbha, kalaśa* and *kapotālī*). The torus (*kalaśa*), inserted to make the *vedībandha* complete, is given an up-turned profile, an early feature that disappears in the eighth century (see fig. 3.2). The mouldings and the square slabs (*bhiṭṭa*) of the platform run round the whole shrine, organically working the open porch (*mukha-catuṣkī*) into the rest of the structure (fig. 2; pl. 1). In the earlier temples at Chapāra, Sānchī and elsewhere the arrangement is more additive. This development indicates an effort to draw the diverse elements of the temple into a coherent design scheme.

On each side of the sanctum at Mahuā the mouldings (*vedībandha*) are subject to offsets (*bhadra*) which are carried up into the wall, entablature and superstructure. This arrangement continues the precedent of the fifth century. The wall (*jaṅghā*) is constructed like the earlier *maṇḍapikā* at Chapāra and the projecting pilasters are carved with similar discs, tongues and drop-finials.

Simple, heavy brackets are placed on top. This pillar type was often used in the fifth and sixth centuries, but the proportions at Mahuā are more stocky than before. Pillars of identical design are used in the porch (*mukhacatuṣkī*), again emphasising the integration of this element into the rest of the structure.

The recessed panels of the wall differ from Chapāra in that they carry sumptuous floral scrolls and, on the cardinal offsets (*bhadra*), images of Gaṇeśa, Māhiṣāsuramardinī and Varāha. This combination of divinities is unusual by eighth-century standards, when Gaṇeśa, Kārttikeya and Pārvatī became the fixed choice for Śaiva temples in Gopakṣetra and other regions of north India. The style of the Mahuā images, like the iconographic programme, is in a formative stage of development. With their occasional distortion, these sculptures bear the impress of late sixth-century art, but instead of rude ballooning forms, the figures are animated by fresh volume and brooding rhythms. The static repose of earlier work is yielding to ongoing and unresolved movement (pls 3, 4). The scrollwork, which fills the corner panels, is no longer stiff but boils upward with erratic agitation. These qualities are equally present in the decoration of the door and its river goddess figure (pl. 5). At times the sculptor's hand moves with easy confidence, at other times it seems halting and unsure. This unevenness is also seen in the handling of the fanciful creatures on the beam ends of the *vedībandha* and in the carving of the doorway (pl. 5).

The pediments (*udgama*) over the cardinal niches (*rathikā*) continue the formative unevenness of the sculptures and ornaments. On the west and north sides the pediments are of a simple type, consisting of an ogee dormer (*candraśālā*) with wings, foliate finial and a quatrefoil opening (pl. 4). Except for the unusual elephants peeping from each side, these *candraśālā*-dormers show little change from the fifth-century examples at Chapāra, Deogarh and Bhumara. The south wall, however, carries a more elaborate type (pl. 3). A face has been placed in the dormer opening, and below is a depressed barrel vault resting on miniature pillars. The outer edge of this barrel vault overlaps the bottom of the *candraśālā* and shows no structural relationship to it. This formal independence of the two parts indicates a move away from the mimetic replication of wooden prototypes and the beginning of the elaborate interweaving that develops with prominent richness in the eighth and ninth centuries (pl. 41). The specifics of this process, first noted by Coomaraswamy, have been traced by Odette Viennot.[5]

The door of the *maṇḍapikā* shows innovations of equal importance (pls 5, 2). The door surround (*mālāśākhā*) and jambs have assumed the flexible arrangement favoured in later centuries. The degree of change since the sixth century is well illustrated by a door jamb from Sānchī with its cramped carving and stereotyped organisation.[6] In the lintel (*uttarāṅga*) there is a definite tension and imbalance between the forms, quite different from the stately order and balance found earlier at Chapāra and other fifth-century sites. In addition, the little temple models on each side show, for the first time in this part of India, a fully fledged curvilinear superstructure (pl. 2). This type of spire, known as *latina*, can only be achieved by moving beyond the crystalline repetition of fifth-century architectural elements.

Returning to the elevation of the *maṇḍapikā*, the entablature (*varaṇḍikā*) consists of a wide, unadorned recess (*antarapatra*) and a heavy roll-cornice (*kapota*). Two rows of dentils (*nīvrapaṭṭikā*) underpin the cornice. Mirroring the decoration of the *vedībandha*, the cornice carries dormers and a peacock with a rich foliate tail. The superstructure consists of three rough slabs, and a serrated crown (*āmalasāraka*), once the topmost roof member, lies half-buried a short distance away. There are no other fragments of a superstructure. A narrative relief from Nachnā showing a pavilion with finials and a *candraśālā*-dormer gives some idea of the upper parts of flat-roofed buildings between the fifth and seventh centuries.[7]

This detailed analysis of the *maṇḍapikā* at Mahuā allows us to summarise its stylistic significance. The shrine shows a debt to the past in typological terms, but the sculptural and architectural forms are animated by a new vigour and pulsate with inventive restlessness. Uneven as the result seems, an effort has been made to control the independent tension of the parts and integrate them into the design scheme. This anticipates the balanced texture that appears in the temples of the late seventh century and beyond.

The *maṇḍapikā* at Mahuā is one of the few complete buildings datable to the first half of the seventh century. Within the Gopakṣetra region the only other antiquity that can be assigned to this period is a hero-stone from Pāroli (pl. 6). This relatively humble work shows the head of a deceased warrior in a simple *candraśālā*-dormer. Like the sculpture of Mahuā, the face combines a brooding plasticity with tense linear accents. In the lower panel the warrior's last military encounter is illusbatrated. The figures in this scene, even in their battered state, display a heavy modelling similar to the *maṇḍapikā*. The formative iconography of the Pāroli stone is also akin to Mahuā; a more detailed and settled formula is evolved for memorial stones in later centuries (pl. 130).

The stūpa at Rājāpur, a short distance from Mahuā, is another monument that has been placed in the first half of the seventh century (pl. 7). The theory sometimes voiced by local historians is that Buddhism flourished during the time of Harṣa (r. AD 606–47) and therefore the stūpa was probably made at that time. Of itself, the monument cannot substantiate this idea. Called simply the *gol maṭh*, or 'round temple', by people in the vicinity, the stūpa is made of rough slabs and has no sculpture associated with it. The closest parallel is found at Sānchī where several stūpas with square bases and similar hammer-dressed masonry were built between the sixth and seventh century.[8]

Seventh Century: Late Phase (*c.* AD 650–700)

A style of vigorous maturity developed in the second half of the seventh century, radically altering the formative characteristics seen in the Mahuā *maṇḍapikā* and other early remains. The most complete building in this mature style is the Śiva temple at Mahuā.[9] This temple is located in the same village as the *maṇḍapikā* and like that shrine is an important monument for the history of seventh-century architecture (pl. 8).

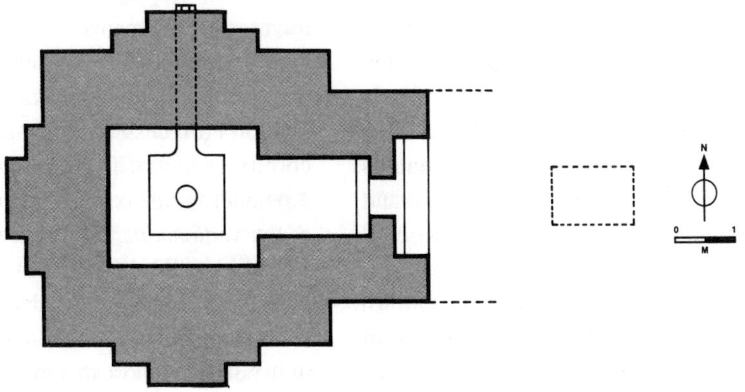

4 Mahuā, Śiva temple, late seventh century

In plan the Śiva temple has three receding faces (*aṅga*) on each side (fig. 4). These are carried up logically from the *vedībandha* into the elevation. In the wall (*jaṅghā*) the faces are further articulated with pilasters and niches. The *vedībandha* rests on two roughly hewn slabs (*bhiṭṭa*); the *praṇāla*, or drain (drawing water from the lustration of the linga inside), pokes through the top *bhiṭṭa* (pl. 8).[10] The mouldings of the *vedībandha* are broad and massive. The *kalaśa* has an up-turned profile and a small concave moulding immediately above it (fig. 3.3). These early features disappear in the eighth century. The dentils (*nīvrapaṭṭikā*) are carved with peacocks and makaras (mythical water creatures) with foliate tails (pl. 10). These sculptures display remarkable richness and clarity beside the fidgety dentil ends of the *maṇḍapikā*-shrine (pls 3, 4).

In the wall section (*jaṅghā*) above the lower mouldings each face is marked off by pilasters of an elaborate order (pl. 9). These carry pots overflowing with flowers and frothy scrollwork, decorative bands with festoons, half-lotus patterns and, in the octagonal sections, flying peacocks holding garlands. The brackets above are carved with palmettes. The pillars are descendants of the type used on the *maṇḍapikā*, but the halting unevenness has been replaced by a resilient balance of parts (pls 9, 1).

The central offsets (*bhadra*) of the Śiva temple carry *rathikā*-niches that project prominently and take the form of miniature blind doors. These are crowned by a triangular pediment (*udgama*) resting on a heavy roll-cornice and a row of lion heads (*siṁhamukha*). The images have been removed from the niches, but the small subsidiary sculptures are preserved, albeit much battered. The figures are heavily cast, but the loose sense of modelling found in the early part of the seventh century has been brought under control. The wide entablature (*varaṇḍikā*) is marked by two cornices (*kapota*) with large dentils (*nīvrapaṭṭikā*). Like the cornices employed on the *rathikā*-niches, this element is not much different from that used on the *maṇḍapikā*, but its overall role in the elevation has been subdued. The recess (*antarapatra*) in the *varaṇḍikā* is strongly marked by simple pilasters and keyhole niches with ogee-shaped tops.

Above the entablature (*varaṇḍikā*) rises the impressive *latina* superstructure, now partly ruined (pl. 8). It logically continues the configuration of the mouldings and wall. Thus the spire corner (*veṇukośa*) springs from the pilaster on the wall corner (*karṇa*), while the subsidiary spire offset (*latā*) springs from the pilaster on the subsidiary wall offset (*pratiratha*). The *latā* repeats the form of the *veṇukośa*, creating what may be described as a 'double *veṇukośa*'. Between the two elements is a deep recess (*salilāntara*) with large aedicules (*bālapañjara*). These features add depth and architectural diversity to the spire. The central spire offset (*madhyalatā*) is covered with a robust mesh of interlocking window motifs (*jāla*). The floor levels (*bhūmi*) of the spire are marked by massive discs (*karṇāṇḍaka*) and by roll-cornices (*kapota*) with large dentils (*nīvrapaṭṭikā*). The cornices echo the *varaṇḍikā* and lend horizontal coherence to the design. The large *āmalasāraka* (serrated crown) sits precariously atop the whole temple. The disc is notable for its bulbous form and powerfully worked flanges; as in other parts of the building, heavy dentils are present.

The temple is placed on a small hill, giving the impression of a high platform. This appears to have been extended on the eastern side to accommodate some form of hall, but no trace of this structure can be found. On the building itself, the east façade and antefix (*śukanāsā*) have collapsed. The temples at Alampur, far to the south on the Tungabhadra, give a general idea of what this side of the building would have been like.[11] The stoutly proportioned door has a T-shape, a type of long-standing popularity (pl. 11). Encircling the whole frame is a voluminously carved door surround (*mālāśākhā*), and within that are a pillar-shaped jamb (*stambha-*

śākhā), a jamb with dancing dwarves (*gaṇaśākhā*) and a floral inner jamb (*pratiśākhā*) carved with lashing vigour. Above in the lintel are flying figures (*vidyādhara*). Large images of Gaṅgā and Yamunā with their attendants occupy the bottom of the jambs. These figures display the same ponderous elegance as the fabric of the superstructure and give the impression of gopis with their imposing volume and fecundity (pl. 12).

This detailed description of the Śiva temple at Mahuā allows us to evaluate its chronological position and stylistic significance. A number of elements are similar to the nearby *maṇḍapikā*, but the way these are used has been changed. The main difference is that the fierce independence of detail has been restrained to create a more ordered and coherent whole. In the *maṇḍapikā* the pilasters, sculptures and mouldings compete for visual dominance; in the Śiva temple the architectural parts are still boldly articulated, but the elements are carefully balanced and orchestrated (pls 1, 8). This difference anticipates the architecture of the eighth and ninth centuries and indicates that the Śiva temple is later in time than the *maṇḍapikā*.

The superstructure of the Śiva temple supports this conclusion. Compared to the models on the *maṇḍapikā* door, the spire has a smoother profile (*rekhā*) and a more masterly juxtaposition of part beside part (pls 8, 2). This difference can be further illuminated by the Lakṣmaṇa temple at Sirpur, which can be assigned, in all probability, to the first quarter of the seventh century.[12] Though geographically removed from Gopakṣetra, the Lakṣmaṇa merits comparison to the Śiva temple as it has the only complete *latina* superstructure that is earlier in date. Some key differences between the two buildings may be briefly noted. In the Lakṣmaṇa the elements of the spire are not strongly tied together. For example, the massive discs (*karṇāṇḍaka*) in the spire corners (*veṇukośa*) indicate the floor levels (*bhūmi*), but the subsidiary offset (*latā*) follows an unrelated scheme. In contrast, the *latā* and *veṇukośa* of the Śiva temple have matching designs and are tied together with broad cornices (*kapota*). This, coupled with similar *kapota*-mouldings elsewhere, produces a more integrated appearance. The central spire offset (*madhyalatā*) adds to this sense of order. In the Lakṣmaṇa the *madhyalatā* is made of superimposed arches with little relation to the floor levels (*bhūmi*); in contrast, the *madhyalatā* of the Śiva temple has become a robust mesh (*jāla*), and the slabs (*kalā*) on which that mesh is placed are the same as those in other parts of the spire. This treatment produces horizontal coherence. Vertical coherence in the Śiva temple is produced by placing convincing supports, in the form of pilasters, below each part of the superstructure. In addition, the *madhyalatā* seems to be a logical extension of the projection (*bhadra*) and pediment (*udgama*) of the wall niche. In the Lakṣmaṇa this sense of support is absent. The walls are heavily worked with *candraśālā*-dormers and other prominent ornaments, and the delicate entablature (*varaṇḍikā*) with its chequer pattern and small cornices seems on the verge of being crushed by the massive superstructure above. These points of difference demonstrate that the rugged configuration of the Lakṣmaṇa (similar in some ways to the *maṇḍapikā* at Mahuā) has been superseded in the Śiva temple by an organised sureness and vital vision of the whole. The change is a harbinger of temple forms in the eighth and ninth centuries and clearly shows that the Śiva temple can be placed after the Lakṣmaṇa in time.

The sculpture of the Śiva temple also points to a date in the latter part of the seventh century. The river goddesses on the door are animated by a sensuous heaviness and vigour, with none of the distortion and uneasy movement seen in the *maṇḍapikā* (pls 12, 3, 4). The floral scrolls have become a frothy, lashing spray and no longer boil with erratic agitation (pls 11, 3). The uneven formal texture present in the first part of the seventh century has been replaced by a sense of clarity, control and wonderful confidence. This stylistic change again foreshadows the future and indicates that the Śiva temple is later than the *maṇḍapikā*. While a general date sometime after the mid-seventh century is thus provided, the further chronological limits can only be set by expanding our corpus of seventh-century material.

The images from the cardinal niches of the Śiva temple have been destroyed, but examples from other sites give an idea of their appearance. The closest cognate is at Deogarh. Inside the hill-fort is a ruined temple dedicated to Viṣṇu's incarnation as Varāha.[13] The main image there has the substantial cast of the river goddesses at Mahuā; this is shown by such details as the sensuous modulations of the limbs, the heavy hands and the ponderously rendered female figure (pl. 13). In the Varāha the rolling power of the torso and limbs are conceived with great sureness and conviction, infusing the image with heroic and unshakeable strength. The same massive sense of volume is found in a figure of Ambikā from Gyāraspur (pl. 14).[14]

These sculptures can be dated by remains at Indragarh, a site in the northern part of the Avanti region. Indragarh is a total ruin and had yielded a variety of items spanning four centuries. Of value for the present concern is a long inscription recording the foundation of a Śiva temple in VS 767/AD 710–11.[15] The epigraph is cut on a slab of buff-coloured sandstone and several images and architectural fragments in the same material may be taken as early eighth-century products. The best preserved is the Gajalakṣmī kept in the Central Museum, Indore (pl. 15). The goddess is shown seated on a lotus which springs from the waters where joyous serpent divinities (*nāga*) stand in rapt attendance. Above, clustered about the nimbus, is a herd of elephants lustrating the goddess. All the forms strike a careful balance between rich modelling and dancing linearism. The details are carefully chiselled but not to the detriment of the plastic sense. A date in the early part of the eighth century for the image is borne out by the few fragmentary figures at Kanswa that belong with an inscription of MS 795/AD 738–9.[16] These images show a tighter treatment of form and more linear outlines.

Parallels to the Gajalakṣmī can be found in Rājasthān, but, rather than developing a chronology there, we may return directly to material of immediate concern. The Ambikā from Gyāraspur provides the closest comparison (pls 14, 15). The full modelling, particularly in the face, shows that these two sculptures are not far removed from each other in time. The Ambikā, however, is more ponderously worked and lacks the restraint and rhythm seen in the Gajalakṣmī. This implies that the Ambikā must be placed before *c.* AD 710: a date somewhere in the latter part of the seventh century seems probable. These observations allow us to come full-circle to the Varāha at Deogarh and, finally, the Śiva temple at Mahuā. They too must be placed sometime in the late seventh century.

The foregoing comparisons, though somewhat complex, provide a reasonably secure date for the Śiva temple at Mahuā. Before leaving this question, we may briefly note the temples at Alampur. The buildings at this site were completed towards the end of the seventh century, as the wall enclosing the precinct is dated AD 713.[17] Caution must be exercised in using this material because of its distance from Gopakṣetra; in addition, Alampur seems removed from its northern prototypes as the sculpture shows accommodation to the indigenous traditions of the south. Still, with these buildings dated before AD 713, it is difficult to place the Śiva temple at Mahuā to any other time than the late seventh century.

Summary

This chapter charted the development of architecture and sculpture in Gopakṣetra from AD 600 to 700. There is little question that this century was marked by changes of fundamental importance; at one end were the last residues of the great fifth-century tradition, at the other a mature and revitalised style resting on entirely new principles. Developments during the first half of the seventh century (the 'early phase') were characterised by the *maṇḍapikā*-shrine at Mahuā (pl. 1). The architecture and sculpture of the shrine, while related to the rugged forms of the late sixth century, exhibited a brooding plasticity and vigorous independence of detail. In the second half of the seventh century (the 'late phase') the uneven qualities of earlier work were restrained and ordered in a creative flowering of startling force. The Śiva temple at Mahuā and the Varāha at Deogarh exemplified the maturity and breadth of vision found in this period (pls 8, 13). The images and architectural forms bristled with astonishing vitality and power, while the decorative scrollwork was brought to an exuberant and frothy boil (pl. 11). With these qualities we left behind the legacy of the fifth century and entered a new formal order, in which stately calm and lyrical repetition were superseded by dynamic tension and rhythmic complexity. This was a crucial turning point and the beginning of a new dispensation in the art of India.

Notes

1 Patil, *Descriptive and Classified List*, no. 944. For the epigraph, see *Inscriptions of Gopakṣetra*, p. 114. In S. Sankaranarayanan and G. Bhattacharya, 'Mahua Inscription of Vatsarāja', EI 37 (1967–8): 53–5, the authors have confused Krishna Deva's description of the larger Śiva temple at Mahuā with the *maṇḍapikā* and this has garbled their arguments; see Krishna Deva, *Temples of North India*, p. 16. The term *maṇḍapikā* commonly refers to customs-houses (D. C. Sircar, *Indian Epigraphical Glossary* [Delhi: Motilal Banarsidass, 1966], s.v. 'maṇḍapikā'). In addition to references given by Sircar, see EI 5 (1898–9): 210, n. 3.

2 P. V. Kane, ed., *The Harṣacharita of Bāṇa* (Bombay, 1918): 89. For additional discussion of Īśāna, see V. S. Agrawala, *The Deeds of Harṣa; being a Cultural Study of Bāṇa's Harshacarita* (Vārānasī: Prithivi Prakashan, 1969), p. 34. The identification of the Īśāna in the Mahuā inscription with the Īśāna known from literature was first proposed in my 'Brick Temple at Kherahat', in *Gvāliyar darśan*, p. 332.

3 Krishna Deva, *Temples of North India*, p. 16; M. Meister, 'Construction and Conception: Maṇḍapikā Shrines of Central India', *East and West* 26 (1976): 409–18.

4 *Encyclopaedia of Indian Temple Architecture: North India, Foundations of North Indian Style, c. 250 B.C. – A.D. 1100*, ed. M. Meister, M. A. Dhaky and Krishna Deva (Princeton: University Press and Delhi: American Institute of Indian Studies, 1988), figs 267–9.

5 Ananda Coomaraswamy, 'Early Indian Architecture: III. Palaces', *Eastern Art* 3 (1931): 199–205. Viennot, *Temples de l'Inde centrale et occidentale.*

6 John Marshall and Alfred Foucher, *The Monuments of Sanchi*, 3 vols (London: Probsthain, 1940), vol. 3, pl. 127(e).

7 J. G. Williams, *The Art of Gupta India: Empire and Province* (Princeton: University Press, 1982), pl. 170.

8 Debala Mitra, *Sanchi* (Delhi: Archaeological Survey of India, 1973). Stūpa 7, 12, 13, 14 and 16 are assigned to the sixth or seventh century; stūpa 6 is older but received a new casing and square base in the sixth or seventh century.

9 Patil, *Descriptive and Classified List*, no. 945.

10 M. A. Dhaky, 'The "Praṇāla" in Indian, South-Asian and South-East Asian Sacred Architecture', in *Rūpa Pratirūpa: Alice Boner Commemoration Volume*, ed. Bettina Bäumer (Delhi: Biblia Impex, 1982), 119–66.

11 B. R. Prasad, 'Temples of the Latina Form at Alampur', JISOA 5 (1972–3): 53–75; P. R. Ramachandra Rao, *Alampur* (Hyderabad: Akhara, 1977).

12 For the Lakṣmaṇa temple inscription, see EI 11 (1911–12): 184–201; EI 27 (1947–8): 319–25; and EI 35 (1955): 60–65. For illustrations and a summary of views regarding the temple's date, see Williams, *Art of Gupta India*, p. 160, also *Encyclopaedia of Indian Temple Architecture*, figs 464–5.

13 P. C. Mukherjee, *Report on the Antiquities in the District of Lalitpur, N. W. Provinces, India* (Roorkee: Tamason Engineering College, 1899), pls 2 and 25 (showing subsidiary figures intact). The Varāha temple is in ruins and is of a later date than the main image discussed here. N. R. Banerjee, 'New Light on the Gupta Temples at Deogarh', JAS 5 (1963): 37–49 gives an account of the temple but his attempt to date it to the Gupta period is misguided.

14 Thakore, *Catalogue of Sculptures in the Archaeological Museum, Gwalior*, room 10, no. 20.

15 EI 32 (1957–8): 112–17. The inscription is now in the Central Museum, Indore.

16 IA 19 (1890): 55–62; Meister, 'Forest and Cave: Temples at Candrabhāgā and Kansuan', AAA 24 (1981): 56–73.

17 EI 35 (1963–4): 121–4.

Chapter 3

Regional Architecture in Maturity

Surviving monuments and inscriptions indicate that there was a substantial increase in temple building during the eighth century. While construction took place throughout northern India, in Gopakṣetra an especially large number of temples have been preserved. Ranging from simple shrines to the largest structures built in north India at the time, these temples represent the culmination of the regional tradition before it was absorbed into the more homogeneous architectural style that appeared in the ninth century. Although dated material is scarce, three phases between AD 700 and 800 emerge with clarity and are termed here 'early', 'middle' and 'late'.

Eighth Century: Early Phase (*c.* AD 700–735)

A standing goddess from Kota is an appropriate place to begin an outline of early eighth-century sculpture and architecture (pl. 16).[1] This image is a form of Brāhmī to judge from the rosary, pot and lotus that she holds. The goddess retains the heavy modelling of the late seventh century, especially in the arms and face. Compared to Mahuā, however, there is a clearer definition of outline and a linear crispness in the ornaments (pl. 12). The opulent modulations of surface have also been toned down and the heavy volume of the drapery significantly reduced. Also belonging to the early eighth century is a sculpture of Gaṇeśa recovered from Gaṅgola Tāl on Gwalior Fort (pl. 17).[2] In this little masterpiece there is a careful balance between fullness of form and tension of surface. The body retains its plasticity and the ornaments their richness, but compared to seventh-century sculpture both have been quietly subdued.

The difference between sculptures from Gwalior and the surrounding countryside is illustrated by a linga at Bārāhet (pl. 18).[3] The Gaṇeśa is identical to the Gaṅgola Tāl example but more ruggedly executed. The trunk and body have a decidedly angular outline, but the same plasticity and tension of surface informs both images. That this is a difference in level of production rather than date is shown by the other figures on the linga (pl. 19). These have the less opulent modelling just discussed. In addition, the attendant figures have a clumsy construction like those on the stele from Kota (pl. 16).

The village of Bārāhet rests on a high mound untouched by excavation. Assorted ruined temples are found in the vicinity, but the only piece belonging to the early eighth century seems to be a fragment bearing a *candraśālā* which apparently formed part of a temple superstructure (pl. 20).

Other early eighth-century architectural fragments have been recovered on Gwalior Fort. One of the finest was once part of a *rathikā*-niche, as can be seen by comparing it to the Śiva temple, Mahuā (pls 21, 10). The overflowing-pot motif used in the Gwalior fragment is close to Mahuā in design, but it shows a lighter and more restrained treatment of form. A number of pillars in the Archaeological Museum, Gwalior, also belong to the early eighth century (pl. 22). Again these are related to Mahuā but display flatter and more precisely chiselled surfaces. These fragments show there were several significant temples built on Gwalior Fort at this time.

The objects examined so far allow us to evaluate the temple at Dāng (pl. 23). Like the Bārāhet linga, this temple is removed from Gwalior Fort and other important centres in the region. It is, consequently, best understood as a relatively humble production. This explains such oddities as the tops of the pediments (*udgama*), which are shown as incised lines on the entablature (pl. 26). Despite such features, the temple merits scrutiny as the only surviving building of the early eighth century.

The temple is dedicated to Śiva and rests on a low slab (*bhiṭṭa*), a common feature of eighth-century temples in Gopakṣetra. The illusion of a high platform has been created by erosion which has exposed the foundation. The temple's plan shows three receding faces (*aṅga*) on three sides and a small porch (*prāggrīva*) projecting to the east

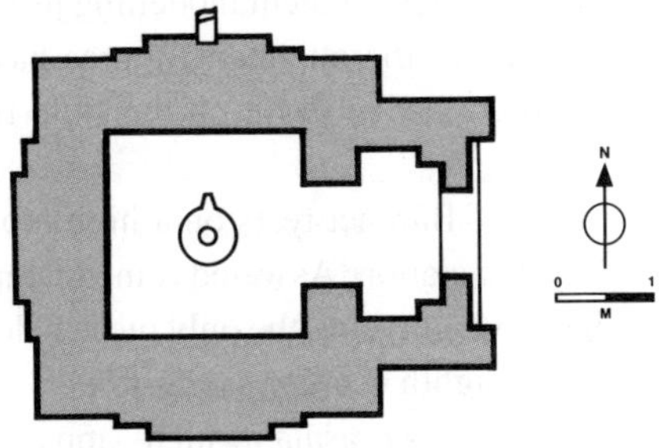

5 Dāng (Bhind), Śiva temple, early eighth century

(fig. 5). The massive *vedībandha* is relieved by dentils (*nīvrapaṭṭikā*) decorated with scrolls, diamond patterns and symmetrically disposed flowers. The diversity of motifs in some ways recalls seventh-century buildings, but the carving is flatter and more precisely rendered. The top moulding (*kapotālī*) carries *candraśālā*-dormers and randomly placed scrolls and peacocks with foliate tails (pl. 24). Beside contemporary pieces from Gwalior Fort this work is somewhat cramped and rugged in character (pl. 21).

The wall section (*jaṅghā*), constructed of large blocks of stone, has offsets (*bhadra*) on each side with *rathikā*-niches in the form of small blind doors (pl. 23). This type of niche was seen earlier at Mahuā (pl. 8). Around the inside of each niche is a floral jamb (*pratiśākhā*) surrounded by an astragal and a laborious lotus moulding. A row of lion heads (*siṁhamukha*) runs across the top. The pediments (*udgama*) are heavily rendered and clearly show the small supporting pillars inside each arch. This again recalls seventh-century work, but the playful sumptuousness seen earlier is lacking. As already noted, the tops of the pediments project into the cornice where they are shown with incised lines. Other notable features include the lotus flowers that sprout from each side of the pediments. While this is found in eighth-century temples at Osiān, the sole comparison in Gopakṣetra are the elephants that peep from behind the pediments of the *maṇḍapikā*-shrine at Mahuā (pl. 3). Enshrined in the cardinal niches are images of Gaṇeśa, Kārttikeya and Pārvatī. The Gaṇeśa (pl. 26) is carved with the same plasticity and tension of surface as the Bārāhet linga (pl. 18). The construction of the figure is additive and imbued with a dancing movement that tends to break down the integrity of the form.

The subsidiary offsets of the wall (*pratiratha*) are narrow and completely taken up by attached columns (pl. 23). This continues the practice of articulating the wall surface with pilasters as seen at Mahuā (pl. 9). However, the role of the pilasters at Dāng has been significantly reduced, a treatment that points toward the eventual elimination of this feature in some buildings (pl. 71). Like the decorations of the *vedībandha*, the *pratiratha* pilasters have a fascinating variety of detail, each with a different bracket, decorative panel and bird perched on the overflowing pot. This variety would seem to be a throw-back to the seventh century, were not all the pieces firmly sublimated to the overarching architectural scheme. The scrollwork and other elements have lost their frothy exuberance to a more precisely chiselled surface where light and dark are accentuated rather than the overall sense of plastic volume.

The corner sections (*karṇa*) carry framed niches with guardians of the directions (*dikpāla*). Similar niches on the wall of the porch (*prāggrīva*; pl. 24) contain figures that show subdued modulations in the treatment of the flesh and broad sweeping forms as found on the Bārāhet linga (pl. 19). The *rathikā*-niches have a robust pediment (*udgama*) resting on a heavy lotus moulding, richly carved dentils and a *kapota*-cornice. The floral decorations on the dentils and *rathikā* pilasters are flat and have a frilly edge with incised lines and drilled holes. This is similar to the fragments on Gwalior fort, but at Dāng the execution is much simpler.

The wall section (*jaṅghā*) is topped by a *śiraḥpaṭṭī*, a running festoon of pearls, bells and flowers. Over this is the entablature (*varaṇḍikā*). Only a single *kapota*-cornice remains, except on the east side where the broad recess (*antarapatra*) is filled with miniature pillars and niches with ogee-shaped tops; this configuration was seen earlier in the Śiva temple at Mahuā (pl. 8). The spire, a later replacement in brick, calls for no comment except for three panels on the east side (pl. 27). These seem to have come from other buildings of the same period that have disappeared. The Kārttikeya is well preserved and in the same style as the sculptures on the temple. More interesting from an iconographical standpoint are the scenes from the life of Lord Kṛṣṇa. The pediments on these panels continue the rustic quality of the temple proper; in the panel carrying a serpent divinity (*nāga*) the single miniature pillar supporting the lower arch of the *candraśālā* has the naiveté often found in folk art.

The door frame has been repeatedly whitewashed and all the sculptures are badly worn (pl. 25). From what can be seen of the dancing figures at the top of the *mithunaśākhā*, or 'amorous couple jamb', it seems they have the same characteristics as other early eighth-century work. More generally, this door shows a suppression of sculptural texture compared to late seventh-century examples (pl. 11). Emphasis is now placed on architectural simplicity – the river goddesses are contained in panels and reduced in scale; there is also a distinct stress on architectural parts rather than rippling ornamentation. This is most apparent in the lintel (*uttarāṅga*) with its prominent lotus moulding, cumbersome *candraśālā* and large aedicules on the top of the pillar jamb (*stambhaśākhā*).

The aedicules on the door call for comment because they indicate the possible appearance of the original superstructure. They do not seem to be the usual *latina*, as found on most eighth-century temples, but a type known as *phāṁsanā*. This form of spire is made of horizontal slabs stacked one above the other. Usually the *phāṁsanā* was placed on temple entrance halls, but sporadically it also appears over the main sanctum. Models suggest this use from as early as the fifth century and complete examples, dating from the ninth to the thirteenth centuries, are found at Badoh, Naresar, Khojra, Deoguna and elsewhere.[4] The aedicules at Dāng indicate the use of the *phāṁsanā* in the eighth century and remind us that the history of Indian temple forms is often fragmentary.

While considering the Dāng doorway, we may note that it does not have the usual T-shape. This might be interpreted as an early attempt to eliminate this configuration, but it is actually the result of making the *mithunaśākhā* the outermost jamb and omitting the door surround (*mālāśākhā*). Because the T-shape is not actually discarded until the tenth century, what we see at Dāng is best understood as a form of rustic shorthand. This explanation is supported by the perfunctory door sill (*udambara*) and the other rugged features, such as the *udgama*-pediments already noted.

Finally, we may note the features of the temple interior. The vestibule has been partially rebuilt, particularly the roof. The sanctum (*garbhagṛha*) contains a linga and is quite plain except for the ceiling. A lotus moulding supports slabs set diagonally to create a diamond-shaped coffer; inside the coffer is a lotus flower.

The Śiva temple at Dāng prompts a brief consideration of regional styles and their character. As we have seen, the prevalent style of any given period was often found at a number of sites in Gopakṣetra. Cognates could also be located in neighbouring provinces, and such examples as necessary for this regional history have already been noted. Dāng adds a further dimension to this picture. The temple displays a style of the early eighth century, but it is removed from the main centres and somewhat rustic in character.[5] To simply call this 'provincial' is not adequate because humble and fine workmanship was often produced at the same site. Differences are not strictly geographical but involve levels of production and patronage. For this reason the terms 'regional' and 'sub-regional' are preferred here. As the eighth century progresses, sub-regional idioms become especially evident. There was some hint of the phenomena in earlier periods, but the extensive corpus of eighth-century temples in Gopakṣetra clearly document sub-regionalism for the first time. As we shall see, this terminology continues to be of use into the ninth century.

The chronology of the temples and sculptures so far discussed is fixed in an approximate way by remains in the Avanti region. Indragarh and the various images that can be linked to an inscription of VS 767/AD 710–11 have already been mentioned.[6] Returning to the Gajalakṣmī, we find a careful balance between rich modelling and taut dancing rhythms that is analogous to the goddess from Kota (pls 15, 16). The figures in the pedestal of the Gajalakṣmī may be compared to the Sūrya and Viṣṇu on the Bārāhet linga for their simple yet masterful treatment of surface (pls 15, 19). Also of some use in dating is the ruined temple at Kanswa near Kota, securely fixed by an inscription to MS 795/AD 738–9.[7] The sculptures there show a tighter and more controlled sense of form and thus confirm our chronology of the early eighth century.

Eighth Century: Middle Phase (*c.* AD 735–65)

Many temples and sculptures have come down to us from the middle decades of the eighth century. This quantity of material makes for an increasingly rich and complex architectural history. The range of workmanship, from humble to fine, gives the impression of a baffling variety of styles, but this is readily understood as a manifestation of regionalism and sub-regionalism.

The temples in the gorge at Naresar (ancient Naleśvara) serve as a convenient point of entry into the architecture and sculpture of the mid-eighth century. Six temples of Śaiva dedication were built there, and from their general similarity it appears that they were all constructed within a few years of each other (fig. 6; pl. 28).[8] As a group, these buildings are critical for illustrating how the sub-regional style of Gopakṣetra developed after the Śiva temple at Dāng. We may begin with the temple carrying a label recording its dedication to '*śrī bhītuprene*[*śvaradeva*]'.[9] The most striking difference between Dāng and the Bhītupreneśvara is the decisive reduction in the richness and variety of detail (figs 7, 5; pls 29, 23). The *vedībandha* is

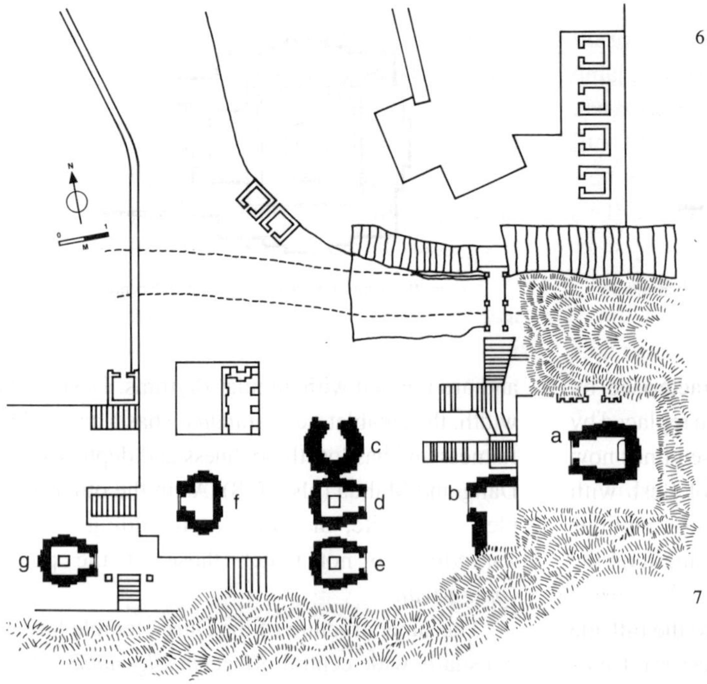

6 Naresar (Morena), site map showing location of temples: (a) Durgā, (b) Śītaleśvaradevī, (c) twelfth-century temple, (d) Krakoṭakeśvara, (e) Bhītupreneśvara, (f) Mātā kā Mandir, (g) Śiva

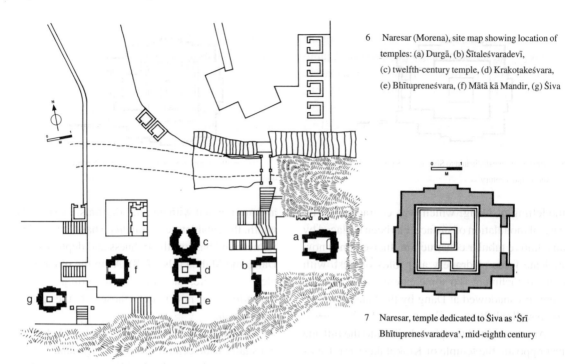

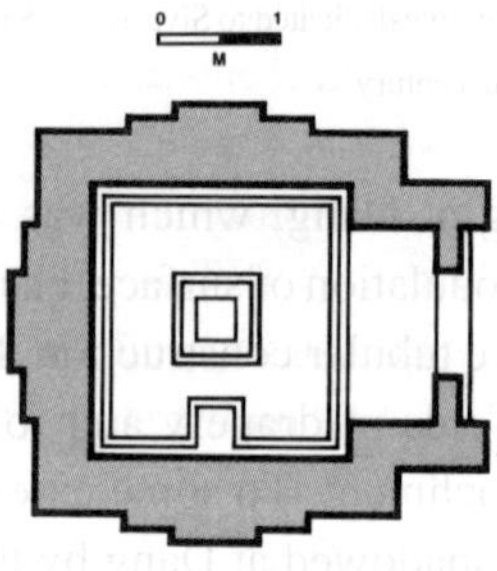

7 Naresar, temple dedicated to Śiva as 'Śrī Bhītupreneśvaradeva', mid-eighth century

compressed and no longer adorned with different floral scrolls and birds. The *candraśālā*-dormers and dentils (*nīvrapaṭṭikā*) that do appear are left flat or are incised in a simple manner. In the wall the subsidiary offset (*pratiratha*) is still treated as a pilaster, but the details have been regularised. The *rathikā*-niches in the main offsets (*bhadra*) follow the design of the simpler subsidiary niches at Dāng, but again the variety of motifs has been reduced (pls 30, 23). In the entablature (*varaṇḍikā*) the roll-cornices (*kapota*) are less massive, and the recess (*antarapatra*) with miniature pilasters and ogee arches has been omitted. In a similar manner, the entrance door at Naresar shows a significant reduction in the role of sculpture (pls 31, 25). The more architectonic treatment is heightened by flat, starkly worked floral scrolls and other details.

Immediately beside the Bhītupreneśvara is a second temple carrying a dedicatory label that reads '*śrī krakoṭakeśva*[*ra*]*deva*' (fig. 8; pl. 32). Although this temple is similar to its neighbour, some of the differences between the two buildings may be noted to illustrate the scope of design in the Naresar temples. In the wall section (*jaṅghā*) the pilaster in the subsidiary offset (*pratiratha*) has been eliminated, and the elaborate running festoon (*śiraḥpaṭṭī*) is interrupted by the door frame (pl. 33). The bulky spire is the same except for the antefix (*śukanāsā*). Here the *candraśālā*-dormer is larger and the depressed barrel vault has been replaced by a single slab of stone. The doors of the two temples have a generic similarity, but in the Krakoṭakeśvara the lintel (*uttarāṅga*) is simplified. The sculptures of both buildings vary slightly in iconography but are executed in an identical style.[10]

On a platform below the Bhītupreneśvara and Krakoṭakeśvara is a third temple. Although it lacks an inscribed label, the standard iconographic programme of Gaṇeśa, Kārttikeya and Pārvatī shows it was a Śaiva dedication. The building is in the same style as those discussed, but only one side is well preserved (fig. 9; pl. 34). The images on the door show the same sort of reduction we have noted in the architectural forms at Naresar.[11] The full-bodied

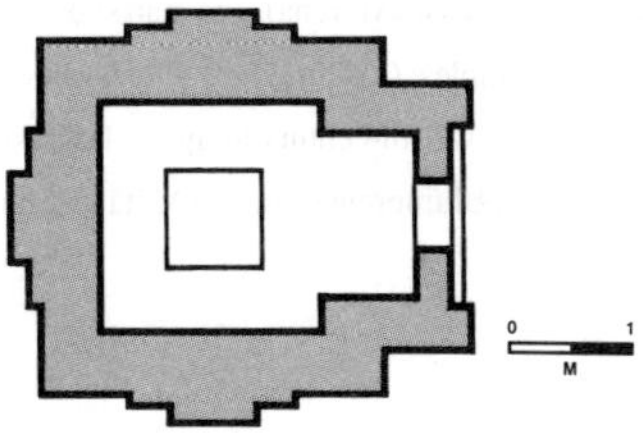

8 Naresar, temple dedicated to Śiva as 'Śrī Krakoṭakeśva[ra]deva', mid-eighth century

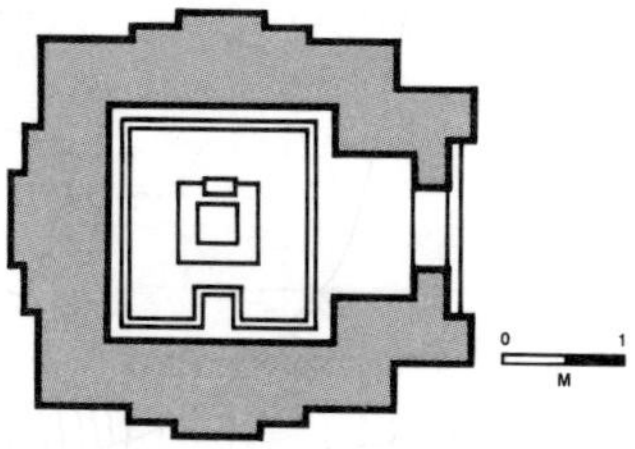

9 Naresar, Śiva temple, mid-eighth century

modelling at Dāng, which was characterised by careful modulation of surface, has been replaced by an additive tubular construction. Incised lines now indicate folds of drapery and folds of flesh with equal detachment. To some extent these qualities were foreshadowed at Dāng by the Gaṇeśa on the south wall (pl. 26).

Another ruined temple is built onto the hillside just opposite the temple of Krakoṭakeśvara. Dedicated nowadays to Śītaleśvaradevī, the shrine was evidently constructed to shelter a cave that serves as the sanctum. The rugged doorway to the cave is probably the lowest common denominator of subregionalism during the mid-eighth century (pl. 35). On a stone slab used in the construction of the shrine is an inscription in characters of about the ninth century recording a donation of land (pl. 36).

On higher ground above the temples just described is a small platform cut out of the hillside. The main temple of Naresar is situated there (figs 6, 10; pl. 37). This building was dedicated to Durgā, as can be seen from a relief of Siṁhavāhinī in the antefix (*śukanāsā*) and a large broken image of Māhiṣāsuramardinī in the sanctum. Like the other buildings at Naresar, the Durgā temple shows advances over the Śiva temple at Dāng. The *vedībandha* is compressed, the wall is simple and the variety of architectural ornament reduced. The result is a starker and more architectonic surface. The same holds true for the doorway, with its austere design and simply modelled sculpture (pl. 38). The images have an ungainly tubular construction and are imbued with angular rhythms. Despite its width, the entablature (*varaṇḍikā*) has a controlled flatness and has lost the richness and depth seen at Dāng and Mahuā (pls 37, 8). As in the other temples at the site, the complex mouldings of the *varaṇḍikā* do not match those of the porch (*prāggrīva*).

The superstructure of the Durgā temple has an unusually wide central offset (*madhyalatā*), a feature also seen in the other buildings at Naresar. This configuration is due to the fact that both the mouldings and the complete wall section (*maṇḍovara*) have three receding faces (*aṅga*) while the spire itself has only two. This accounts for the disproportionate broadness of the *madhyalatā*. Considering both earlier and later buildings in Gopakṣetra, this seems to be a quirk of the craftsmen who made these temples and not any special indicator of date.

The superstructures of the Naresar temples, and that of the Durgā temple in particular, warrant com-

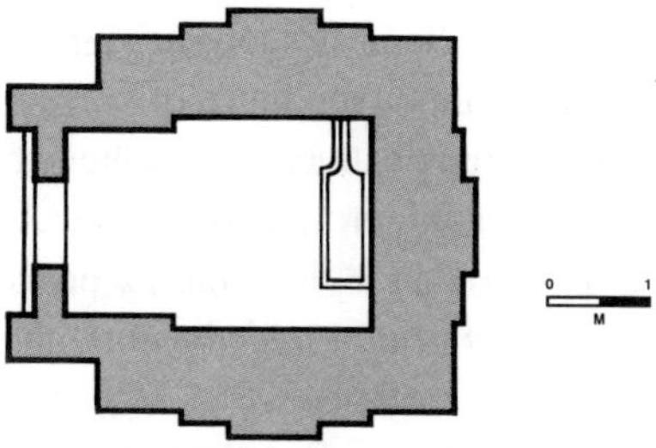

10 Naresar, Durgā temple, mid-eighth century

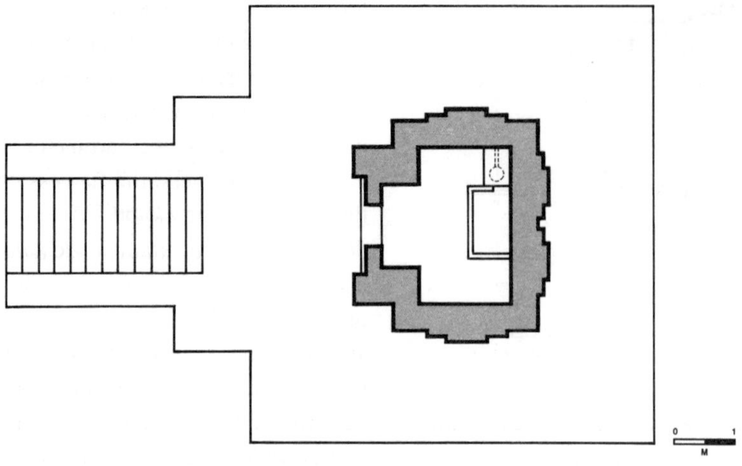

11 Naresar, Mātā kā Mandir, mid-eighth century

parison to the Śiva temple at Mahuā. This is because a comparison between Mahuā and Naresar (making due allowance for the level of production) summarises what happened to the *latina* form between the late seventh and mid-eighth century. The differences are considerable (pls 37, 8). At Naresar the whole fabric of the superstructure has assumed a chaste texture. The corner discs in the spire (*karṇāṇḍaka*) are compressed and the intervening slabs (*kalā*) are less prominent. The mesh pattern (*jāla*) laid on the *kalā*-slabs and on the central offset (*madhyalatā*) is flatter and more intricate (pls 41, 8, 26). The aedicules (*bālapañjara*) in the vertical recess (*salilāntara*) also play a less significant visual role. Finally, the serrated crown (*āmalasāraka*) is proportionately smaller and treated in a less bulbous way, though caution must be exercised regarding this element because the top of the Durgā temple has been rebuilt and the *āmalasāraka* may not be original. A larger *āmalasāraka*, also an eighth-century product, lies on the lower platform beside one of the later temples (pl. 28).

Directly beside the Durgā temple is a niche flanked by pillars and pierced screens (*jālī*). Inside the niche is a slab resting on miniature pillars, while at the extreme ends are *rathikā*-niches like those on the temples (pl. 42). This construction served as an elaborate seat, to judge from later buildings with balconies and parapets (*kakṣāsana*). It is the earliest known example of this architectural type.

The only other eighth-century building at Naresar is the temple known as Mātā kā Mandir (mother-goddess temple). This building has a rectangular plan (fig. 11), a type developed for rectangular idols such as a reclining goddess, a row of Mātṛkā figures or Śeṣanārāyaṇa. The sanctum is empty now, but a number of seated goddesses dating to the twelfth century were collected at Naresar and attest to the prevalence of goddess-worship there.[12] The elevation of the Mātā kā Mandir is similar to the other temples at the site, the short sides (*pakṣabhadra*) each having a single offset and niche (pl. 43). The long back wall (*pṛṣṭabhadra*) accommodates a pair of offsets and niches of the same design. As is common with rectangular buildings, the roof has a *valabhī* or barrel-vaulted shape. This is underpinned with one storey (*bhūmi*) of the *latina* type of superstructure, creating what is known in architectural manuals as a

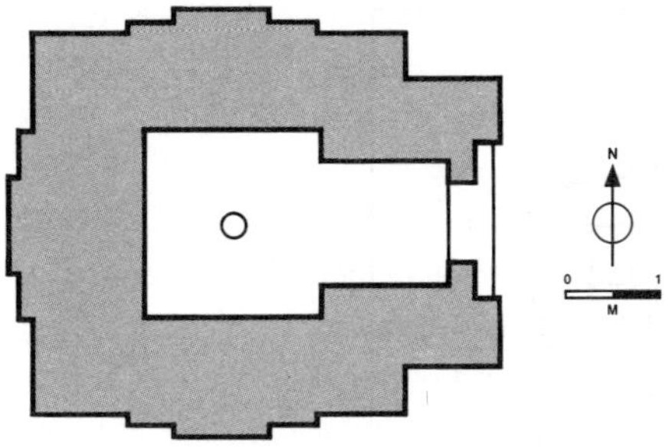

12 Amrol (Gwalior), Rāmeśvar Mahādev temple, mid-eighth century

miśraka, or mixed mode. Other temples of this class are known, the most famous being the Telī kā Mandir on Gwalior Fort (pl. 84). The *valabhī* was used all over India when a temple had to be made for a rectangular type of image.

The Mātā kā Mandir shares many stylistic features with the other Naresar temples but is more finely executed. Thus while the doorway of the Mātā kā Mandir is almost identical to the Durgā temple in configuration, it shows a more accomplished hand at work in the carving of sculpture (pls 44, 38). Architectural elements, such as the pediments, are also less rugged and given to elaboration. Lastly, the wide entablature (*varaṇḍikā*) is carefully worked in to the elevation but, as in all the Naresar temples, it still stops abruptly where it meets the porch (*prāggrīva*).

From the sub-regional style of the various temples at Naresar, it is a considerable jump to the Rāmeśvar Mahādev at Amrol (ancient Āmardaka).[13] This temple exhibits a fine level of workmanship without immediate parallel. Close examination shows, however, that it belongs in the middle part of the eighth century. Beginning with the plan, we see that the temple, like those at Naresar, has three receding faces (*aṅga*) and a narrow porch (*prāggrīva*) on the eastern side (fig. 12). The *vedībandha* mouldings retain something of the massiveness of the early eighth century; note especially the concave moulding directly above the torus (*kalaśa* ; fig. 3.12). Although this is an early feature, often favoured in the seventh century, the mouldings are otherwise treated in the standard mid-eighth-century way. Detail is everywhere suppressed, such as in the perfunctory handling of the *candraśālā*-dormers, the flatness of the scrolls on the top moulding (*kapotālī*) and the omission of dentil ends (*nīvrapaṭṭikā*) in the *kalaśa* (pl. 46). This is quite different from the sumptuous flourish seen in the early eighth-century temple at Dāng (pl. 24). The wall section (*jaṅghā*) shows the same kind of reduction and simplification. Certainly the blunt austerity of Naresar is not seen in the variety of the pediments (*udgama*), but the fussy plasticity and enrichment at Dāng (in such things as the detailing round the *rathikā*-niches) has completely disappeared (pls 47, 24). In the subsidiary wall offset (*pratiratha*) the absence of pilasters adds to the stark simplicity of surface.

The sculptures in the *rathikā*-niches at Amrol follow the usual eighth-century programme, that is Gaṇeśa, Kārttikeya and Pārvatī. The subsidiary niches contain Śiva's attendants (*gaṇa*), while guardians of the directions (*dikpāla*) are found in the niches of the porch (*prāggrīva*). Most of the images are sadly damaged, but enough is left of the Īśāna on the north side to see that it displays the subdued modelling of the mid-eighth century (pl. 50). Beside early eighth-century work, like the linga at Bārāhet (pl. 19), Amrol has a tighter surface, precision of line and less lateral expansion.

A comparison of images at Amrol and Naresar underlines the range of sculptural workmanship during this period. Placing a Śiva *gaṇa* from the Rāmeśvar beside a similar figure from the Durgā temple shows the ruggedness of the Naresar carving (pls 49, 40). This is a difference of quality rather than kind. Both sculptures display a restrained tension of surface and a noticeable move away from the rich modulations found at Dāng and other early eighth-century monuments (pl. 24). The Gaṇeśa on the south wall of the Rāmeśvar temple helps close the gap between Amrol and the subregional style of Naresar (pl. 47). If we recall the Gaṇeśa from Gwalior Fort dating to the early eighth century, we can see how far the style has come (pls 47, 17).

The door of the Rāmeśvar conforms to the type seen at the Bhītupreneśvara at Naresar, but it is more elegantly designed and executed (pls 48, 31). Something of the heaviness of earlier work is retained by the conspicuous dentils (*nīvrapaṭṭikā*), but the brisk precision of the scrolls and simple modelling of the figures in the couple jamb (*mithunaśākhā*) are clear traits of the mid-eighth century. It is one of the peculiarities of Gopakṣetra in this period that the door sill (*udambara*) is left plain whether the building is humble or fine.

The wide entablature (*varaṇḍikā*) of the Rāmeśvar is directly comparable to the Durgā temple at Naresar (pls 46, 37). In both cases it is equal in width to the wall section (*jaṅghā*) and not logically continued into the porch (*prāggrīva*). The superstructures at Amrol and Naresar are also comparable in that they show an analogous compression and abstraction beside the late seventh-century Śiva temple at Mahuā (pl. 8). Of course Amrol is not identical to Naresar, the significant difference being that the offsets of the spire match those of the wall and mouldings. Thus there is a subsidiary spire offset (*latā*) composed of heavy blocks (*kalā*) and covered with large and intricately worked *candraśālā*-dormers. This is the earliest move toward the elimination of the 'double *veṇukośa*', the matching design found on both the spire corner (*veṇukośa*) and the adjacent offset (pl. 8). The same move towards the elimination of the double *veṇukośa* is made at Naresar by simply widening the central spire offset (*madhyalatā*) and omitting one of the receding faces of the superstructure.

The foregoing descriptive analysis shows that the Rāmeśvar Mahādev at Amrol can be placed in the mid-eighth century. A pilgrim's record confirms this, since epigraphically it does not seem to be later than the mid-eighth century.[14] A few features of the Amrol temple, such as the *vedībandha* profile, wide *varaṇḍikā*, variety of *udgama*-pediments and heavy *kalā*-blocks in the superstructure suggest it might be earlier, perhaps even antecedent to the main Durgā temple at Naresar. Amrol could therefore be pushed back in time and serve as a transitional monument between the early and middle phases of eighth-century architecture. Considering, however, that Amrol is stylistically later than Dāng and has many features of the mid-eighth century, and considering also the relative scarcity of complete buildings and dated material, any attempt at a tighter and more complex chronology will remain hypothetical and beyond substantial proof.

The high level of production seen in the Rāmeśvar Mahādev may make it seem aberrant, but such an impression has been created solely by the temple's chance survival. This is readily shown by a study of architectural fragments at Gwalior. These show that a Śiva temple of equal standard was built in the fort in the mid-eighth century. All that remains of the Gwalior temple are a few pieces in an unusual dark grey sandstone, a material not used in any other monument.[15] The best preserved shows a beautifully carved head of Śiva in a *candraśālā* (pl. 51). The delicacy of the modelling parallels the best work at Amrol (pl. 49). The dark stone used in the construction was an especially apt choice for the god who was sometimes called Kāla, the swarthy, and thus identified with time (*kāla*) as the destroyer of all things.

Also from Gwalior, but not so accomplished, are two panels that formed the walls of a shrine (pl. 52). The treatment of the pediments (*udgama*) and the modelling of the figures compare with Naresar, especially the Mātā kā Mandir (pl. 45). These panels are important for they show that various levels of production existed side by side at the same place. Even the rugged workmanship at Naresar is only 15 kilometres from Gwalior Fort. This means qualitative differences are not the result of geographical factors and thus cannot be characterised as 'provincial' – hence the terminology regional and sub-regional used here.

None of the monuments discussed so far have major sculptures connected with them. This is due to the reduced role of figural sculpture in architecture, something made clear by fifth-century buildings like the Daśāvatara temple at Deogarh. Nevertheless, monumental sculpture continued to be carved and these items were usually installed in temple sanctums. Five such monumental images are the Mātṛkā figures from Kota, a village near Shivpuri.[16] The figures of Indrāṇī and Kaumārī are the best preserved and show that large cult figures display a level of workmanship seldom found in temple niches (pls 53, 54). The modelling of the goddesses has the simple, uncluttered treatment seen in the Rāmeśvar Mahādev at Amrol and the Gwalior temple fragments (pls 50, 51). The substantial volume often found in the early eighth century has been quietly discarded and replaced by a taut surface and firmer outline (pls 53, 16). A date in the mid-eighth century for the Mātṛkā figures is best confirmed by their similarity to the river goddesses at Naresar (pl. 45).

Standing figures of Śiva (pl. 55) and Skanda were also recovered from Kota and have the same reduction of plastic volume as the Mātṛkā figures.[17] The awkward tubular construction of the limbs preserves a quality found in the sculptures at Naresar (pl. 39). The most impressive image from Kota, however, is a colossal Gajāntaka (pl. 56).[18] This figure shares the angular outline and elliptically rendered torso of the standing Śiva (pl. 55). As a group, the Kota figures show considerable change compared to early eighth-century sculpture. The forms are now less fully modelled and the details decidedly less sumptuous. They are tempered with an austere grace, like most work in Gopakṣetra. A head of Śiva in the Archaeological Museum, Gwalior, also belongs with these sculptures in the mid-eighth century (pl. 57).[19] The closest parallels are with the Īśāna at Amrol and the small head of Śiva in the *candraśālā* at Gwalior (pls 50, 51).

A few fragments from neighbouring regions may be briefly mentioned to provide a wider context for the Kota images. From Tumain come two dancing Mātṛkā figures, preserved only from the waist down (pl. 58). These are almost identical to the Kota sculptures and may be placed with them in the mid-eighth century. A head of Śiva from Tumain in the National Museum of India also belongs in this period.[20] In this bust the more controlled surface that typifies mid-eighth-century sculpture is clearly seen; it is not yet brittle but still more subdued than during the early part of the century. Mid-eighth-century sculptures are also found at Deogarh, as for example the extensive collection of images built into the wall surrounding the main temple. These sculptures vary considerably in age, quality and state of preservation, but the Jaina goddess shown here in plate 59 is one of the finest and least damaged. Despite the harsher conception and crisper line, it is close in style to the Mātṛkā images from Kota (pl. 53).

From further south in the Ḍāhala country comes a stele that helps fix the chronology of the sculptures and temples discussed in the preceding pages. This piece is a panel from Sāgar carved with images of donors.[21] Making due allowance for slight regional differences, we can see that the figures on the stele have the same taut surface and tubular construction as work in Gopakṣetra. It is not necessary to labour the formal similarities. The panel is inscribed in the reign of Śaṅkaragaṇa, and studies of the historical and epigraphical evidence have placed this ruler in the mid-eighth century.[22] Consequently, the Sāgar panel indicates that the stylistically coherent group of monuments presented in this section belongs in the middle decades of the eighth century.

Eighth Century: Late Phase (*c.* AD 765–800)

As we move into the latter part of the eighth century, temples and sculptures continue to survive in considerable numbers. As in previous phases, the range of production varies, but the difference between regional and sub-regional idioms becomes less pronounced. Dating continues to be problematic, but a relative chronology is possible on the basis of surviving monuments.

Of the many temples in Gopakṣetra, the best indicator of architectural developments in the late eighth century is the Batesar Mahādev near Pāroli (fig. 13; pls 60, 62).[23] Comparing this temple to earlier ones at Naresar and Amrol elucidates the fundamental difference between mid- and late eighth-century architecture (pls 62, 37). In general terms, the Batesar Mahādev shows that the steady process of abbreviation and compression continued unabated over the entire course of the eighth century. Specific points in the spire illustrating this are the subsidiary discs (*karṇāṇḍaka*) and intervening slabs (*kalā*) which are now flatter than before. The *candraśālā* motifs applied to the spire are thin, intricate patterns rather than bold dormers. Similarly, the central spire offset (*madhyalatā*) has been covered with a true *jāla*, or net-like pattern. The aedicules (*bālapañjara*) are tightly knit into the fabric of the superstructure. The elegant antefix (*śukanāsā*) has been scaled down compared to earlier buildings and is logically bonded to the rest of the structure (pl. 61). The end result of these changes is that each architectural part has a precisely defined role in the building and contributes to a careful balance of vertical and horizontal lines. This integration of design stands in contrast to the awkward juxtaposition that is often found in temples of the mid-eighth century (pl. 37).

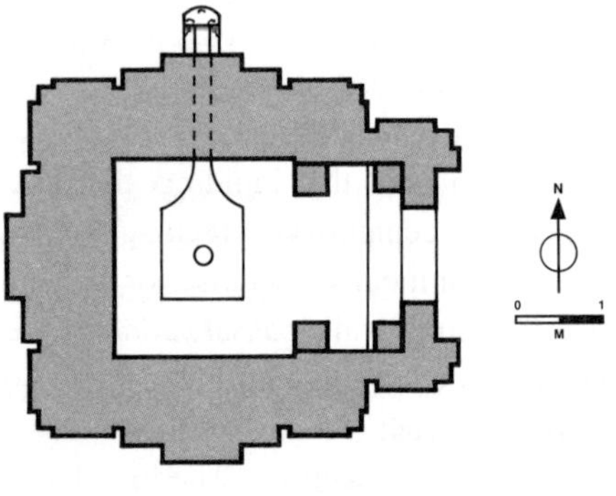

13 Pāroli (Morena), Batesar Mahādev temple, late eighth century

The immediate area around the Batesar Mahādev was enclosed at a later time, obscuring much of the entablature (*varaṇḍikā*) and shutting the mouldings and wall in a dark ambulatory passage. In plate 63 the compressed roll-cornice (*kapota*) and some of the dentils (*nīvrapaṭṭikā*) are visible. The dentil ends are carved with a rich variety of animal figures, including monkeys. Some may be identified as Hanumān and are among the earliest-known representations of this divinity. A similar row of dentils, from a ruined shrine, lies a short distance from the temple. The wall section (*jaṅghā*) of the Batesar Mahādev carries *rathikā*-niches on the central offsets (*bhadra*), corners (*karṇa*) and porch (*prāggrīva*). As can be seen from plate 63, the niches carry tall pediments (*udgama*), the first appearance of this configuration in Gopakṣetra. The *candraśālā* motifs are interwoven with each other and precisely carved with a bevelled edge to heighten the vibrant play of light and dark over the pediment surface. The closest precedent is at Amrol, but there each *candraśālā* remains distinct and the overall shape is still triangular. The *vedībandha* of the Batesar Mahādev is of the standard eighth-century type and calls for no special remarks (fig. 3.11). The low plinth (*pīṭha*), customary in the temples of Gopakṣetra, has been obscured by paving stones and debris.

The sculptures on the *rathikā*-niches have been defaced, but the door is reasonably well preserved (pl. 64). In contrast to the rest of the temple, it is

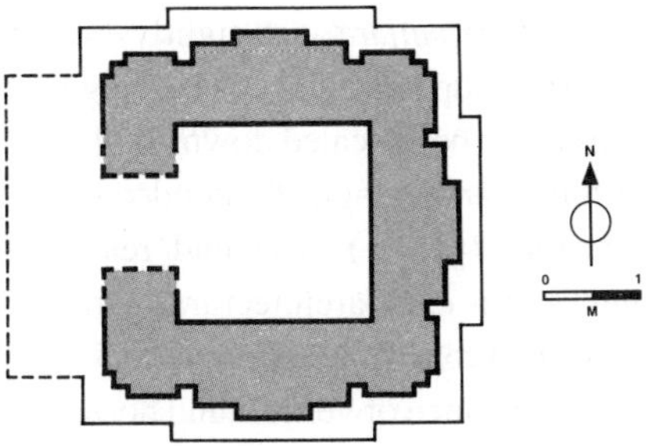

14 Amrol (Gwalior), Dhane Bābā temple, late eighth century

ruggedly executed, but still shows innovations of the sort seen in the spire. For the first time in Gopakṣetra a row of interlocking serpents (*nāga-pāśa*) has been introduced between the inner jamb (*pratiśākhā*) and couple jamb (*mithunaśākhā*). Although this is a small change, it indicates a move toward more elaborate door designs. The sculptures of Gaṅgā and Yamunā at the base of the door are rendered with less clumsiness than during the mid-eighth century (pl. 39).

Another building belonging to the late eighth century is a ruined temple near the village of Amrol. It is known locally as Dhane Bābā kī Maṛhī (fig. 14; pl. 83).[24] An elegant temple like the Batesar Mahādev, it has three receding faces (*aṅga*), a low plinth (*pīṭha*) and narrow offsets (*bhadra*). The *vedībandha* is of the usual type. The wall, also like Batesar, carries *rathikā*-niches with tall pediments (*udgama*). The Dhane Bābā is ruined on one side and there is no trace of the porch or door frame. A battered Nandi, however, still sits in front of the sanctum. A brief comparison between the Dhane Bābā and the nearby Rāmeśvar Mahādev (pl. 46) re-emphasises the characteristics of the late eighth century. The pediments (*udgama*) no longer stand out as three-dimensional forms but are regularised and flattened; the running festoon (*śiraḥpaṭṭī*) is much less sculpturesque. The entablature (*varaṇḍikā*) has been reduced to just three parts, a roll-cornice (*kapota*), a lotus or *padma* moulding and a set of dentils. In the spire the corner discs (*karṇāṇḍaka*) and slabs (*kalā*) are compressed and the mesh pattern (*jāla*) given a reticulated surface. Like the Rāmeśvar Mahādev, the Dhane Bābā has no grooved discs in the subsidiary offset. However, instead of large, simple *candraśālā*-dormers and heavy *kalā*-slabs, the Dhane Bābā has intricately worked elements set against thin slabs. This anticipates the ninth century when the *jāla* spreads from the central offset (*madhyalatā*) to the subsidiary offset (*latā*).

The Dhane Bābā faces west, an orientation often found in Śaiva temples in Gopakṣetra, and shows the usual programme of Gaṇeśa, Kārttikeya and Pārvatī. The corner sections (*karṇa*) carry the regents of the directions (*dikpāla*), an arrangement evidenced earlier at Dāng. The figures show advances over mid-eighth-century work, but they are so damaged as to be of little interest from the stylistic point of view.

The survey of the eighth century given so far provides the requisite data for assessing the Telī kā Mandir (pl. 84).[25] Placed on high ground at a central point in Gwalior Fort, the Telī temple rises to a height of 24.4 metres and its broad outline is visible for a considerable distance in the surrounding countryside. As the grandest building of the period and the largest temple to survive in north India before the tenth century, the Telī kā Mandir merits detailed examination.

The Telī temple is rectangular in plan with a large porch (*prāggrīva*) on the east side. The earlier Mātā kā Mandir at Naresar exhibits a similar arrangement on a smaller scale (fig. 11). As noted in our discussion of that building, the type was developed to accommodate rectangular images such as a row of mother-goddesses or a recumbent divinity. The short wall (*pakṣabhadra*) of the Telī temple is divided into the customary main offset (*bhadra*) and corner (*karṇa*), these sections being subject to minor projections. The long back wall (*pṛṣṭhabhadra*) is similarly treated, but a subsidiary offset (*pratiratha*) has been added to fill the required space. The exterior of the *prāggrīva* is subject to projections like the main offsets and corner sections of the temple proper.

The whole building rests on three roughly hewn slabs (*bhiṭṭa*). Although these are large in themselves, in proportion to the rest of the elevation they are relatively small and thus continue the practice of the low plinth (*pīṭha*) favoured in the eighth-century temples of Gopakṣetra. A battered animal-headed spout (*praṇāla*) pokes through the top *bhiṭṭa* on the north side. We should note that the impression of a high plinth has been created by the exposure of ragged foundation stones during clearing and restoration.

The tall *vedībandha* is exceptional but not unique (pl. 87). The type, which omits the torus (*kalaśa*), was common in the fifth century and was used sporadically after that time; examples are found in some of the small shrines at Batesar and in temple 12 at Deogarh (fig. 3.8). On the Telī temple the wide recess (*antarapatra*) is elaborately carved and divided into two equal sections by pilasters with cruciform brackets. These carry flat half-lotus patterns (*ardhapadma*) and dense palmettes (pl. 92). Between the pilasters are small panels filled with sculptures of bearded Śaiva ascetics and a variety of other divinities. The ascetics typically have a hand raised in reassurance (*abhayamudrā*) and hold a gourd, club or trident. Similar images are found at Khajurāho.[26] Other Śaiva images include Gajāntaka, Ekapāda, Lakulīśa, Gaṇeśa, Kārttikeya and Śiva. Viṣṇu Trivikrama, Vāyu, Agni, Kubera, Brāhma, a *mithuna* couple and a flying *vidyādhara* also appear; there is even one standing Tīrthaṁkara tucked deep into a corner on the south side (between the *prāggrīva* and *karṇa*). A number of the finer images bear craftsmen's names, and in plate 92 one of these labels can be seen on the projecting bracket to the left of Lakulīśa. All the sculptures are mutilated, making it difficult to assess their style, but they seem to show a reduction of modelled volume compared to Amrol and Naresar.

Above the pilasters and sculptures just mentioned is a frieze carrying grotesques (*kīrtimukha*) and a wonderful variety of animals amidst a jungle of floral scrolls. This work lacks the supple plasticity found at Dāng and Amrol, and is executed with the same lashing precision and crispness as the pinnacle of the antefix (*śukanāsā*) at Batesar (pls 92, 61). The *vedībandha* is topped by two rows of finely worked dentils (*nīvrapaṭṭikā*) and a block-like top moulding (*kapotālī*) with *candraśālā* ornaments.

The wall section (*jaṅghā*) continues the projections of the plan and *vedībandha*. The large *rathikā*-niches on the cardinal offsets (*bhadra*) are given the form of doors and cut through the *vedībandha* down to the foot moulding (*khura*). These mock doors have a configuration similar to the Rāmeśvar temple at Amrol, but the roll-cornices (*kapota*) in the over-door are lighter, and the *candraśālā* ornaments are more delicately rendered (pls 86, 48). As in most buildings of the mid- to late eighth century, there is an increase in the number of door jambs (*śākhā*). Above is a row of lion heads (*siṁha-mukha*) and above that again an elaborate pediment (*udgama*) of interwoven *candraśālā* arches with beaded edges. This mesh pattern (*jāla*) is close to that on the spire of the Durgā temple at Naresar, but it is more intricately and precisely done (pls 86, 41). Like the main offsets (*bhadra*), the porch (*prāggrīva*) of the Telī temple carries *rathikā*-niches shaped like doors, but the upper parts forming the pediments are given the shape of fully fledged *latina* spires (pl. 88). The only other eighth-century building that carries similar models is the brick temple at Nimiya Khera near Kānpur.[27] The remarkable model on the Telī temple is a complete elevation in every detail and may be compared to the Batesar Mahādev (pl. 62). Although the Telī temple exhibits a certain robustness, both show the compression and abstraction that characterise the *latina* spire during the late eighth century. Looking back to Naresar, we see that the antefix (*śukanāsā*) of the Telī model displays more linear precision and a delicate decorative propensity (pls 88, 37). The entablature (*varaṇḍikā*) of the model is reduced to three mouldings as in the Dhane Bābā temple at Amrol (pl. 83). The aedicules (*bālapañjara*) in the vertical recess (*salilāntara*) are omitted, an especially telling abbreviation that foreshadows developments during the ninth century (pls 104, 113). The Gaṅgā and Yamunā sculptures on the door of the temple model, in contrast, show little movement beyond the awkward tubular rendering found at Naresar (pls 91, 39, 45).

In the *rathikā*-niche on the south side of the porch (*prāggrīva*) there are a number of eighth-century inscriptions. The longest is part of a verse describing Durgā.[28] The record suggests that an image of this goddess was once installed there, but no trace of it can be found. In his report on the restoration of the Telī temple Keith mentioned discovering images in the debris that had accumulated around the plinth.[29] I have been unable to trace these sculptures and can suggest no candidates, whole or fragmentary, that may have been originally installed in the niches.

The corner sections (*karṇa*), like the porch, carry niches with pediments in the form of *latina* temples. On the long back wall (*pṛṣṭhabhadra*) the original intention seems to have been to put similar models on the subsidiary offset (*pratiratha*), but this was changed to tall pediments (*udgama*) as the work went forward (pls 84, 87). On the east façade the *rathikā*-niches flanking the entrance door show a similar tall-pediment design. It is worth noting that the *rathikā*-niches are not consistent throughout the building. On the north side the niche openings are like doors, complete with jambs, over-door and little figures of Gaṅgā and Yamunā. On the south side the openings are more perfunctory, consisting only of columns ornamented with overflowing pots, garland festoons and the bell-and-chain motif (pl. 87). A further oddity is found higher up on the building in the running festoon (*śiraḥpaṭṭī*) at the top of the wall. This consists of two courses on the south side but only one course on the north. They meet on the long back wall (*pṛṣṭhabhadra*), causing the lowest moulding of the entablature (*varaṇḍikā*) to be visibly askew (pls 87, 84). These observations show that two different teams of craftsmen worked on the building, a practice that was widespread in India. This helps explain the mismatching of the *vedībandha* on the north-east corner of the building.[30]

The entablature (*varaṇḍikā*) of the Telī temple consists of five mouldings, close in design to the Rāmeśvar at Amrol but occupying proportionately less space in the elevation and substantially reduced in visual significance. Like the Batesar Mahādev, some of the mouldings of the *varaṇḍikā* are carried into the porch (*prāggrīva*). Over the *varaṇḍikā* rises the massive superstructure. The lower portion shows two storeys (*bhūmi*) of the *latina* type, marked by compressed corner discs (*karṇāṇḍaka*). The discs appear on the inner offsets as well, creating a double *veṇukośa*. The intervening space is filled with aedicules (*bālapañjara* ; pl. 85). On the back side of the temple (*pṛṣṭhabhadra*) the grooved discs on the inner offsets do not line up with those on the corners; a muddled appearance is the result (pl. 84).

The central offsets are surmounted by prominent arched gables (*śūrasenaka*). Inside the *śūrasenaka* on the south side is an eight-armed image of Durgā seated on a lion. The corresponding image on the north side shows a four-armed god seated with a *yogapaṭṭa* tied around the knees and a rosary (*akṣamālā*) in the upper right hand. It may be either Lakulīśa or Śiva Dakṣiṇamūrti (pl. 85). The latter has a long history in northern India going back to its fifth-century appearance in Vārāṇasī.[31] On the long side of the temple (*pṛṣṭhabhadra*) the damaged *śūrasenaka*-gables seem to have been filled with architectural motifs rather than sculpture. Behind and above these gables were two rows of pillars and ogee-shaped arches. Above this there seems to have risen an arched gable of large proportions which reached the summit of the roof (pl. 84).

Two *kapota*-mouldings terminate the *latina* body and mark the transition to the crowning superstructure. The depressed barrel vault (*skandhavedī*) carries dormer-like *rathikā*-niches on the long sides while the ends take the form of an enormous open arch with sumptuous beadwork, lozenges and floral appendages. The barrel-vaulted crown (*valabhī*) has similar decorations. Though this part of the roof is much restored, the screens (*jālī*) in the circular opening on the north side are original (pl. 85).[32] The ridge of the *valabhī* roof probably carried a row of finials and a pair of lions.[33] A lion head was incorporated into the gate-house built in front of the Telī temple in the late nineteenth century.

Turning to the porch (*prāggrīva*) and the east façade of the Telī temple, we find that its upper sections have been completely rebuilt. Where we see the triangular mass of plain masonry, we must imagine a massive antefix (*śukanāsā*) shaped like the arched gables elsewhere on the building. The monumental doorway has been partially blocked up, but the original frame, rising to a height of 10.66 metres, is fully visible (pl. 89). It is a more imposing version of the mock doors of the principal niches. The door has five elaborately carved jambs (*śākhā*) with the inner three continued across the lintel. At the centre, Garuḍa grips the snakes that make up the *nāgāśākhā*, or 'serpent jamb'. As already noted in the discussion of Batesar, the interwoven snake motif (*nāgapāśa*) first appears in Gopakṣetra during this period. The richly carved pillar jamb (*stambhaśākhā*) ends in a palmette bracket that supports the broad over-door (*uttarāṅga*). The *uttarāṅga* carries spire models of the type found on the building's exterior walls. Continuing the elaborateness of the door, the door surround (*mālāśākhā*) is made of two mouldings rather than one. Running across the top of the door is a row of lion heads (*siṁhamukha*), a motif of long-standing popularity.

At the base of the jambs are figures of Gaṅgā and Yamunā with their attendants (pl. 90). Nandi and Mahākāla stand as door guardians (*dvārapāla*), while in the clouds above are *vidyādhara* figures and sages attending on Lakulīśa. Though damaged, these river goddesses merit attention because they are the only large sculptures still attached to the building. They display the kind of constrained linear tension observed at Batesar; compared to earlier work, the forms have gliding curves and a taut economy of modelling. The subtle undulations seen in the figures on the Mātā kā Mandir at Naresar have been substantially eliminated (pl. 45).

Moving beyond the door to the interior, we find that the vestibule (*antarāla*) has been heavily restored, but some badly worn female figures flank the entrance to the sanctum (*garbhagṛha*). These may be an additional set of Gaṅgā and Yamunā images or female door guardians (*dvārapalikā*).[34] The sanctum is empty except for eight pillars carved with various designs and the flat ceiling that carries traces of lotus flowers and grotesques (*kīrtimukha*) in low relief.

With the sanctum we are brought to a consideration of the original dedication of the Telī temple. This may be reconstructed from a summary of the pertinent iconographic, epigraphic and architectural data. First there are the images in the *vedībandha*, predominantly Śaiva ascetics and various Śaiva divinities. The inscription in the *prāggrīva* niche describing Durgā suggests an image of that goddess was once installed there. On the main door Mahākāla and Nandi serve as guardians; above them is a small figure of Lakulīśa. On the temple niches some of the pediments carry small lingas and *gaṇas*; there is also a single-faced Śiva linga in one of the half-niches on the long back wall (*pṛṣṭhabhadra*). In the arched gables of the superstructure are Siṁhavāhinī and a damaged image, possibly Śiva Dakṣiṇamūrti. This evidence taken together indicates the building was Śaiva in dedication. The rectangular shape of the temple further suggests the original cult image was rectangular. As it was Śaiva, we can choose between a row of Mātṛkā figures or a reclining goddess. Both were popular in the region. A damaged set of Mātṛkās lies outside a small rectangular shrine at Batesar and recumbent goddesses are seen at Gwalior (outside Urwāhī Gate in a rock-cut niche and on the Caturbhuj temple). More distant, but also important in this regard, is the Gadarmal at Badoh, a rectangular building that once contained a reclining mother-goddess.[35]

Views on the chronological position of the Telī temple have varied considerably. Earlier writers placed the building in the tenth or eleventh century, but their opinions were based on ill-informed guesswork and need little attention.[36] More recently, Krishna Deva has placed the Telī temple to the middle of the eighth century.[37] With the detailed survey of the period provided in this chapter it is possible to refine the dating further. To do this, it is necessary to abstract the relevant points from the description of the Telī temple given above. Beginning with the superstructure, we find a greater degree of compression and abstraction than at Amrol and Naresar. This points to a date in the late eighth century. Other elements supporting this chronological horizon include the entablature (*varaṇḍikā*), which has a less significant role in the elevation than featured in mid-eighth-century monuments; indeed, in the temple models on the wall (*jaṅghā*) the entablature is reduced to just three mouldings. Another late feature of the models is the elimination of the aedicules (*bālapañjara*), a change directly anticipating ninth-century practice. The various pediments (*udgama*) and arched gables (*śūrasenaka*) follow established patterns but are marked by a delicate decorative propensity that is rather different from what is found in the first half of the eighth century. On the subsidiary offsets (*pratiratha*) the pediments are given the tall proportions as found at Batesar and other late eighth-century buildings. The entrance door and the mock doors of the *rathikā*-niches both show a proliferation of jambs (*śākhā*); individual elements are also lighter and more finely worked than during the mid-eighth century. The figural sculpture, though damaged, displays a reduction in volume compared to Amrol and Naresar. The main figures flanking the entrance participate in the late eighth-century style in having smooth outlines and a taut economy of modelling. The floral scrolls, like Batesar, are carved with crisp precision. This evidence suggests that the Telī temple should be placed in the late eighth century. Other factors, however, cannot be ignored. For example, some of the figures on the *vedībandha* maintain the over-accentuated contraposto and awkward tubular construction found at Naresar. The different pediments (*udgama*) on the back wall (*pṛṣṭhabhadra*) may be seen as marking a transition from the triangular shape at Amrol to the tall, slender form at Batesar (pl. 84). Though the entablature (*varaṇḍikā*) is reduced in visual significance, it still consists of five mouldings, as in earlier temples. The spire shows advances over mid-eighth-century examples but retains the robust double *veṇukośa* and has yet to assume the sleek balance of horizontals and verticals we find at Batesar (pl. 62). Taking this stylistic information as a whole leads us to conclude that the Telī temple marks a transition from the mid-eighth-century style of Amrol and Naresar to the fully fledged late eighth-century style as evidenced by the Batesar Mahādev.

The Telī kā Mandir is the largest temple of the eighth century, but the Gargaj Mahādev at Indor represents a higher order of regional production and a continuation of the standard found earlier at Amrol and Mahuā (pl. 93). The Gargaj Mahādev has a circular plinth (*pīṭha*) consisting of two *bhiṭṭa*-slabs. As on the Telī temple, an animal-headed spout (*praṇāla*) pokes through the top *bhiṭṭa* on the north side. Over the *bhiṭṭa*-slabs rises the *vedī*-

15 Indor (Guna), Gargaj Mahādev temple, late eighth century

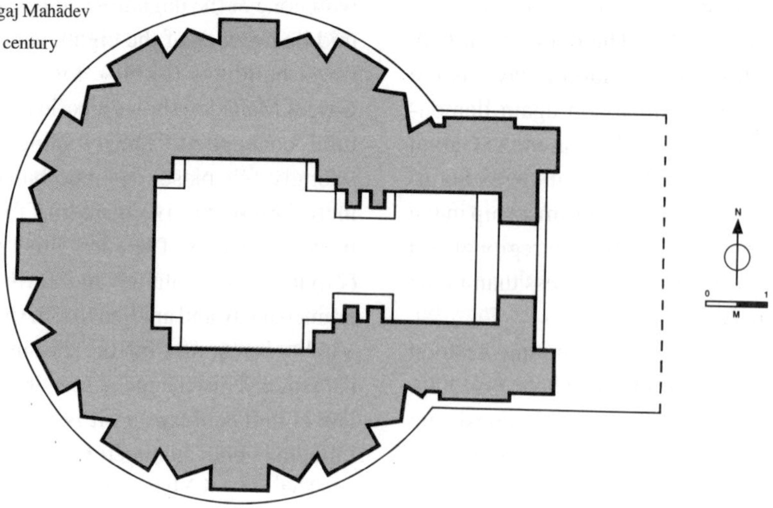

bandha which marks the transition from circular to stellate (fig. 15). Nine offsets are arranged around the sanctum with the intervening spaces filled with projecting corners (*pallava*).[38] This yields the stellate shape in which square and acute projections are carried up through the whole structure. This configuration is often found in the early brick temples in Madhyadeśa and Ḍāhaladeśa and anticipates the complex *bhūmija* temples of the eleventh century.[39]

The *vedībandha* is massive and clearly ornamented with *candraśālā*-dormers and the occasional floral scroll. The mouldings have the usual profile, though in size they approach the Telī temple (fig. 3.7). The wall (*jaṅghā*) carries *rathikā*-niches on all nine offsets. At the cardinal points are images of Gaṇeśa, Kārttikeya and Pārvatī; the subsidiary niches carry regents of the quarters (*dikpāla*). This iconographic programme is in consonance with the usual arrangement for Śaiva temples in Gopakṣetra during the eighth century. Each image is sheltered by a *kapota*-cornice with a row of lion heads (*siṁhamukha*; pls 95, 96). As previously noted, the tall slender pediments (*udgama*) are characteristic of the late eighth century. The individual *candraśālā* motifs making up the pediments have sharply raised edges that accentuate the vibrant play of light and dark over the surface. The treatment is similar to the Batesar Mahādev (pl. 63). The larger niches of the porch (*prāggrīva*) contain images of Indra and Īśāna, continuing the *dikpāla* theme (pl. 95). The modelling of these superlative sculptures shows a subtle tension and crispness of line that is analogous to the linear precision that appears in the architectural forms of the period. The niches on the porch (*prāggrīva*) have wide pediments (*udgama*) close to those on the principal offsets (*bhadra*) of the Telī temple (pl. 86).

On the east side is the doorway, notable as the finest eighth-century example still standing in northern India. In design it is comparable to the Telī temple, but whereas that door is attenuated to the point of absurdity, Indor displays sober proportions and a balanced elegance (pl. 94). The figural carving of the door participates in the late eighth-century style, but, compared with contemporary sculpture at other sites, the outlines are handled with masterful ease and the modelling with consummate efficiency. The sharp, frilly scrolls have the lashing briskness of those on the antefix (*śukanāsā*) of the Batesar Mahādev (pl. 61), but they are of a more elaborate order. Both seem drained of supple plasticity when compared to earlier work at Amrol (pl. 48). The door sill (*udambara*), carved with lions and floral sprays, is the same as Batesar; this comparison again demonstrates the higher level of production in the Gargaj Mahādev. The difference shows that there continued to be a substantial range of workmanship in the late eighth century; the gap between regional and sub-regional idioms was, however, less than in the early eighth century.

The door is topped by a running festoon (*śiraḥpaṭṭī*) that goes round the whole building. Over this is the entablature (*varaṇḍikā*), consisting of two heavy *kapota*-cornices with a row of dentils (*nīvrapaṭṭikā*) in between. The reduction in the number and relative size of these mouldings is like other late eighth-century temples, such as the Dhane Bābā at Amrol (pl. 83). The scrollwork on the dentil ends displays the variety and flourish seen in the Telī temple *vedībandha*, but the carving is of a more exquisite order.

Between the *varaṇḍikā* and superstructure is a recess with small pilasters and niches filled with Śiva attendants and other figures. This brings the *vedībandha* of the Telī temple to mind, but it is more directly descended from the pillared recess (*antarapatra*) in the same position at Mahuā and Dāng (pl. 8). At Indor the treatment is subdued and carefully integrated into the elevation, in accord with the architectural style of the late eighth century. Above rises the ruined spire. Enough survives to show that the portions above the projecting corners (*pallava*) were treated like spire corners (*veṇukośa*), while the portions above the square offsets (*bhadra*) were treated like subsidiary spire offsets (*latā*). The mesh patterns (*jāla*) have the reticulated surface of the Batesar Mahādev (pl. 63).

This descriptive analysis shows the Gargaj Mahādev temple can be placed in the latter part of the eighth century. Like the other buildings of this period, especially the Batesar Mahādev, the temple shows a stately balance of horizontals and verticals, with none of the ungainly additiveness found in the middle decades of the eighth century, even in the finest buildings (pl. 46). More significantly, the Gargaj Mahādev shows a basic change in architectural conception. The building is no longer a strongly felt plastic volume but is becoming an increasingly passive backdrop for the display of intricate designs. The energy that previously gave conviction to volume and form is now subtly drained away and applied to rich rhythmic surfaces. Vitality is retained, but the shift in emphasis is fundamental. This change is seen in all temples of the late eighth century and it is a transformation that influences both architecture and sculpture.

The Gargaj Mahādev has the best preserved *in situ* sculpture of the late eighth century and these images are valuable for dating pieces separated from their context. Ones such fragment is a head of Pārśvanātha on Gwalior Fort (pl. 97). Comparing the Pārśvanātha to the Īśāna at Indor we see the faces are virtually identical (pl. 96). Both have precisely chiselled eyebrows, narrow eyes and a subtly hardened treatment of the flesh. Note how the gentle volume of the form has been tightened compared to the mid-eighth-century Śiva head in the Archaeological Museum, Gwalior (pl. 57). The assembly of semi-divine beings behind Pārśvanātha's serpent canopy show a concern with rippling surface patterns, a feature seen in contemporary architecture. A hero-stone from Pāroli shares all the qualities of the Pārśvanātha (pl. 6). At the top is an idealised bust of the deceased warrior, with panels below showing his last battle, death and heavenly felicity in Goloka. These lower panels are more schematically carved than the bust and may be compared to the figures on the Telī temple (pl. 92). Similar hero-stones are found at Bārāhet but they are not so well preserved. The Kalyāṇasundara panel at Batesar also belongs with the sculptures just discussed (pl. 81). The faces of Śiva and Pārvatī are worn and the work is not so fine as Indor, but the modelling of the forms, especially the legs, is sufficiently alike to allow a date in the late eighth century.

Dating the remains of the late eighth century with any exactitude is difficult. The only monument from the last half of the eighth century relating to the problem is the Mahāvīra temple at Osiān. An inscription of VS 1013/ AD 956–7 records that the original construction took place in the time of Pratīhāra Vatsarāja (*c.* AD 777–808).[40] Although this might appear valuable, the Mahāvīra has been substantially rebuilt and those parts that belong to the late eighth century are either without direct parallel or in such a local style that they cannot be compared to the late eighth-century monuments of Gopakṣetra. We might be in a position to suggest parallels between these regional traditions if a complete history of temples in Rājasthān was available. While M. A. Dhaky has furnished a valuable beginning, such a history has yet to be written.[41] Consequently, what we see at the Mahāvīra cannot be suitably applied to the chronology of the late eighth century in Gopakṣetra.

Summary

The eighth century in Gopakṣetra, the focus of this chapter, was marked by a measured consolidation of seventh-century achievements. There were few dramatic departures, only steady elaboration and development with each passing generation. Three phases were discernible. In the early phase architectural and sculptural forms were substantially lightened. The plastic independence of detail found in late seventh-century temples yielded to a carefully chiselled surface and an effort to fit each architectural part into the design scheme (pl. 23). In sculpture this produced subdued volume and a toning down of the rippling modulations of the flesh so conspicuous in seventh-century images (pl. 16). The increased number of survivals showed a range of workmanship, effectively illustrated by comparing the Gaṇeśa from Gwalior with the Gaṇeśa on a linga at Bārāhet (pls 17, 18). Dating the early phase with exactness was problematic but was fixed in an approximate way by sculptures referable to an inscription of AD 710–11 at Indragarh in the Avanti region (pl. 15).

In the middle phase an increase in the number of surviving temples emphasised the variety of work produced in Gopakṣetra (pls 37, 46). Because fine and humble work was often found at the same site, this variety could not be explained as 'provincial'; the terms 'regional' and 'sub-regional' were used instead. Despite the range of style, all the work of this period could be seen as continuing and amplifying trends evident in the early phase. Compression and regularisation were found everywhere. Pillars, pediments and other elements were standardised and many details were eliminated. Decorative motifs like the mesh pattern (*jāla*) became flattened and more intricately worked. The result was that temples began to assume a chaste and noticeably architectonic texture (pl. 30). In sculpture an analogous tension and rhythm of surface appeared, accompanied by the elimination of the fussy plasticity of the early phase (pl. 53). Often the forms had an awkward tubular construction (pl. 55). Dating the middle phase with exactitude was difficult, and we were forced to look at remains from neighbouring regions. A stele from Sāgar inscribed in the reign of Śaṅkaragaṇa (*c.* AD 750) allowed this phase to be placed in the middle decades of the seventh century; also of value was the ruined temple and associated sculptures at Kanswa dated AD 738–9.

The late phase was ushered in by the Batesar Mahādev near Pāroli, the Dhane Bābā temple at Amrol and the Gargaj Mahādev at Indor (pls 62, 83, 93). These temples displayed a stately balance of horizontals and verticals and a linear precision of detail. The ungainly and additive quality found in the middle phase, even in the finest buildings, entirely disappeared (pl. 37). More significantly, the temple was no longer a strongly felt plastic volume, but an increasingly passive backdrop for the display of intricate surface designs. The energy that previously gave conviction to volume and form was subtly drained away and applied to rich rhythmic surfaces (pl. 94). Vitality was retained, but the shift in emphasis represented a fundamental change in architectural conception. This transformation influenced both architecture and sculpture (pl. 96). As in previous phases, humble work continued to be produced, but the gap between regional and sub-regional styles started to narrow (pl. 6). It was from this beginning that the polished and homogeneous style of the ninth century was to emerge. Dating the late phase with exactitude was not possible. The only dated monument from the last half of the eighth century, the Mahāvīra temple at Osiān built in the time of Vatsarāja (*c.* AD 777–808), has been substantially rebuilt and the surviving parts could not be compared to late eighth-century monuments in Gopakṣetra.

Notes

1 Thakore, *Catalogue of Sculptures in the Archaeological Museum, Gwalior*, room 10, no. 8.

2 Harihar Nivās Dvivedī, 'Gaṅgolātāl ke gaṇapati', in *Gvāliyar darśan*, pp. 353–6.

3 Rāmavatār Śarmā, 'Bārāheṭ se prāpta ek vilakṣaṇa śivaliṅga', ibid., pp. 297–8.

4 For fifth-century examples, see Williams, *Art of Gupta India*, pl. 233; for Khojra, see Mukherjee, *Report on the Antiquities in the District of Lalitpur*, pls 66–7; the temples at Deoguna (near Jaso in District Satna) appear to be unpublished.

5 The word *dāng* means 'jungle' in the Gwalior dialect. Although the area is now agricultural, the name suggests the place was once isolated in forest.

6 EI 32 (1957–8): 112–17.

7 IA 19 (1890): 55–62; for the application of Kanswa to the history of sculpture in the Gangetic plain, see *The Dictionary of Art* 15: 479

8 The temples added to Naresar in later centuries are outside the scope of the present study; see my 'Architecture in Central India under the Kacchapaghāta Rulers', pp. 28–30.

9 *Inscriptions of Gopakṣetra*, p. 116. The inscription is written in characters of about the eleventh century. The temples are best referred to by their inscribed names (even if later in date) as opposed to an arbitrary numbering system. For assistance with the Naresar inscriptions, I am grateful to Richard Salomon and R. N. Misra.

10 Trivedi, *Temples of the Pratīhāra Period*, pl. 7, shows one of the sculptures before it was defaced.

11 Aschwin de Lippe, *Indian Medieval Sculpture* (Amsterdam: North Holland Publishing, 1978), pl. 35. The Yamunā figure illustrated has been removed by vandals, who have also been responsible for defacing the images on the other temples.

12 Thakore, *Catalogue of Sculptures in the Archaeological Museum, Gwalior*, room 22, nos 5–9 and 11–19. *Inscriptions of Gopakṣetra*, pp. 10 and 116

13 This is a reconstruction of the ancient name; compare Vatodaka and Badoh, Khajūravāhaka and Khajurāho, Pṛthūdaka and Pehoa, and Agrodaka and Agroha. The location of Āmardaka is of some interest as it appears to have been an early seat of Śaiva Siddhānta; it is mentioned as a seat of ascetics (*āmarddaka santāna*) in the Haddala plates; see IA 12 (1883): 190–95 and, for larger religious and historical context, Davis, *Oscillating Universe*, pp. 14–15.

14 *Inscriptions of Gopakṣetra*, p. 105.

15 The fragments of this temple that I have been able to trace are: (a) large battered head of Śiva, Scindia School; (b) *candraśālā* with a lion face, principal's garden, Scindia School; (c) fragment of a *candraśālā* built into the north side of the Sās Bahu temple; (d) *candraśālā* illustrated here, principal's garden, Scindia School.

16 Thakore, *Catalogue of Sculptures in the Archaeological Museum, Gwalior*, room 10, nos 5, 6, 7, 9, 10. Illustrations in S. Kramrisch, *Manifestations of Shiva* (Philadelphia: Museum of Art, 1981), no. 58; also K. A. Harper, *The Iconography of the Saptamatrikas* (Lewistown, NY: Edwin Mellen, 1989), figs 80–83.

17 Thakore, *Catalogue of Sculptures in the Archaeological Museum, Gwalior*, room 10, nos 2, 4.

18 Ibid., room 10, no. 18.

19 Ibid., room 10, nos 1, 1(b). Thakore's descriptions are not detailed enough to settle the provenance.

20 Harihar Nivās Dvivedī, 'Gvāliyar rājya meṁ prācīn mūrtikalā', in *Vikrama Smṛti Grantha* (Ujjain: Scindia Oriental Institute, vs 2001): 667–708. The head is not from Gwalior as sometimes stated.

21 Illustrated in Donald M. Stadtner, 'The Śaṅkaragaṇa Panel in the Sāgar University Art Museum', in *Indian Epigraphy: Its Bearing*

on the History of Art, ed. Frederick M. Asher and G. S. Gai (Delhi: American Institute of Indian Studies, 1985), pp. 165–8; also in Stadtner, 'Nand Chand and a Central Indian Regional Style', AA 43 (1981–2), fig. 6.

22 CII 4, no. 35; further discussion in Stadtner, 'Nand Chand', p. 132.

23 Patil, *Descriptive and Classified List*, no. 1274.

24 Ibid., no. 57.

25 The popular name Telī kā Mandir literally means 'oil-grinder's temple'. This has no historical significance. C. E. Luard, *Gwalior State Gazetteer* (Calcutta: Superintendent Government Printers, 1908), p. 227, mischievously suggested that the name derives from Telingana Mandir and that the temple was designed by some courtier from Telingana, possibly in honour of a southern queen of the Kacchwaha chiefs. This is a nonsense that has given rise to a 'tradition' repeated by tour-guides and popular writers.

26 Pramod Chandra, 'Kaula-Kapālikā Cults at Khajurāho', *Lalit Kalā* 1–2 (1955–6): 98–107.

27 See my 'Brick Temple of the Ninth Century', AA 52 (1992), pl. 13.

28 *Inscriptions of Gopakṣetra*, p. 108 and pl. 4.

29 J. B. Keith, *Preservation of National Monuments: Gwalior Fortress* (Calcutta: Superintendent of Government Printing, 1883), p. 34. The restoration was begun in 1880.

30 Ajaṇṭā, cave 14, has a door with two entirely different designs on each side. M. Meister, 'Geometry and Measure in Indian Temple Plans: Rectangular Temples', AA 44 (1983): 266–96, does not fully account for these facts.

31 Ananda Krishna, 'The Gupta Style of Sculpture from the City of Benares', in *Rūpa Pratirūpa*, pp. 87–98.

32 For a photograph taken before late nineteenth-century restorations, see Percy Brown, *Indian Architecture (Buddhist and Hindu Periods)* (Bombay: D. B. Taraporevala, 1956; reprint edn, 1971), pl. cxvi; for an older view, Fergusson, *History of Indian and Eastern Architecture*, p. 453.

33 The Navadurgā temple at Jageśvar preserves these elements on its *valabhī* roof. K. P. Nautiyal, *The Archaeology of Kumaon* (Vārānasī: Chowkhamba Sanskrit Series, 1969), pl. 7.

34 Krishna Deva, *Temples of North India*, p. 23.

35 Coomaraswamy, *A History of Indian and Indonesian* Art (New York: Karl Hiersemann, 1927), fig. 178. Thakore, *Catalogue of Sculptures in the Archaeological Museum, Gwalior*, room 10, no. 19.

36 Among the views expressed, the most influential have been Fergusson, *History of Indian and Eastern Architecture*, p. 453 (tenth or eleventh century); A. Cunningham, ASIR 2 (1862–5): 357 (ventures no date for the building but inscriptions are of the 'ninth or tenth centuries'); Brown, *Indian Architecture*, p. 128 (eleventh century).

37 Krishna Deva, 'Telī-kā-mandir, Gwalior', in *Indian Epigraphy*, pp. 161–3.

38 I am grateful to M. A. Dhaky for informing me that the proper term for the acute projection in a stellate plan is *pallava*.

39 Krishna Deva, 'Bhūmija Temples', in *Studies in Indian Temple Architecture*, pp. 90–113.

40 ASIAR (1908–9): 208–13; JRAS (1907): 1010.

41 Dhaky, 'Genesis and Development of Māru-Gurjara Temple Architecture', in *Studies in Indian Temple Architecture*, pp. 114–65.

Chapter 4

The Gurjara-Pratīhāra Age

Temple architecture in northern India entered a period of increasing elaboration and decorativeness during the ninth century. Continuity with the past was a keynote, but entrenched regional idioms and their sub-regional variants began to loose vitality. By the end of the ninth century a new unity had emerged in which regional idioms came to closely resemble one another and were more homogeneous within themselves. This new style has been attributed to the rise of the Gurjara-Pratīhāra rulers who established control over most of northern India in the time of Nāgabhaṭṭa II (*c.* AD 810–33). While there is a general correlation between the rise of the Pratīhāras and the ninth-century style, an examination of inscriptions shows that this was not due to the agency of imperial patronage.[1] Developments in ninth-century architecture fall into three discernible phases: early, middle and late. Fixing the chronological horizon of these phases is facilitated by dated monuments which appear for the first time in Gopakṣetra and neighbouring areas.

Ninth Century: Early Phase (*c.* AD 800–825)

The stylistic changes that mark the early ninth century are best introduced by numerous small shrines at Batesar. As we have seen in the previous chapter, the main temple of Batesar Mahādev was built in the late eighth century (pl. 62). The subsidiary shrines added to the site are undated but appear to have been started soon after the main temple was complete. This can be seen from the Śiva temple placed immediately to the west of the Batesar Mahādev (pl. 65). This building differs from the main temple in a number of details, such as the elimination of the aedicules (*bālapañjara*) in the spire's vertical crevices (*salilāntara*). This does not immediately alter the style of the superstructure, nor is it especially innovative, because slow compression and abstraction of the *latina* form had been going on for several centuries. Nevertheless, the cumulative effect of subtle changes like this generated a significant shift in architectural style. Small shrines to the north of the Batesar Mahādev illustrate this point (pl. 70). At first glance these buildings do not seem to have developed much beyond the Śiva temple just discussed, but, compared to the Batesar Mahādev itself, they show more tightly ordered superstructures and, in the lower portions, a flattening of the *rathikā*-niches and mouldings (pls 71, 62). The subsidiary grooved discs (*karṇāṇḍaka*) are less rounded, and the recesses between them and the *kalā*-slabs are not so deep as before. The breadth of the vertical crevice (*salilāntara*) is also reduced. These are changes of the first importance, preparing the way for the mature ninth-century spire. This form of spire, as we shall see, is a single architectural form as opposed to a balanced assembly of independent parts. A little shrine built adjacent to the Batesar Mahādev, now half-buried in rubble, may be taken as another ninth-century example that shows a greater evenness of overall texture beside its eighth-century counterparts (pl. 69). The omission of the aedicules (*bālapañjara*) adds to this effect.

The other temples clustered around the Batesar Mahādev vary considerably in design and quality of workmanship. The shrine directly east of the main temple exhibits a sub-regional style of humble character (pl. 66). As in many structures of the early ninth century, the form is beginning to show a definite smoothness and uniformity, but the wide central spire offset (*madhyalatā*) and simple *candraśālā*-dormers continue mid-eighth-century conventions found at Naresar (pl. 30). The temple placed immediately to the north of the Batesar Mahādev has a more sophisticated superstructure but still displays a number of rustic features (pls 67, 68). Flying *vidyādhara* figures are simply placed on the wall on each side of the door; these and the other sculptures are crudely carved. The large ungainly loops of the running festoon (*śiraḥpaṭṭī*) become suddenly compressed over the door where they are interrupted by a frieze of *navagraha* ('nine planets'). The craftsmen apparently had difficulty dealing with this new iconographic element and, bound to an old formula for doors, could do nothing but place the *navagraha* over the *śiraḥpaṭṭī*.

Other temples added to the Batesar complex in the early ninth century are more carefully designed and finished. The best preserved are a group of shrines on the hillside to the north-east of the main temple (pl. 74). This group shows the tenacious continuity of the *maṇḍapikā*, a type that first appeared in Gopakṣetra during the seventh century (pl. 1). As we have seen, *maṇḍapikā*-shrines are characterised by a wall (*jaṅghā*) composed of alternating pillars and recessed panels. The Batesar group continues the essentials of the type, but everything is cast in the early ninth-century style. The *rathikā*-niches, for example, display considerably less plastic texture than those on the Batesar Mahādev (pl. 63). The pillars making up the wall are decorated with a conspicuous variety of floral rosettes; these are the last vestige of the discs, tongues and pendants that often appear on pillars between the fifth and eighth centuries (pl. 3). Resting on the pillars are palmette capitals. Such capitals were common in the eighth century, but in the Batesar *maṇḍapikā*-shrines the motif is more flatly rendered (pl. 92). The intervening panels are also substantially different from eighth-century workmanship. The scrolls now have the appearance of soft curling leaves as opposed to a lashing spray with frilly jagged edges (pls 61, 92).

The doors of the Batesar *maṇḍapikā*-shrines vary, but all are derived from types found in Gopakṣetra during the eighth century. The main iconographic innovation is the incorporation of the *navagraha* and Mātṛkās over the door and, in the sill (*udambara*), a lotus-shaped central projection (*mandāraka*) flanked by elephants (pl. 75). Stylistically, the sculptures show a coherent elegance and easy fluidity beside eighth-century work (pl. 48). The T-shape is discarded, as often happens in small buildings, and the whole door acquires a rich evenness, removed from the bold independence of elements found in the eighth century. This is directly analogous to the overall uniformity that begins to appear in the *latina* type of superstructure during this period. Another door of the early ninth century stands at the edge of the tank beside the Batesar Mahādev temple (pl. 78).

In most of the *maṇḍapikā*-shrines at Batesar the entablature (*varaṇḍikā*) has a sloping awning (*chādya*) and a recess (*antarapatra*) decorated with step-pyramids and triangular floral panels. The *chādya* is a new feature, and the portions projecting out over the door indicate that small open porches (*mukhacatuṣkī*) originally stood in front of these shrines. One such *mukhacatuṣkī* is preserved to the south-east of the Batesar Mahādev, but there the shrine itself has collapsed (pl. 76). Another ruined porch nearby is notable for the lotus decoration in its ceiling (pl. 77). Early ninth-century *maṇḍapikā*-shrines are common in the neighbourhood of Batesar. A partially ruined example stands immediately beside the Batesar Mahādev temple and in the outskirts of Pāroli village there are several other examples.[2] That many of these shrines once carried *latina*-type spires is evidenced by the fragments that lie scattered beside them.

A ruined temple south-east of the Batesar Mahādev belongs in the early ninth century with the *maṇḍapikā*-shrines just discussed (pl. 79). Although little is left of this building, the fragments display a high standard of workmanship recalling Indor and Amrol; despite the different configuration, the temple can be viewed as a descendant of those eighth-century masterpieces. The *vedībandha* is similar to Indor, with the top moulding (*kapotālī*) having *candraśālā*-dormers, floral ornaments and a block-like profile. The treatment of the decorative devices, however, is more refined than in the late eighth century (pl. 95). The one *rathikā*-niche on the principal offset (*bhadra*) that has been preserved is shaped like a small door; above is a row of lion heads (*siṁhamukha*), a roll-cornice (*kapota*) and a pediment (*udgama*). Again these elements show a debt to the eighth-century repertoire, but compared to Indor the forms are more delicate and have an even finish. The corner section (*karṇa*) carried niches, and the rest of the wall (*jaṅghā*) was filled with pilasters and panels carved with elaborate scrollwork. This type of construction looks back to Mahuā, but now the scrolls have the soft, lyrical style seen in the wall panels of the Batesar *maṇḍapikā*-shrines (pls 74, 75). This confirms an early ninth-century date for the ruin. It is worth noting that the projecting pilaster on the wall carries a little appliqué niche; this is a configuration that appears here for the first time and is used later at Gwalior, Markhera and Barwa Sāgar (pl. 108).[3]

The only other part of the ruined temple that still stands is the doorway (pl. 80). The jambs (*śākhā*) are all well-established types, but the fluted bell-capital on the pillar jamb (*stambhaśākhā*) is unusual in the architecture of Gopakṣetra. The form makes an embryonic appearance in the *maṇḍapikā* at Mahuā (pl. 5), but the closest contemporary parallel is found at Roda in the Medapāṭa region.[4] Like the wall construction with its echoes of the seventh century, the bell-capital emphasises that many architectural forms have long histories that are unknown to us. Stylistically, however, the position of the doorway is clear: compared to late eighth-century work, it shows increasing refinement and deliberate precision in the carving of details. The scrollwork in particular has lost its lashing vigour to a carefully measured richness (pls 80, 94).

The last temple examined at Batesar is a rectangular shrine, unusual because the stone is cut in flat slabs imitating brick.[5] The upper portion of the shrine has disappeared, but enough remains to show that it was of the barrel-vaulted type (*valabhī*). As we have seen, temples with this shape were commonly dedicated to the goddess. At Batesar itself there is a fragmentary row of the Mātṛkās, lying just beside the entrance to the main complex (pl. 82). This was probably the cult image originally installed inside the shrine.[6] Battered though the figures are, they display an internal coherence and softly modelled elegance, removed from the awkward construction often found in the eighth century.

A more complete sculpture showing the same qualities is an image of Kubera and his consort Ṛddhi (pl. 98). Like the Mātṛkās, this image has a smooth coherence in the modelling of the forms and a lyrical richness of detail. The subtle elegance of the ornaments, a hallmark of early ninth-century work, is especially betrayed by such things as the delicate twist of the garland falling between

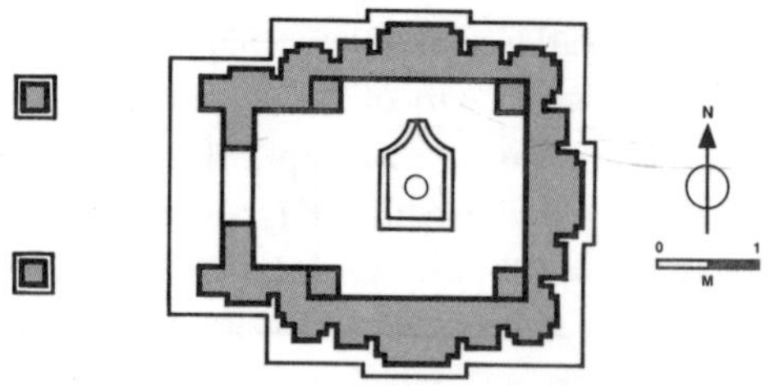

16 Terāhī (Shivpuri), Śiva temple, early ninth century

Ṛddhi's breasts. An elaborate stele with seated Tīrthaṁkaras on all four sides also belongs in this period (pl. 99). The mid-ninth-century temple at Bānpur (District Tīkamgarh) suggests this piece was once installed in a shrine of the *caturmukha* type.[7]

In the southern part of Gopakṣetra there are more early ninth-century remains. The most important is the Śiva temple at Terāhī which stands beside a monastic structure (*maṭha*) once used by Śaiva Siddhānta ascetics (pl. 100). The temple faces west and rests on a platform paved with stone slabs. Debris and rubble from the crumbling *maṭha* have partially obscured this platform. The building has three receding faces (*aṅga*) which are subject to a number of minor offsets (fig. 16). The result is a more complex plan than found in the eighth century at Amrol, Naresar and Batesar (figs 10, 12, 13). This increasing complexity parallels the elaboration we have already seen in early ninth-century architectural and sculptural ornament.

Reflecting the plan, the diminutive *vedībandha* has been given a number of projections and further differs from earlier examples in being less robustly carved (fig. 3.13; pl. 101). Similar qualities are found in the highly ornamented wall (*jaṅghā*). The tall pediments (*udgama*) on the corner sections (*karṇa*) have an intricate, flat finish like the early ninth-century additions at Batesar (pls 69, 74). The subsidiary offsets (*pratiratha*) are taken up by pillars richly decorated with floral panels and overflowing pots. On the pillars rest palmette brackets and grooved abaci. The principal offsets (*bhadra*) have wide *rathikā*-niches with massive awnings (*chādya*) that embrace each projection and shelter the images. This is repeated on the vestibule wall (*kapilī*). This use of the *chādya* is a new feature that appears for the first time in this building. The elaborateness of surface is enhanced by the proliferation of small offsets, floral panels and slender mock-niches. Amidst all this there is little room for the running festoon (*śiraḥpaṭṭī*), but where space is left, the loops and bells can be seen.

The images continue the established iconographic programme of Gaṇeśa, Kārttikeya and Pārvatī, but they are so battered that they cannot be used to illustrate stylistic developments. The entablature (*varaṇḍikā*) is composed of two cornices (*kapota*) and a row of dentils (*nīvrapaṭṭikā*) carved with floral patterns and grotesques (*kīrtimukha*). Compared to earlier examples, the cornices are more compressed and the sculptural variety of the dentil decoration reduced. In addition, the miniature dentils under each cornice have been eliminated and there is a sharper distinction between the wall (*jaṅghā*), entablature (*varaṇḍikā*) and spire (*śikhara*; pls 100, 83). Over the vestibule wall (*kapilī*) the space between each cornice has been widened and filled with a chequer pattern (pl. 101). This is another feature appearing for the first time.

The superstructure shows the compression and flattening of form seen elsewhere in the early ninth century, most notably in the additions to the Batesar complex (pls 100, 71). To re-emphasise the difference between the late eighth and early ninth century, we may compare Terāhī and the Batesar Mahādev (pls 100, 62). The most obvious difference is the elimination of aedicules (*bālapañjara*). This substantially alters the proportion of the spire and permits greater evenness of texture. Individual elements have less independence, as can be seen from the subsidiary grooved discs (*karṇāṇḍaka*) which do not stand out with the same vitality. The central spire offset (*madhyalatā*) also carries a more intricate and complex mesh pattern (*jāla*).

On the west side of the Śiva temple is an open porch (*mukhacatuṣkī*) with richly carved pillars (pl. 100). As in the attached pilasters of the wall (*jaṅghā*), the soft curling scrollwork is identical to the panels on the Batesar *maṇḍapikā*-shrines (pls 103, 74). Above the open porch is the antefix (*śukanāsā*). It consists of one floor level (*bhūmi*) of the *latina* mode, topped by a depressed barrel vault. The crowning arch, containing an image of Naṭeśa, lies on the ground to the east of the temple. With it are two miniature spires (*kūṭa*) which may have formed part of the porch roof. In these elements we again find more compression and attention to detail than in the Batesar Mahādev.

The door of the Terāhī temple has five jambs (*śākhā*), all more delicately carved than late eighth-century examples. The pillar jamb (*stambhaśākhā*) has attenuated proportions and the serpent jamb (*nāgaśākhā*) a slender refinement not evidenced previously (pl. 102). The image of Viṣṇu on Garuḍa placed on the centre of the lintel is damaged, as are the other sculptures, but the smooth treatment of form characteristic of the early ninth century is clearly present. Next to late eighth-century work, the Terāhī door ornaments have an easy rhythmic unity (pls 102, 64). The overall impression is one of a rich, even surface, similar to the later doors at Batesar (pl. 75). Above the entrance is an over-door (*uttarāṅga*) with blind arcading and triangular pediments (*siṁhakarṇa*). The row of lion heads (*siṁhamukha*) beneath the arcading is hardly recognisable and shows that the popularity of this motif was beginning to wane.

Buildings like the Śiva temple at Terāhī were once common, to judge from the ruins at different sites. For example, at a place called Satanwārā near Narwar there are a number of pillars, lintels, *rathikā*-niches and *vedībandha* fragments that appear to be products of the early ninth century.[8] The ruined Śiva temple at Kheldhar (fig. 17) is

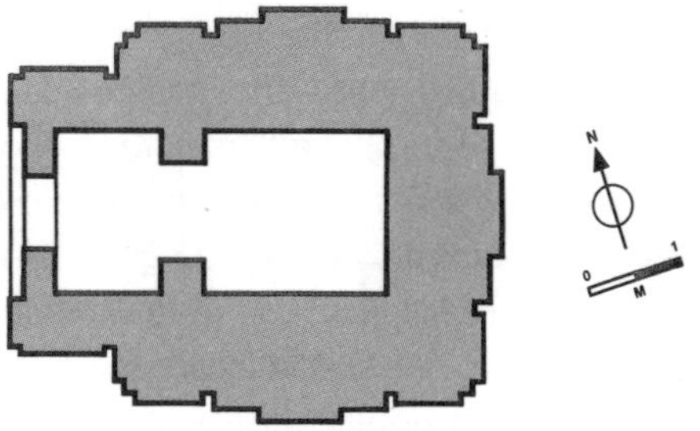

17 Kheldhar (Guna), Śiva temple, early ninth century

coeval.[9] At Gwalior stray pillars at the south end of the fort (some incorporated into small pavilions) indicate that temples were also built there at this time. The appearance of these buildings can be gleaned from a pair of miniature shrines (pl. 104).[10] Being large models, they have all the details of full-scale buildings. Like the Śiva temple at Terāhī, they show the elimination of aedicules (*bālapañja-ra*) and the accompanying compression and flattening of details in the superstructure. A miniature spire (*kūṭa*), also from Gwalior Fort, participates in the stylistic traits of the models (pl. 105). Like the miniature spires at Terāhī, it suggests multi-spired superstructures were under formulation in the early ninth century.[11] To judge from the Caturbhuj temple (dated AD 875–6), such spires may have been used on the outer corners of a hall roof (pl. 107). Once such a usage became entrenched, it was a small step for these elements to be clustered around the main superstructure, creating a multi-spired form (*anekāṇḍaka* or *śekharī*).

The diversity of architectural types, now all but lost, is further indicated by an important ruin at Sihoniyā. Located in the middle of the village, this building shows the town was established well before it rose to importance in the eleventh century under the name Siṁhapānīya.[12] The outer wall of the hall and a few stray fragments are all that remains of this early ninth-century structure (pl. 106). The wall carries *rathikā*-niches with pediments (*udgama*) and figural sculptures executed in a style close to the Śiva temple at Terāhī. Above these are grooved discs which apparently served as bases for squat pillars in the balcony. In the central section is the sloping parapet seat (*kakṣāsana*) flanked by projecting elephant heads. This arrangement, found also in the Gadarmal at Badoh, becomes standard in later temple architecture.[13] Below the sloping splat is a large *rathikā*-niche with a heavy awning (*chādya*) sheltering an image of Māhiṣāsuramardinī. On either side are subsidiary *rathikā*-niches. This rich ornamentation of the wall recalls the Terāhī temple and shows a growing intricacy simultaneously combined with a reduced sense of plasticity. The apposition is entirely characteristic of the ninth century. The Sihoniyā hall was of the closed type (*gūḍhamaṇḍapa*), so called because the interior was lit only by the balcony openings. The ninth-century Mālā Devī temple at Gyāraspur, in the Vidisha region, preserves a hall of this kind in its entirety.[14] In Gopakṣetra, however, Sihoniyā is the only surviving *gūḍhamaṇḍapa* from before the eleventh century.

Ninth Century: Middle Phase (*c.* AD 825–75)

In the half century between AD 825 and 875 a rich maturation comes to the architecture and sculpture of northern India. During this period the monuments of Gopakṣetra are executed in a style that begins to resemble those in neighbouring areas; at the same time sub-regional idioms begin to falter and gradually disappear. The resultant homogeneity makes for a less problematic chronology. The key monument for an understanding of the middle part of the ninth century is the Caturbhuj temple at Gwalior. According to inscriptions incised on the building, the temple was cut out of the rock in VS 932/AD 875–6 at the order of Alla, a feudatory of the Pratīhāra monarch Mihira Bhoja.[15] This is the

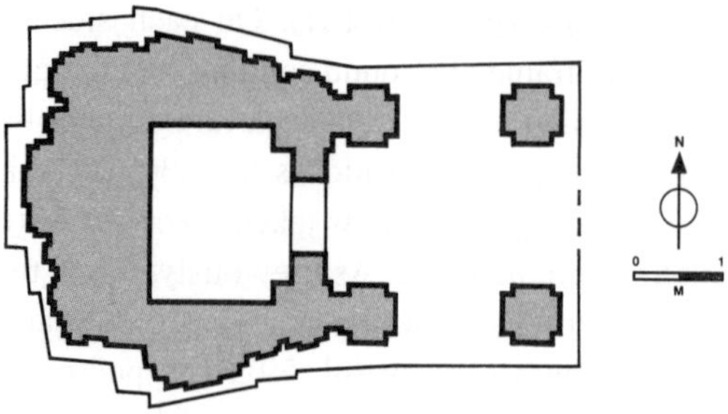

18 Gwalior (Gwalior), Caturbhuj temple, dated VS 932/AD 875–6

earliest dated temple in Gopakṣetra and as such is an important instrument for our chronology.

The Caturbhuj temple is a small monolithic building excavated in the cliff-face of Gopādri (pl. 107). Seated lions, also carved out of the rock, once flanked the temple, but one was destroyed by later renovations and the other is so weather-worn as to be hardly recognisable. The smooth upper section of the superstructure is a restoration of the twentieth century.[16] The temple proper shows three receding faces (*aṅga*) in plan with an open porch (*mukhacatuṣkī*) resting on pillars before the entrance (fig. 18). The low plinth (*pīṭha*) consists of a single slab (*bhiṭṭa*) and a lotus moulding. This *padma*, or 'lotus moulding', is a new feature in the temples of Gopakṣetra and is often used in late ninth and early tenth-century buildings (pl. 108).[17] On the plinth rests the *vedībandha*. The tendency to compress these mouldings, which appeared in the early ninth century at Batesar and Terāhī, is here carried further (pls 108, 71). The *vedībandha* carries appliqué niches on each projection, a feature not found previously in the region.

Moving to the wall section (*jaṅghā*), we find it has broad *rathikā*-niches that completely cover the wall surface. In the main niches are figures of Varāha, standing Viṣṇu and Trivikrama (pl. 110). The guardians of the directions (*dikpāla*) appear on the corners (*karṇa*).[18] Awnings (*chādya*) shelter the battered images. Compared to earlier examples, the awnings are not so broad and the individual ribs less emphatic (pls 108, 101). On each side the images are framed by round columns and rampant griffins (*vyāla*), a significant departure from the flat pilasters used in earlier niches (pl. 63). The subsidiary offset (*pratiratha*) is taken up by a pilaster with an appliqué niche. As previously noted, this particular arrangement first appeared at Batesar in the early ninth century (pl. 79). The pediments (*udgama*) on the Caturbhuj are relatively squat and on the central projections (*bhadra*) they almost have a triangular shape (*siṁhakarṇa*). This is not a retrograde feature, going against the tall *udgama* that is generally favoured from the late eighth century, but merely a result of the narrow wall. The decorative mesh (*jāla*) on the pediment confirms this by its delicacy compared to the robust, plastic treatment common in the early ninth century (pls 108, 101). The entablature (*varaṇḍikā*) is marked off from the wall by a narrow recess (*antarapatra*) and is made up of two cornices (*kapota*) and a row of dentils (*nīvrapaṭṭikā*). The compression and precision of these parts echo the handling of the *vedībandha* mouldings. A second *antarapatra* marks the transition from entablature to superstructure.

Like the lower section of the temple, the superstructure of the Caturbhuj is significantly different from those dating to the early ninth century. The changes in style may be cogently summarised by comparing the spire with the examples at Terāhī and Batesar (pls 109, 71, 100). The most obvious difference is the elimination of the double *veṇukośa*: now a flat and finely woven mesh (*jāla*) spills over from the central spire offset (*madhyalatā*) to cover the subsidiary offset. The vertical crevices (*salilāntara*) are reduced to narrow slits, and in the spire corners (*veṇukośa*) the discs (*karṇāṇḍaka*) are less plastically carved. The recesses between the slabs (*kalā*) and other parts are also substantially reduced. Like the *maṇḍovara* (plinth to entablature inclusive), the whole spire displays a penchant for flat, intricate surface. This quality is found in the early ninth century, but with the Caturbhuj every part is strictly controlled and sublimated to the architectonic scheme.

The large antefix (*śukanāsā*) abutting the spire documents changes analogous to those seen in the rest of the building (pl. 107). Looking back to the early ninth-century additions at Batesar or the miniature temples from Gwalior Fort, we find the bold single arch crowning the *śukanāsā* has been replaced by an intricate pattern of wavy lines (pls 65, 104). The depressed barrel vault, making up the lower section, is still recognisable, but compared to the Śiva temple at Terāhī, the parts have no convincing architectural purpose and are important only for their surface effect.

The porch before the entrance has four cruciform pillars, each set on a base moulded after the fashion of a *vedībandha*.[19] The pillars have overflowing pots (*ghaṭapallava*) and small *rathikā*-niches containing figures and diamond-shaped lozenges. From the mouths of the grotesques (*kīrtimukha*) come chains with bells on the end. A complex abacus, capital and bracket rest on top. These pillars are more elaborate than those at Terāhī and mirror the rich decorativeness that is prominent in the rest of the Caturbhuj. On the inside edge of the lintels of the porch are damaged reliefs showing scenes from the life of Kṛṣṇa. Externally, the porch roof is also damaged, but there are traces of several horizontal tiers (*phāṁsanā*), each separated by a recess carrying a chequer pattern. On each side of the roof there are projecting triangular pediments (*siṁhakarṇa*), and on the corners there are miniature spires (*kūṭa*). As already noted, this arrangement seems to have appeared in the early ninth century at Terāhī. The awning (*chādya*) that skirted the edge of the roof is almost entirely broken away. Few roofs of this type survive from before the time of the Caturbhuj and its significance can only be appreciated with reference to later buildings such as the Lakṣmaṇa temple, Khajurāho.[20]

The door of the Caturbhuj is worn, but merits

attention as the first dated example in Gopakṣetra (pl. 111). The sill (*udambara*) shows kneeling devotees beside a central projection (*mandāraka*) and two reclining lions at the outer edge. Figures of Gaṅga and Yamunā and their attendants flank the opening. In their present condition it is impossible to comment on the sculptural style. The jambs (*śākhā*) follow the customary arrangement in Gopakṣetra, the closest precursor being found at Batesar (pl. 78). The over-door (*uttarāṅga*) is decorated with rampant lions, *rathikā*-niches and temple models; it projects beyond the jambs to create the usual T-shape. Even though the sculptures are unrecognisable in their present condition, the general appearance of the over-door shows an increased elaborateness and richness of surface beside early ninth-century examples (pl. 102).

The Caturbhuj has been discussed in detail because the building is dated AD 875–6. With the help of the stylistic data that the temple provides, monuments that appear to be earlier in time can be described. This approach allows us to form a general picture of temple architecture in the middle part of the ninth century. Of the many buildings that belong in this time frame, the most important and complete is the Sun temple at Khiaoda (pls 112, 113).[21]

The chronological position of the Khiaoda temple can be established by a synopsis of its features in relation to the Caturbhuj on the one hand and early ninth-century temples on the other. Beginning at the bottom with the mouldings, we see the *vedībandha* is given a massive treatment and carries dentils (*nīvrapaṭṭikā*) carved with grotesques (*kīrtimukha*). On the *vedībandha* rests a string-course (*mañcikā*), richly carved with floral scrolls and drop-pendants. Both these features are found on the Gadarmal at Badoh, a building of the early ninth century. The wall (*jaṅghā*) is filled with broad and elaborate *rathikā*-niches. The prominent openings on the cardinal offsets (*bhadra*) are shaped like miniature doors and flanked by both pilasters and round columns. The pilasters and door-like niches have been inherited from the early ninth century, but the columns with their grooved abaci look ahead to the Caturbhuj (pl. 108). The subsidiary niches, containing Gaṇeśa, regents of the quarters and other figures, are framed with similar round columns and, on the porch (*prāggrīva*), with both columns and rampant griffins (*vyāla*). In this last type we see a direct forerunner of the *rathikā*-niches on the Caturbhuj temple. Like the Caturbhuj also, the subsidiary offsets (*pratiratha*) are filled with a pilaster carrying an appliqué niche. All the images are sheltered by prominent awnings (*chādya*), as heavy as those of the early ninth century but lightened by drop-pendants along the awning-edge. The pediments (*udgama*) are extended up to the entablature (*varaṇḍikā*), but the broadness of the niches and the narrow wall gives them a triangular shape, just as at the Caturbhuj. On the porch (*prāggrīva*) the pediments are shaped like a temple superstructure, an unusual configuration that recalls the Telī kā Mandir at Gwalior (pl. 88). Although this is the last appearance of this kind of pediment, it is probably not a deliberate anachronism, but simply the only surviving example of a form that was in use since the eighth century.

The entablature (*varaṇḍikā*) of the Khiaoda temple consists of two roll-cornices (*kapota*) and a wide recess (*antarapatra*) articulated with stocky pilasters and little keyhole niches. While the cornices are not much different to the Caturbhuj, the conspicuous recess looks back to earlier buildings. In the well-preserved spire (pl. 113) a mesh (*jāla*) has been placed on both the central and subsidiary offset, replacing the once-popular double *veṇukośa* (pl. 100). The arrangement looks ahead to the Caturbhuj and beyond, but the various parts of the superstructure retain a rippling, plastic texture that is reminiscent of early ninth-century temples.

The foregoing analysis shows that the Khiaoda temple has some features that recall early ninth-century buildings, while others anticipate the

Caturbhuj temple of AD 875–6. This mixed repertoire is coupled with an overall organisation that has yet to show the rigorous architectonic order in evidence at the Caturbhuj and beyond. These facts indicate that Khiaoda is prior to the Caturbhuj and that it dates to the middle part of the ninth century.

On Gwalior Fort there are numerous architectural fragments and sculptures that date to the same period. A large Tīrthaṁkara, now in the Archaeological Museum, may be taken as representative (pl. 114).[22] In this stele Mahāvīra is shown seated in *padmāsana* on a lion throne with two whisk-bearers at his side. The oval nimbus behind his head carries a lotus and is ringed with floral scrolls. *Vidyādhara* figures hold a garland and canopy above. The torso and limbs of the Jina's body are arranged with unfaltering assurance and carved with the same sort of balanced linear grace as contemporary temple forms. Compared to early ninth-century sculptures (pl. 99), the Jina has more carefully controlled volumes and a restrained, sheer surface. Everywhere delicacy and excellence are coming to the fore; this is especially apparent in such details as the brocade pattern on the cushion. The back of the Jina's throne takes the shape of an elaborate image-frame (*prabhāvallī*) and is crowned by temple models. In these models we see something of the intricacy and compression of the Caturbhuj superstructure. There are other Jaina sculptures at Gwalior that belong with this image in the mid-ninth century. One of the finest is the rock-cut Tīrthaṁkara near Urwāhī gate (pl. 115). There, the Tīrthaṁkara stands in a shallow cave flanked by two attendants; *vidyādhara* figures with garlands fly in the clouds above.

A *vyāla* (griffin) figure, also from Gwalior Fort, shows the same controlled sense of form as the Jaina images just mentioned (pl. 116). The curling leaves on the griffin's horns have the flat restraint typical of all mid-ninth-century scrollwork. To judge from the tenon at the top, this piece served as a bracket or strut in a temple entrance hall. No trace of this building remains, but there are numerous fragments built into the walls of Gwalior Fort that date to the same period. Evidently many temples were built in the fort at this time.

In contrast to Gwalior Fort, the immediate countryside has yielded few pieces dating to the mid-ninth century. An image of Viśvarūpa from Sihoniyā is the most important and best preserved (pl. 117).[23] The restrained volume and smooth modelling of the forms are identical to the Gwalior Jinas (pls 114, 115). The style of these sculptures is manifestly elegant and assured, and readily recognisable wherever it appears.

Farther south in Gopakṣetra representatives of the mid-ninth-century style are found at Sakarra. Two shrines were built facing each other on the edge of a large tank (pl. 118). Each building has three receding faces (*aṅga*) with a vestibule (*antarāla*) and small open porch (*mukhacatuṣkī*). The shrines rest on several roughly hewn slabs (*bhiṭṭa*). Above, the finely cut *vedībandha* mouldings show the same sort of precise reduction and compression as the Caturbhuj, but an austere note is struck by the absence of dentils (*nīvrapaṭṭikā*) and appliqué niches. The narrow *rathikā*-niches on the offsets (*bhadra*), also of chaste design, are less prominent than early ninth-century examples and carry pediments (*udgama*) with an intricate flat finish like the Caturbhuj temple. The figural sculpture, all Śaiva in character, displays the even, controlled form of the Gwalior and Sihoniyā images just mentioned (pl. 119).[24] Beside earlier work the figures show the substantial reduction of plastic volume that is characteristic of the mid-ninth century. The subsidiary niches at Sakarra, as well as the running festoon (*śiraḥpaṭṭī*), have been left as unfinished blocks. The doorways are also uncarved except for the sills and figures of Gaṅgā and Yamunā. Returning to the elevation, we see the entablature (*varaṇḍikā*) is composed of two roll-cornices (*kapota*) and a finely carved row of dentils (*nīvrapaṭṭikā*). The arrangement is similar to the

Caturbhuj temple, but the horizontal spaces between the parts are greater, making the whole form more emphatic (pls 118, 108). The superstructures of both the Sakarra temples have fallen, but the moulded bases that are left apparently supported miniature pillars. This suggests a spire similar to the one on the Maṛhiā Dhār near Kuchdon.[25] The pillars of the porch (*mukhacatuṣkī*) carry cruciform brackets carved with palmettes and a sloping awning (*chādya*) with shallow coffers. The configuration of these parts recalls a number of earlier buildings in Gopakṣetra, but the motifs are now rendered with greater flatness and delicacy. In summary, there is a mixture of old and new elements in the Sakarra shrines; the style is decidedly less robust than found in the early ninth century, but the uniform refinement and elaborateness that appear toward the end of the ninth century has yet to be attained.

Humbler work of the mid-ninth century is found at Batesar, the site where so much was built in earlier periods. A row of shrines to the north of the main temple are the best preserved examples (pls 72, 73). Beside earlier buildings these shrines exhibit a penchant for tightly worked patterns and flat architectural components. This is especially clear in the spires that exhibit, albeit in a rustic way, the same basic appearance as the Caturbhuj temple at Gwalior (pl. 107). The Batesar shrines are of the *maṇḍapikā* class, but only half-heartedly so, for the pilasters are weakly articulated and the floral scrolls in the receding panels only cursorily incised. The principal niches are set on wide slabs which take up a larger part of the wall than in earlier temples. This handling of the forms shows a decided weakening of the *maṇḍapikā* type. The *vedībandha* mouldings are cut from single slabs of stone and the ends are not even finished to make the mouldings continuous (pl. 72). The sculptures, little more than stick figures, betray their date only by the reduction of plastic feeling. There are no floral ornaments.

What we see in these mid-ninth-century shrines is the last manifestation of sub-regionalism in Gopakṣetra. Previously the humbler work had an ongoing vitality of its own, no matter how rugged the workmanship. Now the vigour of that tradition is faltering. Not only are the sculptures and ornaments cursorily done, but the *maṇḍapikā* type itself, a mainstay of sub-regionalism, is tending to coalesce with more standard temple forms. Greater uniformity thus emerges in architecture as the sub-regional traditions are absorbed into the mainstream or lapse into unembellished folk art.

Before leaving the mid-ninth century, some dated monuments outside Gopakṣetra may be noted. In Jejākadeśa the most important mid-ninth-century remains are found inside Deogarh Fort in the complex of Jaina temples. The largest building, temple 12, can be linked with an inscription on a pillar incorporated into the hall in the nineteenth century. The record states that the pillar was set up near the temple of Śāntinātha in VS 919/AD 862.[26] Because temple 12 is dedicated to Śāntinātha, the record provides a *terminus ad quem* for the structure. The advances over early ninth-century architecture, and similarities to the Caturbhuj of AD 875–6, fix the date with reasonable security. The pertinent traits, most notably in superstructure, may be briefly detailed.[27] Although the spire was extensively rebuilt towards the top, its lower portions are intact. These show a compression and intricacy not far removed from the Caturbhuj temple at Gwalior. The mesh (*jāla*) is a rich and finely woven pattern that has spread from the central offset (*madhyalatā*) to the subsidiary offset, eliminating the double *veṇukośa*. This organisation is indicative of the ordered subordination of parts to the architectural whole that is characteristic of the mid-ninth century. On the conservative side, aedicules (*bālapañjara*) are still found in the vertical crevices (*salilāntara*) and a pillared recess (*antarapatra*) is placed between the spire and entablature (*varaṇḍikā*). The presence of these features, however, has not diluted the growing sense of uniformity and emphasis on verticality. Especially indicative is the running festoon (*śiraḥpaṭṭī*), now reduced to a tiny frill at the base of the superstructure. This reorganised handling of older features recalls the temple at Khiaoda and confirms a date in the mid-ninth century. The lower parts of temple 12 are unique. The wall (*jaṅghā*) is unornamented and dominated by a tall *vedībandha* with a wide recess; there is no torus moulding (*kalaśa*; see fig. 3.8). The building is surrounded by a curtain wall of post-and-lintel construction. Between the posts are *rathikā*-niches with figures of Jaina goddesses (*yakṣiṇī*) and simple screens (pl. 120). An analogous system of construction was seen earlier at Naresar (pl. 42). The curtain wall rests on a moulded platform and has doors on each side. The sculptural decoration is executed in a rough-and-ready style, but the details flanking the main entrance have been given greater attention (pl. 120). This work amplifies the smooth modelling and steady regularisation that began to appear in the early ninth century. Though the architectural configuration is different, the sumptuous ornamental surface is comparable to other mid-ninth-century temples.

The dated pillar in front of temple 12 is a humble product, but it can be linked to the columns in the curtain wall by the treatment of grotesques (*kīrtimukha*) and the bell-on-rope motif. This link to temple 12 is supported by the palaeography of the inscription which is similar to the labels below the goddesses.[28] Because temple 12 and the dated pillar are close to each other in time, the differences we see are indicative of the range of workmanship that was prevalent in this area during the mid-ninth century. The range is not a large one and is symptomatic of how sub-regionalism was giving way to an idiom of growing homogeneity, a trend already documented in the humbler temples of Gopakṣetra.

Mid-ninth-century remains are also found further south, in the Vidisha region. The most valuable for our concern is a pillar at Badoh locally known as Bhīmgaja. The pillar carries a long inscription that records that the ruler Parabala built a temple to Śauri (Viṣṇu) and caused the pillar to be set up before it in VS 917/AD 861.[29] The pillar, called a *garuḍadhvaja* and a *stambha* in the inscription, stands in the middle of a square platform. There is a projection on one side for a staircase. The platform mouldings are similar to a *vedībandha*, except that the recess (*antarapatra*) has been exaggerated and filled with triangular pendants and inverted step-pyramids. An analogous adaptation of the *vedībandha* is found at the base of the curtain wall of temple 12, Deogarh. The top moulding (*kapotālī*) at Badoh carries a string-course (*mañcikā*) with floral scrolls (pl. 121). This work is close to Deogarh in style, with the flat, feathery qualities particularly evident when we compare it to the earlier scroll decoration at Batesar and Kuchdon (pl. 74).[30]

The Bhīmgaja pillar has lost its crowing sculpture and the Viṣṇu temple built in front of it is ruined. The plinth, *vedībandha* mouldings and some parts of the wall are all that have survived.[31] The entrance hall (*maṇḍapa*) is marked by a few foundation stones. The sculpture on the south vestibule wall (*kapilī*) and the corner section (*karṇa*) is worthy of note, especially the figure of dancing Gaṇeśa. While the modelling of this graceful image is efficient, the forms retain their liveliness and have not been overtaken by the dry line and dynamic rhythm that emerges toward the end of the ninth century. The door of the temple has been reset but is probably original. In the centre is an image of Viṣṇu riding in Garuḍa and, above, a battered frieze of the nine planets (*navagraha*). The closest precursor for the general design is found at Terāhī.[32] Compared to Terāhī, however, the surfaces are richer and the details have acquired a flat tightness. At the bottom the sill (*udambara*) carries a central projection (*mandāraka*) flanked by battling animals and seated figures holding pots. The

Gaṅgā and Yamunā figures are apparently the work of different hands; one side shows the broad expansion of the torso favoured in the eighth century, while the other side is more forward-looking with its coherent rhythm and balance. The division of labour between crews working on different sides of a building was a common practice and seen before in such temples as the Telī kā Mandir, Gwalior.[33]

Ninth Century: Late Phase (*c.* AD 875–900)

In the last quarter of the ninth century the regional styles of northern India become more homogeneous and simultaneously begin to exhibit a more decorative concept of form. The key monument for establishing the chronological horizon of these developments is again the Caturbhuj temple at Gwalior (pl. 107), which can now be used to identify the remains that are either coeval or slightly later in date. Temples of this period are scarce in Gopakṣetra, the only surviving example being located at Sesai.[34] Dedicated to Sūrya, this building has three receding faces (*aṅga*) on each side, with further decorative projections on the vestibule exterior and corners (*karṇa*); a large open porch (*mukhacatuṣkī*) on the west shelters the entrance (fig. 19). Each cardinal offset (*bhadra*) projects in a prominent manner; in the elevation these projections are treated as miniature porches, with small pillars resting on a string-course (*mañcikā*) placed over the *vedībandha* mouldings. A similar configuration is found in the late ninth-century Sun temple at Markhera.[35] Other details show similarities to the Caturbhuj. All the niches in the wall section (*jaṅghā*) are framed by round pillars and those on the vestibule (*kapilī*) have rampant griffins (*vyāla*). The minor niches are filled with diamond-shaped flowers or lozenges, a feature found on the porch pillars of the Caturbhuj. The use of lozenges in lieu of sculpture comes into wide use in the tenth and eleventh centuries. At Sesai niches with diamond-shaped flowers also appear on the *vedībandha* mouldings. As already noted, niches in this location are an innovation of the Caturbhuj. Some aspects of the elevation closely follow the Śiva temple at Terāhī.[36] For example, slender niches are used in the recesses between the offsets, and the entablature (*varaṇḍikā*) is composed of two cornices with an intervening row of carved dentils. Also, like Terāhī, the subsidiary offsets (*pratiratha*) are taken up by pilasters with fluted abaci and palmette brackets; the bases and capitals take the form of overflowing pots and the pilaster faces carry appliqué floral panels. Despite the similarity of arrangement, the Sesai scrollwork has a biting precision quite unlike the soft curling leaves employed

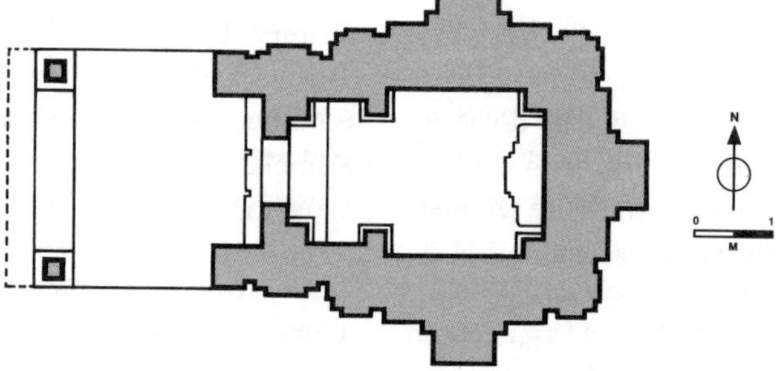

19 Sesai Buzurg (Shivpuri), Sūrya temple, late ninth century

in the early ninth century. The handling of this scrollwork conforms closely to the brisk carving on the late ninth-century temples at Markhera and Umri.[37]

The upper portions of the Sesai temple have collapsed, both over the sanctum and porch. The entrance door, however, is reasonably well preserved.[38] The door is related to types found earlier in Gopakṣetra, but important new features have been introduced. The threshold has been raised by the introduction of a second sill (*udambara*) and this has been fitted with a large semi-circular foot-stone (*ardhacandra*) edged with lotus petals. This is a common configuration in the tenth century, being used in the Śiva temple at Bamora and the hall at Pāroli (discussed below). The framing of the small figures in the figure jamb (*rūpaśākhā*) with round pillars is yet another feature anticipating tenth-century architecture. Furthermore, the *candraśālā*-dormers over the figures are becoming flat, stencil-like patterns for the very first time; this treatment comes to dominate decorative forms in the tenth century. Over and above these specific details, the entire door is animated by a dancing linear rhythm that bends the figures and ornaments according to its demands. The calm elegance of earlier doors is yielding to a rippling linear surface. This is a feature that takes the Sesai temple beyond the Caturbhuj and places it in the latter part of the ninth century.

A notable feature at Sesai is the ceiling in the porch.[39] It consists of a cusped dome with two tiers of curved ribs set against a chequer ground; the drop-finial (*padmaśilā*), which would have been fitted at the apex, has disappeared. The dome is flanked by an elliptical coffer, also with cusped edges and curved ribs. These features are without precedent or parallel in the Gwalior region. Earlier temples generally had flat ceilings carved with lotus flowers and other motifs (pl. 77). The development of domical ceilings is more fully understood in western India where examples are found in considerable number.[40] Had the Sesai temple been destroyed, we would be tempted to assume that such forms were not part of the architectural vocabulary of Gopakṣetra in the ninth century. The ceiling thus underscores a point made elsewhere in this study, namely that the history of many architectural forms is fragmentary.

The date of the Sesai temple, and the late phase of ninth-century art as a whole, is fixed by a monument at Gyāraspur. The freestanding gate known as Hindola Toraṇ and the accompanying ruin called Cār Kambhā ('four pillars') can be associated with an inscription dated MS 936/AD 879–80. The inscription was discovered by Cunningham 'let into a wall near the Toran'.[41] It is now stored in the Archaeological Museum, Gwalior.[42] A second inscription on the same stone belongs to the twelfth-century *mahākumāra* Trailokyavarmadeva and mentions the installation of an image of Cāmuṇḍasvāmideva.[43] The failure to recognise that these are two records has led to some garbled accounts.[44]

As the name implies, the Cār Kambhā consists principally of four pillars. These stand on a ruined platform (*jagatī*) and were originally part of a temple hall. Various fragments lie in the immediate area, including the serrated crown (*āmalasāraka*) and a number of miniature spires (*kūṭa;* pl. 122). These pieces suggest the original building had a multi-spired superstructure (*śekharī*). They are also indicative of the growing precision in the treatment of architectural parts that appears in the late ninth century. Like Sesai, Umri and Markhera, these remains have moved beyond the style found in the Caturbhuj temple, Gwalior. The pillars of the Cār Kambhā confirm this assessment (pl. 123). Compared to the platform at Badoh (dated AD 861), the scrollwork is tightly knit and demonstrates that the easy plastic opulence of the mid-ninth century was becoming more carefully ordered and flattened (pl. 121). Such change would be expected in the twenty years that separate the two monuments.

The chronological horizon of the late phase is further corroborated by the Hindola Toraṇ (pl. 124). The gate rests on large plinth stones, which are edged with a lotus moulding matching that of the Cār Kambhā platform. The individual lotus petals are incised with floral patterns in low relief. The same device is used in temple 45 at Sānchī and is symptomatic of the linear fussiness that develops in the late ninth century. The pillars of the gate sit on *vedībandha*-like mouldings and are elaborately carved with niches, entwined serpents, overflowing pots, grotesques (*kīrtimukha*) and figural panels. Diverse as these elements are, they all cling tightly to the shaft and exhibit the restrained plasticity and dancing rhythm found in the Sesai doorway and other monuments of the late ninth century. The pillars of the gate support brackets which in turn hold chequered pillar extensions (*ucchālaka*) and a cusped floral arch (*vandanamālikā*). This is the first appearance of these elements in mature form, an innovation that parallels the new features introduced at Sesai. Across the top of the Hindola Toraṇ is a heavy lintel similar to those used on the Cār Kambhā. The lintel supports a crowning spire (*kūṭa*); as suggested by the early ninth-century gateway at the Gadarmal, Badoh, crouching lions may have flanked the *kūṭa* on each side.[45]

The monuments examined so far provide a basis for considering the late ninth-century sculpture in Gopakṣetra. One of the finest and best-known pieces is a fragmentary female figure, probably a Jaina goddess (pl. 125). This sculpture, now in the National Museum of India, has been published on several occasions and divergent dates have been proposed for it.[46] The context given here demonstrates that the image belongs in the late ninth century. The detailing is rich and accomplished, as in all ninth-century material, but the treatment of the flesh is starting to congeal. The meticulous finish shows a preoccupation with perfection and clarity, analogous to the Sesai and Markhera temples. A number of Jaina excavations near Urwāhī gate in Gwalior Fort are in an identical style and thus belong with the National Museum's bust at the end of the ninth century (pl. 126).[47] The most interesting cave has a standing Tīrthaṁkara flanked by attendants, flying *vidyādhara* figures and other Jinas, including Mahāvīra and Pārśvanātha (pl. 127). This sanctuary gives some idea of the late ninth-century monuments at Gwalior that have not survived.[48]

A bust of the god Kumāra from Amrol also belongs in this period (pl. 128).[49] In this sculpture there is no clearer indication of how the subtle ups and downs of plastic modelling have been overtaken by a sinuous precision and linear approach to form. The Kumāra was removed from India, but not before its provenance and date were documented.[50] In the large image of Varāha at Hathlau we see an identical sense of modelling, though it has been obscured by surface damage from libation (pl. 129).

These sculptures lead us to a consideration of the various levels of art activity in Gopakṣetra. It will be recalled that in previous periods a considerable amount of humble or sub-regional work was produced in the region. In the late ninth century all the artefacts are executed in a uniform and accomplished manner. The complex of temples at Batesar shows that this does not seem to be the result of limited data. As we have seen, Batesar preserves sub-regional material spanning a considerable length of time. The mid-ninth century additions falter in design and execution, indicating that they are among the last manifestations of sub-regionalism (pl. 72). There is no building activity at Batesar in the late ninth century. When temples are again set up there in the tenth century, they are no longer in a sub-regional idiom but unequivocally representative of the finest work; humbler or more rustic manners are no longer found (pl. 131). This pattern indicates that from the late ninth century all work springs from a homogeneous regional idiom. In addition, this homogeneous idiom has moved closer to the neighbouring regional styles, as evidenced by the remains at Markhera, Umri and Gyāraspur.

Early Tenth Century

In the tenth century there is enough dated material to trace the development of architecture and sculpture with relative ease. Some of the remains, especially the temples at Khajurāho, are published and well known. As a consequence, this section will not be a comprehensive survey but a synopsis aimed at providing a frame of reference for future histories. Particular attention will be given to temples and sculptures that hitherto have been ignored.

An appropriate starting point for the tenth century is a pair of hero-stones from Terāhī dated VS 960/AD 903.[51] These stones, designed as memorials, follow earlier examples in showing various battle scenes with a bust of the deceased warrior at the top. The small subsidiary figures (pl. 130) foreshadow western Indian painting with their wire-like outlines and emphatically sharp noses. The main images are more fully worked, but compared to work of the ninth century, there is no mistaking the abrupt angularity of the poses and the hardening of plastic sense.

The best-preserved building with sculpture comparable to the hero-stones is the open hall (*raṅgamaṇḍapa*) at Pāroli (pls 131, 132). Located in a small fort, the structure stands on a high moulded platform (*jagatī*). The hall itself has an elaborate plinth (*pīṭha*) topped by a *vedikā* (fence-like parapet). The sloping splat (*kakṣāsana*), mostly broken away, carries projecting elephant heads. Inside, there are little shrines beneath the seat slab. This shows an internalisation of the *pañcāyatana*, or five-shrined plan (pl. 131). A similar arrangement is found later in the Sās Bahū temple at Gwalior (dated VS 1150/AD 1093–4). Elaborate square pillars with massive brackets support the lintels and ceilings, all carved with an extraordinary array of sculpture in near perfect condition (pl. 132). All the major gods of the Indian pantheon are represented, along with running friezes of Śaiva rites, events from the life of Kṛṣṇa and scenes of devotional procession and dance.

The iconographic programme of the Pāroli hall has never been studied, but the chronological position can be determined in the context of the present survey. The general sense of elaborateness is comparable to monuments of the late ninth century, but like the Terāhī hero-stones there is an emphasis on repetitive angular forms and complex rhythmic surfaces. The heads of the figures seem proportionately larger than before and the faces are starting to acquire the stereotyped appearance often found in tenth-century sculpture. Close examination often reveals a schematic effort at modelling and a coarsening of detail. These changes foreshadow the degeneration of sculpture into perfunctory architectural ornament during the second half of the tenth century.

The hall has open porches (*mukhacatuṣkī*) on two sides sheltering large foot-stones (*ardhacandra*) flanked by conches. Two freestanding lions originally stood beyond the eastern entrance. Though the lions are still in their original position, they were buried in the glacis when the temple platform was turned into a small fort in the eighteenth century. The roof of the hall was evidently made of horizontal slabs (*phāṁsanā*), but the stones have been stripped away. This part of the building was probably similar to the Mālā Devī temple at Gyāraspur.[52] To the west of the hall is a large, flat space. It is there that the original temple stood, but it has completely perished save for fragments that lie scattered outside the fort or built into its walls. From the preference for Śaiva imagery in the reliefs and the damaged Nandi figures among the loose fragments, we can assume that the building was originally dedicated to Śiva.

The appearance of the Pāroli temple may be

inferred from a ruin at nearby Bhainsorā (pl. 133). This temple, also dedicated to Śiva, has prominent central projections (*bhadra*) and displays an inventiveness of architectural detail, particularly in the plinth (*pīṭha*). Such features are common in the early tenth-century repertoire and are found in buildings like the Jarāi Mātā at Barwa Sāgar.[53] The deep recesses on either side of the subsidiary offsets (*pratiratha*) are decorated with a chequer and carry standing figures and griffins (*vyāla*). Griffins often appear in this location during the tenth century. The individual images are stylistically close to Pāroli. Compared to late ninth-century sculpture they emphasise rhythmic stances and have a reduced plastic feeling. Larger heads, often poorly integrated with the rest of the figure, are a common feature.

Other remains in the vicinity dating to the first part of the tenth century may be mentioned. At Pāroli itself there is a second moulded platform (*jagatī*) not far from the fort. Only the corner of this platform has survived. At Batesar there is a similar *jagatī*; in both cases the temples have disappeared or were never completed. The ruin of a hall, probably once like Pāroli in architectural configuration, is preserved at Bārāhet (pl. 134). A partially ruined temple at Sihoniyā (north-east of the village in a neighbourhood known as Dubalia) shows how the *maṇḍapikā* had declined as an independent architectural type (pl. 135). A shrine dedicated to Śiva at Chhimkā provides another example with a complete doorway (pl. 136). The figural sculpture at Chhimkā is virtually identical to Pāroli and Bhainsorā, a fact that stresses the uniformity of style in the early tenth century.

Remains from the first quarter of the tenth century in the southern part of Gopakṣetra are not common. The only temple is at Kadwāhā, in the group known locally as Morāyat (pl. 137). The name may be a corruption of Mattamayūra, the town in which Śaiva siddhānta ascetics were encouraged to settle and for whom the monasteries at Kadwāhā, Rannod and Surwāyā were built. An early tenth-century date for the Morāyat temple is confirmed by a comparison to Sesai.[54] The *vedībandha* is more compressed and precisely cut, and the entablature (*varaṇḍikā*) has sharper mouldings. Compared to the dated aedicules at Gyāraspur, the spire displays a tighter organisation of its constituents (pls 137, 122). The closest parallel for this handling of the superstructure is the early tenth-century Jarāi Mātā at Barwa Sāgar.[55] The Kadwāhā figural sculpture is identical in style to Chhimkā, though the design of the doorways shows considerable simplification. Of special interest is the stringcourse that runs through the middle of the wall (*jaṅghā*). This type of two-tiered wall (often with two rows of sculpture) is a feature that comes into wide use in the mid-tenth century.

Mid-Tenth Century

The Lakṣmaṇa temple at Khajurāho is not far removed in date or appearance from the monuments just described. The Lakṣmaṇa is the earliest of the Khajurāho series and is assignable to VS 1011/AD 954–5, the date of an inscription found at the base of the building in the nineteenth century.[56] The temple is a massive one, with a central structure and four subsidiary shrines (*pañcāyatana*).[57] The exterior walls of the main temple are ornamented with two tiers of sculpture. Comparing these images to those at Pāroli shows how the forms have changed since the early tenth century (pls 139, 132). The Khajurāho figures have been purged of almost every vestige of plastic feeling, a dynamic play of line being preferred to modelled volume. A harsh metallic quality is often seen in the mask-like faces. The profusion of detail and dramatic postures cannot hide that the sculpture of the Lakṣmaṇa is leading to a simpler and fundamentally debased conception of form. The handling of architectural details also indicates a trend toward simplification. For example, the fence-like parapet (*vedikā*) used on the projecting balconies shows that flat, stencil-like patterns have completely replaced the carved floral scrolls favoured in the early tenth century. Now the elements are viewed as simply receding and dark or projecting and light.

Many of the larger temples of the ninth and tenth centuries have been destroyed, making it difficult to compare the Lakṣmaṇa with earlier buildings. Consequently, the specific changes in architecture evidenced at Khajurāho are best understood if we turn to the subsidiary shrines (*devakulikā*) on the corners of the platform (pl. 138). These structures provide greater continuity with the past in both scale and configuration. A comparison with the Morāyat temple at Kadwāhā shows changes as dramatic as those already noted in the figural sculpture (pl. 137). Mouldings are given sharper profiles and the recesses are accentuated, deepening the shadows between the various parts. This is especially apparent in the entablature (*varaṇḍikā*). While the wall (*jaṅghā*) does not have two tiers of reliefs, it is visually divided by prominent floral panels. These panels are carved with the harsh, stencil-like patterns typical of the mid-tenth century. The sculpture itself is governed by dynamic complications and completely fills the wall surface. The insertion of rampant griffins (*vyāla*) in the crevices is an innovation that first appeared at Bhainsorā (pl. 133). In the spire the horizontal slabs (*kalā*) have sharp profiles and the *jāla* is flattened into a busy mesh. The parts have, in fact, become abstract panels of frosted decoration. Nothing shows more clearly how temple forms have been reduced with painful exactness to simple black and white patterns.

Although the Lakṣmaṇa is an important temple with a secure date, it is simplistic to view all earlier developments leading exclusively to this building. To provide a more balanced picture, we should turn briefly to coeval remains at other sites, particularly those in Gopakṣetra. The most important buildings are the Śiva temples at Surwāyā. Before this complex was turned into a small fort in the fifteenth century, the temples stood in a walled precinct beside a large monastic residence. The oldest and largest Śiva temple belongs to the mid-tenth century.[58] Only the vestibule wall (*kapilī*), open porch (*mukhacatuṣkī*), door and sanctum of this building have survived (pl. 140). The entrance door follows the organisation of jambs favoured during the mid-tenth century; the repetitive rhythms that sweep through the figures are also typical of the period. A comparison of Surwāyā with Pāroli confirms this chronological horizon (pls 140, 131). As Pāroli is the immediate forerunner in the Gopakṣetra region, there are inevitable similarities between the two buildings. A later date for Surwāyā is revealed, however, by the stiffer modelling and stereotyped handling of the postures. Many of the architectural details have a crisp, linear quality beside Pāroli, although the severity and harshness often seen at Khajurāho is avoided.

The spire and exterior walls of the Surwāyā temple have been stripped away, leaving only a ragged masonry core. A temple exterior of the mid-tenth century is preserved, however, at Terāhī in the Mohañjmātā temple (pl. 141). This temple's superstructure has vanished, but the remaining portions are comparable to the *devakulikā*-shrine at Khajurāho (pl. 138). On both buildings the surface is cluttered with tightly modelled images and the wall divided into two levels by stencil-like panels. There is a rigorous contrast of light and dark, both around the images and between the mouldings of *vedībandha* and entablature (*varaṇḍikā*). The freestanding gate before the Mohañjmātā also dates to the mid-tenth century (pl. 142); the changes in this form are illustrated by comparing it to the late ninth-century gate at Gyāraspur (pl. 124).

Summary

This chapter charted the development of architecture and sculpture in Gopakṣetra between AD 800 and 900. Changes were more easily traced in this century because several monuments bear dates; the most notable was the Caturbhuj temple on Gwalior Fort (AD 875–6; pl. 108). With the aid of this and other material three phases of development were mapped out for the ninth century. During the early phase, best exemplified by the Śiva temple at Terāhī, a delicate, even finish emerged in both architecture and sculpture (pl. 100). Each part of the temple began to play a subdued role in the elevation, creating an overall uniformity of texture. In figural sculpture an internal coherence and lyrical richness of detail started to appear (pl. 98). Sub-regional monuments continued to be found, but the humbler additions to the Batesar complex showed that the workmanship was loosing vitality and becoming increasingly rustic (pl. 67).

In the middle phase, datable to the half-century between 825 and 875, a rich maturation came to the temple tradition. Buildings like the Sun temple at Khiaoda showed how every sculpture and architectural element was sublimated to a scheme of extraordinary elegance and elaboration (pl. 113). This was a high point of Indian art (pl. 117), showing a degree of accomplishment and mature assurance unseen since the fifth century. As for sub-regional traditions, they were being rapidly absorbed into the mainstream or were lapsing into unembellished folk art (pl. 72). This resulted in a greater homogeneity of style in northern India.

The late phase after 875 ostensibly continued mid-ninth century conventions with little change, but close scrutiny showed the emergence of sharper distinctions between architectural forms and a biting precision of detail. Scrollwork was tightened and undercut, while sculpture displayed a weakening of plastic feeling (pl. 128). A striving for clarification and disciplined order was everywhere evident. The chronological horizon of this material was fixed by the Cār Kambhā at Gyāraspur, a ruin that can be associated with an inscription of AD 879–80 (pl. 123).

As a postscript to the central consideration of this chapter, a discussion of some tenth-century material was included to carry the chronology forward to the well-known Lakṣmaṇa temple at Khajurāho. The first steps toward the crisp, linear style of the Lakṣmaṇa were taken in the opening years of the tenth century and were particularly apparent in two hero-stones from Terāhī dated AD 903 (pl. 130). The modelling of the figures on the stones showed a harsh angularity beside late ninth-century sculpture; the rhythmic poses appear to be more cursory and stereotyped. In the temple at Kadwāhā architectural forms displayed a tighter and more severe treatment beside ninth-century examples (pl. 137). By the time of the Lakṣmaṇa temple at Khajurāho (datable to AD 954–5) and the monuments that can be grouped with it, an agitated linear style, purged of almost every vestige of plastic feeling had taken over (pl. 139). Flat chisel-work took command of surface, casting a crisp frosting over the entire temple structure (pls 138, 141).

Notes

1 See Chapter 5.

2 One published in Meister, 'Maṇḍapikā Shrines of Central India', fig. 25; see also Meister, *Encyclopaedia of Indian Temple Architecture*, fig. 317.

3 Trivedi, *Temples of the Pratīhāra Period*, pls 149, 189.

4 Dhaky, 'Genesis and Development of Māru-Gurjara Temple Architecture', in *Studies in Indian Temple Architecture*, pl. 69.

5 See my 'Brick Temple of the Ninth Century', AA 52 (1992), pl. 10.

6 For other rectangular temples associated with the Mātṛkās, see J. M. Nanavati and M. A. Dhaky, *The Maitraka and Saindhava Temples of Gujarat* (Ascona: Artibus Asiae, 1969).

7 Illustrated in Mukherjee, *Report on the Antiquities in the District of Lalitpur*.

8 Patil, *Descriptive and Classified List*, nos 1486–89. I am grateful to Donald M. Stadtner for bringing these ruins to my attention.

9 For illustration, see Trivedi, *Temples of the Pratīhāra Period*, pl. 96.

10 Keith, *Preservation of National Monuments*, p. 75, records that these models were found at Surāj Kuṇḍ, Gwalior Fort.

11 The origins of the multi-spired superstructure are briefly discussed in Krishna Deva, 'Mālā Devī Temple at Gyāraspur', in *Śrī Mahāvīra Jaina Vidyālaya Golden Jubilee Volume*, 2 vols (Bombay: Śrī Mahāvīra Jaina Vidyālaya, 1968), 1: 260–69.

12 IA 15 (1886): 33–46 (verses 9–11). Pottery sherds from the large mounds around the present village date from the ninth to fourteenth centuries.

13 For the Gadarmal, see Trivedi, *Temples of the Pratīhāra Period*, pl. 161; in the Gwalior region the form is found in the hall at Pāroli, discussed below.

14 Krishna Deva, 'Mālā Devī Temple at Gyāraspur', for illustrations.

15 *Inscriptions of Gopakṣetra*, pp. 1–2; year [Vikrama] Saṁvat 933 is also given.

16 Old photograph published in ibid., fig. 7, and Archaeological Department, Gwalior, *The History and Monuments of Gwalior Fort* (Gwalior: Alijah Darbar Press, n.d.), p. 30.

17 Trivedi, *Temples of the Pratīhāra Period*, fig. 10.

18 The small niches on the *vedībandha* carry Gaṇeśa, Kārttikeya and Pārvatī, thus continuing the customary Śaiva iconographic programme even though the temple is dedicated to Viṣṇu.

19 Old photographs show that one of the pillars is a replacement of the twentieth century, see *Inscriptions of Gopakṣetra*, pl. 7.

20 Krishna Deva, *Khajuraho* (Delhi: Brijbasi, 1987), plate following p. 127.

21 Khiaoda is located east of Shivpuri, just south of Sirsod; see list of villages and maps in Luard, *Gwalior State Gazetteer*. Also of note is the Viṣṇu temple at Varahavali near Rithorā Kalān which I was unable to visit; however, it is illustrated in Rahman Ali, *Pratīhāra Art in India* (Delhi: Agam Kala Prakashan, 1987), pl. vii, fig. 2.

22 Thakore, *Catalogue of Sculptures in the Archaeological Museum, Gwalior*, room 20, no. 11.

23 Ibid., room 21, no. 12.

24 B. L. Nagarch, 'Temples at Sakarra', JMPIP 10 (1976): 53–7, for an account of the iconography.

25 Illustrated in Meister, 'Maṇḍapikā Shrines of Central India', fig. 16; Meister, *Encyclopaedia of Indian Temple Architecture*, fig. 303.

26 EI 4 (1895–7): 305–10. The date corresponds to 10 September 862.

27 Illustration in Trivedi, *Temples of the Pratīhāra Period*, pl. 81.

28 For readings of some of these labels, H. D. Sankalia, 'Jain Monuments from Deogarh', JISOA 9 (1941): 91–104.

29 EI 9 (1907–8): 248–56 (verses 25–8).

30 For Kuchdon, see Trivedi, *Temples of the Pratīhāra Period*, pl. 92, also Meister, 'Maṇḍapikā Shrines of Central India', fig. 19.

31 Trivedi, *Temples of the Pratīhāra Period*, pls 131–2.

32 Ibid., pl. 133, and our pl. 102.

33 Discussed in detail in Chapter 3.

34 Patil, *Descriptive and Classified List*, no. 1505; Trivedi, *Temples of the Pratīhāra Period*, pls 179–84. See our maps for location.

35 Ibid., pl. 149.

36 Ibid., pl. 179, and our pl. 101.

37 Ibid., pls 111, 154.

38 Ibid., pl. 180.

39 Ibid., pl. 184.

40 M. A. Dhaky, 'The Ceilings in the Temples of Gujarat', *Bulletin of the Baroda Museum and Picture Gallery* 16–17 (1963), provides a comprehensive account. Geographically and chronologically, the closest ceilings to Sesai are found in the Mālā Devī temple, Gyāraspur, and the Jarāi Mātā, Barwa Sāgar; Trivedi, *Temples of the Pratīhāra Period*, pl. 171, and S. D. Trivedi, *The Jarāi Temple at Barwā Sāgar* (Jhansi: The Government Museum, 1985).

41 ASIR 10 (1874–7): 31; EI 19–23 (1927–36), appendix, no. 37. The remains in the immediate area of Hindola Toraṇ are all of one period.

42 ARE (1952–53), B, no. 151.

43 EI 33 (1959–60): 93–4; also in A. C. Mittal, *The Inscriptions of the Imperial Paramāras* (Ahmedabad: L. D. Institute of Indology, 1979), pp. 207–8.

44 Patil, *Descriptive and Classified List*, no. 660; Dvivedī, *Gvāliyar rājya ke abhilekh*, no. 660; Dikshit, *A Guide to the Central Archaeological Museum, Gwalior*, p. 8.

45 James Burgess, *Ancient Monuments, Temples and Sculptures of India*, 2 vols (London: W. Griggs, 1897–1911?), pl. 222. The gate has fallen since this photograph was taken.

46 J. Auboyer, 'Indian Art', in *Encyclopedia of World Art* (New York: McGraw-Hill, 1963) 7, pl. 471, caption reads *c.* eighth–ninth century; *Ancient Sculpture from India*

(Cleveland: Museum of Art, 1964), fig. 93, says eighth to ninth century. Osamu Takada and Teruō Ueno, *Indo bijutsu*, 2 vols (Tokyo: Nihon keizai shimbunsha, 1965), pl. 195, caption says sixth century. M. Meister, 'Āma, Amrol and Jainism on Gwalior Fort', JOI 22 (1973): 354–8, places the bust in the first quarter of the eighth century and suggests it is from the Telī kā Mandir. J. C. Harle, ' The Post-Gupta Style of Indian Temple Architecture and Sculpture', *Journal of the Royal Society of Arts* 125 (1977): 585, remarks only that the piece 'lacks unity of style'. The label in the National Museum of India read (in 1980) first half of the seventh century. S. Huntington, *The Art of Ancient India* (New York: Weatherhill, 1985), p. 453, places the bust in the *c.* seventh century and argues for influences from the Deccan. This diversity of opinion re-emphasises the necessity for a systematic examination of regional styles.

47 Also illustrated in Klaus Bruhn, *The Jina Images of Deogarh* (Leiden: E. J. Brill, 1969), figs. 18–18A.

48 A number of late ninth-century fragments, too small and battered to merit illustration, are preserved in the Scindia School collection.

49 P. Pal, *The Ideal Image* (New York: Asia Society, 1978), no. 43; Kramrisch, *Manifestations of Shiva*, no. 65.

50 GAR (VS 1998–2002/AD 1942–6), pl. xvi; also mentioned in GAR (VS 1986/AD 1929–30), p. 13.

51 *Inscriptions of Gopakṣetra*, p. 2; ARE (1952–3), B, no. 162, suggests the date is *kārttikādi*, in which case the year works out to AD 904.

52 For illustrations, see Krishna Deva, 'Mālā Devī Temple at Gyāraspur', and Trivedi, *Temples of the Pratīhāra Period.*

53 Trivedi, *Temples of the Pratīhāra Period*, pls 188–90; for an account of the temple's name, dedication and iconography, see S. D. Trivedi, *The Jarāi Temple at Barwā Sāgar.*

54 Trivedi, *Temples of the Pratīhāra Period*, pl. 179, and our pl. 137.

55 Ibid., pls 188–9.

56 EI 1 (1889–92): 122–35. The inscription was found sometime after 1843 'amongst the ruins at the base of a temple, known as Lakshmaṇjî'.

57 For further details, see Krishna Deva, *Khajuraho*, pp. 59 ff.

58 M. B. Garde, *Guide to Surwaya* (Gwalior: n.p., n.d.). The temple discussed here is labelled no. 1 in Garde's plan. The monastic residence and other temples are later than the mid-tenth century and thus do not fall within the scope of this study.

Chapter 5

Religious and Royal Patronage in Northern India

The monuments discussed in the foregoing chapters leave little doubt that the building of temples was a leading concern of the Indian people from the seventh century. This is shown not only by the monuments and ruins that have survived but by numerous inscriptions recording the construction and endowment of individual temples. This epigraphic information is particularly important because no archival material from before the twelfth century has been preserved. Despite the important place of temple building in Indian society and the fact that inscriptions are, for the most part, documents of religious giving, the subject of patronage has not been systematically explored.[1]

Direct evidence for patronage first appears in northern India during the third century BC and gifts to temples, particularly in the south, have continued to the present day. In line with the regional focus of the current monograph, this wide field must be narrowed to facilitate examination. Unfortunately there are not enough inscriptions in the Gwalior region to provide a strictly regional history of patronage. We must include examples from across north India if we are to arrive at a balanced evaluation of the data found in individual records. North India is a vast area and the number of inscriptions correspondingly great, but a narrower geographical horizon would not yield a representative sample. Our time frame must also span several centuries. Because standardised formulae dominate epigraphic records, only a broad chronological cross-section can illustrate changes in the anatomy of religious giving.

Inscriptions and the Nature of Religious Gifts

Inscriptions in north India varied considerably between the seventh and tenth centuries, but two basic types were predominant. These were: (a) land-grants on copper plates and (b) eulogistic and commemorative inscriptions inscribed on stone tablets or pillars. Copper-plate inscriptions usually record a king's donation of villages or tax-free agricultural land (*agrahāra*) to members of the priestly class.[2] Revenues from the villages supported Brāhmaṇas and were thus seen as rewarding and perpetuating sacred knowledge. The plates were apparently held by the recipients and have been typically discovered near the villages to which they refer. Stone inscriptions, in contrast, were commonly associated with the foundation of temples. Hundreds of stone inscriptions have been preserved; some are still near temple entrances as originally intended, while others have been recovered from ruins and are now held in museum collections.

Both stone and copper-plate inscriptions are normally written in Sanskrit verse and open with an invocation to a deity such as Śiva or Viṣṇu. This can be followed by an account of the presiding monarch; at times many verses praising the king and his ancestors are included. If the king is not the donor, then the royal eulogy is followed by an account of the donor and his family. The building or grant is then described. In the case of buildings mention is sometimes made of gifts for the temple's maintenance. These gifts could consist of villages, agricultural land or commercial property; the revenue from these sources served as an endowment. An inscription's closing statement often expressed the hope that the temple might long endure and that the endowment might not be disturbed; this could be followed by assorted facts such as the date, the name of the architect (*sutradhāra*), the name of the poet who composed the inscription, the name of the individual who wrote it down and the name of the engraver who incised the record on the stone or plate. While copper plates and commemorative stone tablets are the most common sort of record, other types occasionally provide information about patronage. Pilgrim inscriptions recount visits to holy places and give an indication of the religious importance of certain shrines; memorial inscriptions provide an account of departed relatives or warriors who died in battle and occasionally mention endowments to support the bereaved; cultic inscriptions furnish the pious texts or ritual formulae considered appropriate for a particular place.[3]

Despite standard contents and eulogistic phraseology, each inscription is unique. Just as north Indian temples have a generic similarity but are never actually the same, so each donor emerges from the epigraphic record as a distinct individual. Likewise, each sacred place had its own special history and reservoir of endowments. These endowments, because of their economic value, were given exact descriptions. An inscription from Ahar serves as a useful example. This records a number of transactions in favour of the goddess Kanakaśrīdevī.[4] In one case individuals arranged for rents to be directed to the temple; in another a village council (*mahājana*) donated long-term leases on commercial enclosures (*āvārī*); these properties are described with legal precision and their revenues were placed under the control of a managing board or committee (*goṣṭhī*).

Endowments like those documented by the Ahar inscription were made in substantial numbers before the thirteenth century and were the personal property of the god or goddess enshrined in the building. These deities were not abstract symbols but concrete personalities with clearly defined legal rights to gifted property.[5] A temple was thus a complex institution consisting of one or more gods and a number of social groups who managed the temple's property and controlled the worship of the images. Making a gift to a temple, or more correctly to the god in a temple, was seen as a meritorious act in which all could participate according to their means. Gifts were made by all sorts of people, but most commonly by the ruling nobility. Aside from making gifts, it was incumbent upon rulers to provide a stable environment in which religion could flourish. This meant, in practical terms, the maintenance of established preferments and the protection of temple property from abuse and encroachment. As a consequence, temples came to control an increasing amount of revenue from property. Temples also accumulated important fixed assets such as jewels, bullion and miscellaneous paraphernalia. This paraphernalia might include image-frames, thrones, bells, lamps, censers as well as crowns and vestments for ornamenting and displaying the god.

The end of temple wealth and social prominence was heralded by the violent incursions of Maḥmūd of Ghazna in the early eleventh century. Celebrated religious centres such as Mathurā and Somanātha were ransacked, temple treasuries were looted and much booty removed to Afghanistan.[6] With the establishment of the Sultanate at Delhi in the closing years of the twelfth century, the indigenous ruling élites that built and endowed temples were increasingly circumscribed in power and influence. Temple building declined precipitously, the remaining vestiges being all but swept away by the expansionist policies of the Tughluq dynasty in the fourteenth century. The old temples that survived this cataclysm now stand in secluded spots, their property and revenue sequestered, their rites in abeyance and their very names lost to memory (pl. 60). The inscriptional record helps us recover the ancient life of these hollow shells. It is from the particular facts provided by inscriptions that a history of religious giving can be constructed and it is against these facts that the architectural and sculptural residue of the temple tradition must be measured.

Religious Giving and Temple Patronage

A history of patronage from the seventh century has not been written for a variety of reasons, the most salient being that epigraphic records, like most legal documents, use standard formulae that *prima facie* offer little to the historian. The description of temples and religious gifts changed little over the years and this repetitiveness was coupled with the use of stock phrases that are of little concrete value. For example, so many temples are described as being 'high as Mount Kailāsa' that the words are practically meaningless. In contrast, the factual data provided by inscriptions (such as donor's names and the conditions surrounding an endowment) are so focused on particulars that the information is seldom repeated in other records. Furthermore, many of the temples described, especially those from before the tenth century, are either ruined or unidentifiable. As a result, it is impossible to transform the aggregate of single facts into a connected narrative. However, while the ambition of a history in the traditional sense must be set aside, a modest survey of patronage is nonetheless feasible. With numerous individual inscriptions from which to draw illustrative examples, it is possible present a cross-section of temple building and religious giving. Although this approach has the disadvantage of representing patronage as a static phenomena, it can be justified due to the extremely conservative nature of Indian society, the concepts of innovation and progress having little place in the country's intellectual life before the thirteenth century.[7] A synchronic description is thus appropriate provided it is tempered with vignettes relating to change. Our survey might be criticised as burdened with excessive detail; in fact the details given are but a fraction of what has been preserved. Considerable detail has been retained not only to illustrate the character of inscriptions but to highlight the very information that ancient patrons deemed worthy of record.

Noble patronage

After the seventh century northern India was seldom ruled by a single power, major kings and dynasties emerging only rarely from a matrix of competing clans and principalities. The history of these political entities is not well understood, but surviving inscriptions indicate that religious institutions were vigorously supported by all members of the ruling élite. The first major king to appear after the death of Harṣa Vardhana (AD 606–47) was Yaśovarman of Kannauj (*c.* AD 720–50). Yaśovarman's ancestry is not directly known but, as noted in our historical survey in Chapter 1, he may have come from a Maurya clan that controlled Mathurā in the late seventh and early eighth centuries.[8] Although Yaśovarman was a powerful ruler, little archaeological material can be connected with him. Vākpati's *Gauḍavaho*, a contemporary text recounting Yaśovarman's world conquest (*digvijaya*), states that the king built a temple at

Hariścandranagarī (Ayodhyā).[9] The only other indication of Yaśovarman's architectural activities is given in an inscription from Ghosrāwa.[10] This mentions a location called Yaśovarmapuravihāra, suggesting that Yaśovarman was responsible for a city and monastery in the Rājgir hills where the inscription was found. Yaśovarman's successor Āma (*c.* AD 750–75) had an interest in Jainism and the traditions of that faith credit him with building a temple to Mahāvīra in his capital at Gwalior.[11]

This evidence indicates that the kings who ruled the Gangetic heartland in the eighth century had an active interest in constructing temples. More information is forthcoming about contemporary princes in Rājasthān. An illuminating example of such patronage is provided by the inscription from Kanswa near Kotah.[12] The purpose of this epigraph was to record the establishment of a temple by one Śivagaṇa. We learn from the inscription that Śivagaṇa was the son of king (*nṛpa*) Saṁkuka, himself an ally of king Dhavala. Dhavala belonged to one of the Maurya clans that prevailed in many parts of north India during the eighth century. After a blood-curdling description of the military exploits of Śivagaṇa and Saṁkuka the inscription records that Śivagaṇa built a temple (*bhavana*) of Parameśvara in Kaṇvāśrama, the hermitage of Kaṇva (modern Kanswa).[13] Two villages were given as a perpetual endowment for repairs, lights, incense and other accoutrements of worship. The conclusion of the inscription begins with the customary prayer that the *kīrti* (fame of the builder and thus also the building) might long endure and that this temple (*mandira*) of Śambhu was made to augment merit and fame (*dharmmakīrtivivarddhanaṁ*). Then we find the date, the name of the poet Devaṭa, along with various other people involved in the work, including Ṇaṇṇaka, the architect (*sutradhāra*).

That this sort of patronage continued in later times and was not restricted to deities such as Viṣṇu and Śiva is evidenced by the archaeological material discovered at Ghatiyālā, a site north-west of Jodhpur. Ghatiyālā has a ruined Jaina temple with an inscription stating that it was erected by Kakkuka, a ruler of Pratīhāra lineage, in [v]s 918/AD 861–2. The inscription is in Prakrit but follows established conventions as far as its contents are concerned. Beginning with a genealogy of Kakkuka, the record goes on to state that for the increase of fame Kakkuka founded a market and established two pillars, one at Maḍḍodara (modern Mandor) and the other at Rohinsakūpa (modern Ghatiyālā).[14] Furthermore, Kakkuka commissioned this 'mountain-like temple' (*acalam imam bhavanam*) of the Jina and entrusted it to the care of certain members of the Jaina community. Though inscribed in the reign of the celebrated Pratīhāra monarch Mihira Bhoja (*c.* AD 836–85), the inscription does not mention that king's name. The genealogy provided indicates that Kakkuka was related in some way to the imperial Pratīhāras and that occasionally the two branches of the family seem to have been in conflict.[15]

The pillar mentioned in the Ghatiyālā inscription stands near the ruined Jaina temple and is locally known as Khakhu-devalam. The column is a single piece of stone with a separate crown carved with four images of Gaṇeśa. On the shaft are three ninth-century inscriptions. The inscription on the east side, in Sanskrit prose, gives the genealogy of Kakkuka and again records that he set up two pillars, built a market (*haṭṭa*) and established a community (*mahājana*) in the neighbourhood. The inscription on the west side of the pillar provides further information. This begins with obeisance to Vināyaka (Gaṇeśa) and records that the area was originally inhabited by Ābhīras until Kakkuka routed them, built a market with lovely streets and houses and induced a *mahājana* of Brāhmaṇas and other reputable people to reside in the place.[16]

The degree to which epigraphic records focus on matters of local concern is clearly indicated by Ghatiyālā and further illustrated by an inscription of the Guhila prince Bālāditya from Chātsu.[17] This gives a long account of the achievements of the Guhilas in the service of their Pratīhāra overlords, though it must be noted that the Pratīhāras are barely mentioned. The inscription's main purpose is to record that Bālāditya married a lady named Raṭṭavā and that after his wife's death a temple (*prāsāda*) of Murāri (Viṣṇu) was erected by Bālāditya in commemoration. Another commemorative temple is mentioned in the inscription from Rajor.[18] This describes how a prince named Mathanadeva granted a village to a Śiva temple to maintain the rituals. The temple was known as Lacchukeśvara Mahādeva after Mathana's mother Lacchukā. This naming of temples after a donor or an esteemed person was a long-established practice; it is known from at least the fifth century and has continued down to the present day.[19]

The predominantly local focus of inscriptions, both in recording political events and religious gifts, brings us full circle to the historical considerations explored in Chapter 1. As explained there, a number of models have been put forward to explain internal political arrangements and the constitution of power in ancient India. Whatever methodological course is pursued, it is necessary to set aside the centralised models of state and the idea that political relationships were feudatory in nature. One of the most telling records in this regard is the inscription of king Parabala on the pillar at Badoh.[20] The political and methodological implications of this inscription, and how it shows that north India was more of a political mosaic than previously acknowledged, have already been discussed (p.24). Aside from its historical importance, Parabala's inscription is also an important document of patronage. Its purport is that Parabala built a temple of Śauri (Viṣṇu) and that he caused a Garuḍa pillar (*garuḍadhvaja*) to be set up before the temple. In verse 27 we have a rather eloquent description of the pillar on which the record is incised.

viṣṇoḥ kim caraṇastrivikramakṛteḥ stambhākṛtervvā vapuḥ
sthāṇorbhūvira[rā]tphaṇīndra ripunā śeṣothavā proddhṛtaḥ /
itthaṁ bhūri vi[cāra]yadbhiramarairālokya ni[ścī]yate
stambhaḥ śuddhaśilāmayaḥ parabala [kṣmā]pāla kīrttipradaḥ //

Repeatedly deliberating whether this is Viṣṇu's foot making three strides, or the body of Sthānu shaped like a post, or Śeṣa pulled out of a hole in the ground by the enemy of the serpent king, the gods on viewing it find that it is really a Pillar of pure stone, proclaiming the glory of king Parabala.

While patronage was often dominated by kings like Parabala, we must not neglect the part played by other members of the nobility, especially women of high birth. There is, of course, a long tradition of noble ladies supporting temples and religion in all parts of India. Several inscriptions document that women were important patrons during the period under review. An example from Buchkala may be noted, as the building is well preserved.[21] The inscription states that in the time of Nāgabhaṭṭa II (*c.* AD 810–33) a temple (*devagṛha*) was founded by queen (*rājñī*) Jayāvalī, the daughter of Jajjaka, himself the son of the Pratīhāra prince Bapuka. Slightly older is a fragmentary epigraph from Kāmān (ancient Kāmyaka). This gives the genealogy of a local Sūrasena dynasty over seven rulers and mentions that Vacchikā, the wife of Durgadāman, built a temple to Viṣṇu.[22] The dynasty is otherwise unknown but the record has been dated to the eighth or ninth century on the basis of palaeography.[23]

Inscriptions giving an account of temple construction and endowment are the most common records we have of the Indian nobility. Further information and insight into the ruling class are provided by stelae that carry reliefs depicting noble individuals. Quite often these stelae carry inscriptions of historical value. An illustrative example is a votive slab from Sāgar showing a prince with members of his family.[24] The slab was probably set up in a temple built by the donor and is directly comparable to a later relief in the Gupteśvar temple at Mohangarh. That these were freestanding stelae is shown by the long inscription on the reverse of the Mohangarh slab.[25] Also of a personal character, but still essentially religious in nature, are the memorials that record the death of warriors and occasionally the self-immolation (*satī*) of their widows. The oldest *satī* stone in northern India is at Eran (dated Gupta year 191/AD 510–11), and the practice is subsequently mentioned in the seventh-century *Harṣacarita.*[26] Several eighth-, ninth- and tenth-century memorial stones are known in central India and later examples from Rājasthān survive in large numbers.[27] Elaborate stones have reliefs illustrating such things as the warrior's heroic death in battle and his subsequent enjoyment of heavenly felicity (pl. 130). In some cases the top of the stele carries a bust of the deceased.

Patronage of officers and subjects

From the nobility we may turn to their officers and subjects. These people, like their overlords, supported religious institutions and had their efforts memorialised with inscriptions. A useful example to introduce this level of patronage is found at Gwalior. The Caturbhuj temple (pl. 107) carries two inscriptions describing how it was established by Alla, the warden (*koṭṭapāla*) of Gwalior Fort in the last quarter of the ninth century.[28] From these epigraphs we learn that Alla was the son of Vāillabhaṭṭa and that this Vāillabhaṭṭa had come from Lāṭa (coastal Gujarāt) where he had served as a frontier commander (*maryādādharya*) under the Pratīhāra king Rāmabhadra (*c.* AD 833–6). Alla succeeded to this post and was subsequently appointed to Gwalior by Mihira Bhoja (*c.* AD 836–85). Alla then built this temple of Viṣṇu for the increase of his and his wife's merit, 'a receptacle of his fame, cut by the chisel and marked with his name'. The temple is described as a single piece of rock and a 'great ship for crossing the ocean of existence'. The inscriptions further inform us that the temple was known as Vāillabhaṭṭasvāmin in honour of Alla's father and that Alla built a second temple dedicated to the goddess. (The goddess temple has not survived.) Endowments were lavished on both buildings by various sections of the community and the city council made a grant on behalf of the entire town.

The Caturbhuj inscriptions indicate that this temple was an extremely important building in its day. The Pratīhāra kings valued the fortress of Gwalior because it guarded the territory between Kālinjar and Chittaur and was integral to their campaigns against the Rāṣṭrakūṭas.[29] The warden of Gwalior Fort was therefore a key officer, and a temple built by such a person was the product of a respected and powerful individual. Subsequent members of Alla's family apparently continued in the imperial service at Gwalior, for one of them died facing a Rāṣṭrakūṭa raid. This is evidenced by a hero-stone from Terāhī which records the death of one Allajiyapa, son of Allabhaṭṭa.[30]

In addition to recording Alla's activities, the Caturbhuj temple inscriptions provide a long and informative eulogy of the Pratīhāra dynasty. In contrast, some inscriptions only make passing references to the appropriate overlord. For example, an inscription from the time of Yaśovarman (*c.* AD 720–50) records how his officer Bālāditya built a temple of the Buddha at Nālanda and how it was endowed by Malada, the son of Yaśovarman's minister.[31] Virtually no information is given about Yaśovarman. The same situation is found in the copper plates from Una.[32] These were issued by Balavarman and his son Avanivarman Yoga of Cāḷukya family; they record the gift of villages to a temple of the sun god called Taruṇādityadeva. We are told that the Pratīhāra monarch Mahendrapāla I (*c.* AD 885–910) conferred the title of the 'five great sounds' (*pañcamahāśabda*) on Balavarman and that the gifts were sanctioned by a frontier-guardian (*antapāla*) named Dhīika. This Dhīika appears to have been a representative of Mahendrapāla's court. Despite these imperial connections, a royal genealogy is not given and all the details focus on matters of immediate local importance. The same situation is found in the plates from Haddala.[33] With the example of the nobility before us, we can conclude that officers enjoyed considerable autonomy and that even in the important matter of issuing copper plates they only had to acknowledge the sovereign briefly.

Like the nobility also, the wives of important officers were active patrons. Two examples may be noted which are thematically related to those just discussed. An image of Śiva and Pārvatī from Gwalior carries an inscription that records that it was commissioned by Ṛjjūkā, the wife of Śrī Rudra.[34] This married couple are otherwise unknown, but the record mentions that Śrī Rudra bore the 'five great sounds', making it probable that he was a Pratīhāra officer. Another inscription, of unknown provenance but now in Udaipur, records the activities of a lady named Yaśomatī in [v]s 718/AD 660–61.[35] She was the wife of Varāhasiṁha, a commander in the service of the Guhila prince Aparājita. Having considered the inherent vanity of life, Yaśomatī built a temple of Viṣṇu in order to cross the sea of worldly existence. Though separated by two centuries, both the Caturbhuj and Udaipur inscriptions describe temples as a means of crossing over this world. This serves as a reminder of how little inscriptions and their contents changed with the passage of time.

The foregoing examples are fairly simple in that they represent donors constructing individual temples or making individual grants. Religious centres of importance, however, often attracted an extended series of temples and endowments. This could lead to complicated inscriptions recording numerous gifts by a range of individuals over a span of time. Such collective records are known from Kāmān, Ahar, Partābgarh and Siron.[36] All record a variety of gifts or temple-building projects by a number of persons, some of whom were important officers. For example, the inscription from Siron (ancient Sīyaḍoṇī) mentions that a military commander named Undabhaṭa made a gift to a Viṣṇu temple in VS 964/AD 907–8.[37]

The Siron inscription lists additional grants by persons without title. This forms an appropriate bridge to the lowest level of patronage.[38] Temple gifts at this level often consisted of plots of land, the rents from which were intended to benefit a particular god. Land was not, however, the only source of temple revenue. This is shown by an inscription at Delhi dating to Mihira Bhoja's time which records the gift of rent-money from a house for lamps, sandal paste, flowers and worship at some shrine.[39] Similar, but somewhat unusual, is a gift of wine every month for the worship of Viṣṇu (probably in the tantric fashion).[40] That some kind of tithing was used to support temples is shown by a number of records, the most detailed instance being an inscription from Pehoa (ancient Pṛthūdaka).[41] This recounts how a group of horse-traders imposed certain taxes upon themselves and upon their customers, and how the proceeds were to be distributed to certain temples in fixed proportions.

Individuals without title constructed temples as well as endowed them. This is shown by a second inscription from Pehowa recording that three brothers built a temple (*āyatana*) of Viṣṇu.[42] Each brother's contribution to the work is described as follows:

goggena kāritaṁ madhye pūrṇarājena pṛṣṭhaḥ /
purato devarājena ghanāndhatamasacchide //

In the middle it was made by Gogga, the back by Pūrṇarāja,
The front by Devarāja, for destroying the cloud of intense ignorance.

Common devotion did not always express itself as a complete monument. A pillar at Deogarh dated [v]s 919/AD 862 is one of a pair at the site and these seem to have been part of a gate or gate-house before the main temple.[43] The inscription explicitly states that 'this pillar' was set up 'near the temple of Śāntinātha (*śrī śāntyāyata[na] [saṁ]nidhe*)' by Śrī Deva, a disciple of Kamaladeva.[44] This suggests the gate may have been the collective gift of several individuals. Places like Deogarh, which had an established reputation, were naturally subject to embellishment. Another good example of this is the roadway cut into the east face of Gwalior Fort. The Caturbhuj temple, already discussed, was the most important addition, but there were also a number of small rock-cut shrines and little niches with Hindu and Jaina images. These embellishments continued into the sixteenth century.

Apart from epigraphic documentation of this type, many sites possess material indicative of the patronage of ordinary people. Perhaps the most revealing site in this regard is Batesar, a collection of shrines located near the village of Pāroli. A Śiva temple was built near the tank at Batesar towards the end of the eighth century and a complex of small shrines subsequently developed in the immediate neighbourhood (pl. 70). These shrines were laid out in clusters and are indicative of building activity at a very humble level. There is not a single record stating who commissioned these shrines, but more recent sites readily explain them. An analogous temple-city grew up at Sonāgir (ancient Suvarṇagiri) during the nineteenth century, each addition a product of the individual devotion and means of its patron.[45] The miniature monolithic temples found at many places in northern India are of the same character. An example in the Bhārat Kalā Bhavan, Vārāṇasī, carries an inscription that may be read: *oṁ bāleśvaraḥ*. This means the shrine was dedicated to Śiva, lord of Bāla, the donor. This illustrates the custom of naming the enshrined divinity in honour of the patron or an esteemed family member. This long-standing tradition shows that the Bhārat Kalā Bhavan shrine and other examples like it were bona fide temples in miniature and represent what persons of humble means could add to sacred sites for their own religious merit. The two examples from Gwalior now in the Archaeological Museum (pl. 104) are unparalleled for their architectural accuracy and excellent state of preservation.

That grants to religious establishments by ordinary people were growing in number after the seventh century is evidenced by the increasing mention of the administrative boards or committees (*goṣṭhī*) that were set up to manage endowments. These boards ensured that the funds were directed to the stipulated purpose. Inscriptions give the impression that the wealth of temples from minor grants was considerable and that the administrative boards supervised significant investments and expenditures. Expenditures involved repairs to temples and at times the construction, so some account of these boards is necessary for a complete picture of temple patronage. A good indication of how boards were formed is given by the Kāmān inscription, dated Harṣa year 263/AD 869.[46] This begins by naming the board members (*goṣṭhika*) and recording that three brothers built a tank (*vāpī*) and a temple (*maṭha*) and further arranged for *piṇḍa* rites, the offerings to deceased parents. The brothers then formed part of the board that was set up to manage the shrine and the offerings. A second Kāmān inscription, carrying various dates between Harṣa year 180 and 279/AD 786 and 885, mentions a variety of gifts to different gods, the most important of which was Śiva as Kāmyakeśvara. Several of these grants were instituted or managed by board members.[47] The Pehoa inscription records how some horse-dealers distributed income to various shrines and ends with an exhortation to the board members to manage the grants in accordance with the terms set down.[48]

Royal Patronage in the Age of Pratīhāra Supremacy

Among the competing principalities of the eighth century were the Gurjara Pratīhāras, a clan whose power was centred in the Maru country of Rājasthān. During the time of Nāgabhaṭṭa II (*c.* AD 810–33) the Pratīhāras were able to assert control over most of the ruling families in northern India.

An important step in the expansion of Pratīhāra power, and one that was celebrated in Pratīhāra-period inscriptions, was the capture of Kānyakubja (modern Kannauj), a city long regarded as the imperial centre of the Gangetic heartland. A considerable number of inscriptions survive from Pratīhāra times, some of which have already been mentioned. These inscriptions provide enough documentation to allow a tentative reconstruction of imperial patronage during the ninth and tenth centuries.

The largest corpus of imperial Pratīhāra records are copper plates recording gifts of villages to Brāhmaṇas.[49] In several cases we learn that the king made the grant for the religious merit of his parents, a formula of long-standing popularity.[50] These records contain the royal genealogy and are often interesting for references to the deities that were the object of each monarch's special devotion. An imperial gift is also recorded in the stone inscription from Partābgarh, but in this case the village was given to a temple rather than to Brāhmaṇas. The details are that Mahendrapāla II (*c.* AD 943–46) granted a village to Vaṭayakṣiṇidevī, a goddess whose shrine was under the care of the monastery (*maṭha*) of Haryṛṣīśvara.[51]

Records such as these demonstrate that the imperial Pratīhāras were active patrons of both Brāhmaṇas and notable temples. There are no epigraphs, however, that state that the Pratīhāras supported the actual construction of temples. The only evidence for imperial building activity is given in an inscription found at Sāgar Tāl, a large tank on the outskirts of Gwalior.[52] Beginning in the usual way, the epigraph opens with an invocation to Viṣṇu and a verse in his praise. There follows a twenty-four-verse account of the Pratīhāra family and their noble achievements. The actual object of the inscription is then mentioned in verse 26, which is that the Pratīhāra king Mihira Bhoja (*c.* AD 836–85) erected a city for his seraglio in the name of Viṣṇu. The key verse is as follows:

rājñā tena svadevīnāṁ yaśaḥ puṇyābhivṛdhhaye /
antaḥpurapuraṁ namnā vyadhāyi narakadviṣaḥ //

To increase the fame and merit of his queens,
The king built a harem-city in Viṣṇu's name.

The inscription closes with a prayer for the longevity of this noble building (*āryakīrti*) and mentions the name of the poet Bālāditya. The crucial phrase is *antaḥpurapuram*. The word *antaḥpura* is well known from inscriptions and its interpretation in this context as 'royal harem' or 'seraglio' is not contentious.[53] The word *pura* means 'city' or 'fort', and taking the whole compound as appositionally defined (*karmadhāraya*), we can render it 'a city for the royal harem'. This may be interpreted as a palace complex. The appearance of this complex is unknown because the site of Sāgar Tāl, where the inscription was discovered in 1896, has only one battered fragment of ninth-century date. It served as the wall section of a small shrine that stood beside the tank. Everything else has vanished and the tank itself was rebuilt in Mughal times. During that period, if not before, Sāgar Tāl's original character as a palace site was transformed when it became part of the necropolis of Islamic Gwalior.

Other inscriptions, while not imperial, give incidental details about the building activities of the Pratīhāra kings. The inscription from the shrine of Garībnāth at Pehowa records grants to a series of temples; one was the temple of Viṣṇu Garuḍāsana built by the Brāhmaṇa Bhūvaka on the banks of the Gaṅgā in Bhojapura near Kannauj.[54] This Bhojapura has not been located, but it was probably a suburb established by Mihira Bhoja near the imperial capital. We have already noted how Yaśovarman established Yaśovarmapura in eastern India. Further evidence of royal patronage is provided by the Caturbhuj temple inscriptions at Gwalior. As already noted, the primary purpose of these inscriptions was to record the establishment of the Caturbhuj.[55] In the process of detailing this foundation the inscription mentions that the temple was built 'on the descent of the roadway of Śrī Bhojadeva' (*śrībhojadevapratolyavatare*). This expression refers to the steep road cut into the cliff-face of Gwalior Fort and shows that it was made, or substantially expanded, by Mihira Bhoja. The road originally consisted of a series of wide steps and some are still visible beside the gravel and paving stones laid down in the mid-nineteenth century to facilitate vehicular traffic.[56]

The words 'on the descent of Bhoja's road' suggest that the roadway led to an important Pratīhāra structure of some kind. Examination of the fifteenth-century Mān Mandir, which now crowns the fort, shows that Bhoja's road led to a ninth-century palace. Some sumptuously carved pilasters of great size that belonged to the original structure were reused when the Elephant Gate was reconstructed. From the description of Ibn Baṭṭūṭa, who visited Gwalior in the fourteenth century before the rebuilding began, we know that a life-size image of an elephant and mahout stood outside the entrance.[57] The palace must have been a spectacular structure, but all that remains are the reused pilasters and, on the south side of the entrance, about forty courses of ashlar relieved by a number of cornices (*kapota*). Attention may also be drawn to a double lion capital, now in the National Museum of India. This unique sculpture was found near Tikonia Tāl on the fort and may have crowned a pilaster in the Pratīhāra palace complex.[58] These remains are of considerable importance, there being little known about palace architecture before the Islamic conquest. Further information on early secular architecture is provided by the Sola Khambi at Badoh.[59] This building is placed on a knoll overlooking a lake and apparently served as a pleasure pavilion. It consists of an open pillared hall conforming to the type placed before temples; no inscriptions shed light on the structure but it may be dated on architectural grounds to about the tenth century.

A notable observation to be made from ninth- and tenth-century inscriptions is that the Pratīhāra monarchs were not involved in commissioning temples or images. This is illustrated most clearly by the inscription of Bāuka, a prince belonging to the local royalty at Mandor (ancient Māṇḍavyapura).[60] The epigraph, dated VS 894/AD 837–8, gives a long account of Bāuka's family and culminates with a ghoulish description of his victory in a battle. The celebration of this victory and the praise of Bāuka's lineage is the sole purpose of the inscription; no temple was built and no grant of villages made. Bāuka was a Pratīhāra prince but did not belong to the main imperial line. During the setbacks that marked the reign of Rāmabhadra (c. AD 833–6) Bāuka asserted independence and laid claim to the full range of royal titles. Though his political ambitions were soon suppressed by Mihira Bhoja, Bāuka's inscription is imperial in aspiration and general character.[61] Records of this type were probably once common in the capital at Kannauj before that city was completely destroyed in the eleventh and twelfth centuries. The fairly wide use of such laudatory inscriptions is evidenced by a eulogy (*praśasti*) of the Rāṣṭrakūṭa monarch Kṛṣṇa III (*c.* AD 939–67).[62] This inscription has no purpose but to laud the king; its political overtones are evident both from the use of the Kannada language and from its location at Jura in the Ḍāhala country, an area traditionally under the sway of northern rulers.

The non-involvement of the imperial Pratīhāras in temple building can be understood in various ways. The Vedic rituals that formed a crucial part of early Indian kingship represent the most antique aspect of the problem. These elaborate performances, particularly the horse sacrifice (*aśvamedha*) and royal consecration (*rājasūya*), were widespread in the two centuries before and after Christ. The rituals were seen as propelling the king into a heavenly sphere and infusing him with divine power. This had the effect of simultaneously giving the king a mandate to rule and placing him above the numerous sects and classes over which he had to preside. Ritual performance was therefore the primary and most appropriate focus of royal patronage. Kings were dependent on Brāhmaṇas in this scheme, for Brāhmaṇas alone were qualified to carry out the prescribed rituals. Consequently Brāhmaṇas had to be supported through village grants and other gifts. Royal sponsorship of Vedic ritual declined after the fifth century AD and royal patronage of temples and images clearly emerged under Harṣa Vardhana (*c.* AD 606–47) and his contemporaries in Tamilnadu and the Deccan.[63] In northern India this proved a short-lived innovation, for inscriptions show that the Pratīhāras stood aloof from temple building. While Vedic performances were not reinstated, grants to Brāhmaṇas continued in recognition of their learning. This indicates that the preservation of Vedic knowledge through recitation (*svādhyāya*) was valued apart from its application to specific rituals (*prayoga*). Of this there can be little doubt because each copper plate recording the gift of a village describes the particular Vedic school in which the recipient was an expert.[64] While further conclusions on the basis of the limited corpus of plates are bound to be problematic, the findspots tend to show that Brāhmaṇas with an impressive store of Vedic knowledge were not necessarily given villages close to important centres. Many factors can be suggested to account for this, such as the holding of villages *in absentia* or the simple lack of documentation, but the implication seems to be that the Vedas and attendant Śrauta rituals had declined in importance and that outside their theoretical value as the source of tradition, they had ceased to impinge on day-to-day affairs.

The reluctance of the imperial Pratīhāras to become involved in temple building can also be explained by the nature of temple architecture itself. We have already commented on how a deity in a temple had rights to property; like the learned Brāhmaṇa who received villages from the king, a deity could also receive and hold gifts as a bona fide legal entity. A different relationship was created, however, when a ruler actually constructed a shrine and thus established a divine personality. Inscriptions from as early as the seventh century show that warrior families could be linked to particular temples.[65] Such temples were often patronised by subsequent nobles of the clan; officers and subjects could add subsidiary shrines and endow them with property. A few examples of these clan shrines may be noted: a Cāhamāna family that ruled parts of Mālwa in the tenth century was closely associated with a temple of the sun god that one of their forbears had built at Partābgarh; another Cāhamāna group, also ruling in the tenth century, was intimately connected to the Śiva temple of Harṣadeva which they established and endowed; the Candellas are connected with Maniyāgarh, their family deity being Maniyā Devī.[66] The relationship between such shrines and the clan could be extended to the point where the deity was seen as the true ruler and the prince merely a minister or representative of the god. One of the best-known instances of this is the Lakulīśa temple at Ekalingji which contains the patron-deity of the Guhilas of Medapāṭa (modern Mewar).[67] While the complete subordination of the king to the god was not elaborated in epigraphic records until well after the disintegration of Pratīhāra power, close ties between temples and their founders are indicated by the naming of divinities after specific individuals. This practice goes back to at least the fifth century as has already been mentioned (note 19). Building a temple was thus a meritorious deed that tangibly linked an individual and his clan to a particular place. Not all temples were like this, of course, but those founded by members of the ruling élite could easily assume this character. It was precisely this localisation of power and particularisation of identity that the imperial Pratīhāras sought to avoid. The Pratīhāras belonged to a recognised clan, yet claimed hegemony over all their contemporaries.Temple building and its inevitable ties were seen by the Pratīhāras as something that would only impede their efforts to control the nobility of northern India, a nobility that had a sufficient history of factionalism and violent competition.[68]

This interpretation could be subverted by excavations at Kannauj and the discovery of inscriptions showing that the Pratīhāras built temples in the capital. Pending such excavations, two pieces of indirect information supporting the position argued here may be noted. The first is found at Gwalior. As already mentioned, Gwalior possessed two royal palaces and other remains connected with the ninth-century aristocracy. In addition, there is a monumental relief of Śiva killing the elephant demon (Gajāsuravadha) that is carved into the cliff-face not far from the Caturbhuj temple.[69] Although this relief is almost entirely effaced, surviving details suggest that it is a product of the ninth or early tenth century. Given its great size and prominent position, the relief could be interpreted as making an allegorical statement, that is, drawing a comparison between the prowess of the ruler and Śiva's act of killing the demon. Such an allegory cannot be substantiated, however, because the Pratīhāras seem to have favoured the goddess Bhagavatī.[70] Mihira Bhoja carried the epithet Ādivarāha and Vāraha is depicted on his coins. One such coin is in the British Museum (Marsden Bequest, MXXI.C). This seems to be an echo of earlier traditions that associated the king with this manifestation of Viṣṇu.[71] There is, however, no evidence to link the Pratīhāras with Śiva as Gajāsuravadha and this, in turn, supports the contention that the Pratīhāras were not directly involved in the establishment of images and shrines.

Other information sustaining this conclusion is provided by the Cambay plates.[72] These belong to the Rāṣṭrakūṭa dynasty, the Pratīhāra's most bitter and long-standing foe. One of the events recorded in the Cambay plates is a raid led by Indra III against northern India in the early tenth century. Indra's rampage northward is celebrated in the following verse.

yanmādyaddvipadantaghataviṣamam kālapriyaprāṅgaṇaṁ tīrṇṇā
yatturagair agādhayamunā sindhupratispardhinī /
yenedaṁ hi mahodayārinagaraṁ nirmūlam unmūlitaṁ nāmnādyāpi
janaiḥ kuśasthalam iti khyātiṁ paraṁ nīyate //

After the courtyard of the temple of Kālapriya was knocked
askew by the strokes of his rutting tuskers,
His steeds crossed the bottomless Yamunā, which rivals the sea,
and he completely devastated the hostile city of Mahodaya,
Which even today is renowned among men by the name Kuśasthala.

The temple of Kālapriya was located at Kālpī near the Yamunā river.[73] Mahodaya was, of course, the capital city of Kannauj. The important point to note is that while the temple at Kālpī was singled out for destructive attention, there seem to have been no temples at Kannauj meriting similar treatment. If the Pratīhāras had a temple in the capital that was associated with their clan and a focus of their patronage and power, surely the Rāṣṭrakūṭas would have destroyed it and taken special delight in recording its desecration. Not only are the Cambay plates silent in this regard, but the Sanjān, Rādhanpura and Waṇi plates, in recording earlier defeats of the Pratīhāras, do not mention the destruction of temples, but rather state that the Pratīhāra king was forced to ritually attend upon his Rāṣṭrakūṭa rival.[74] That no account of temple destruction is found suggests once again that the Pratīhāras were not involved in temple building.

Dynastic Temples after the Disintegration of Pratīhāra Hegemony

In the first half of the tenth century the Gurjara Pratīhāras declined and strong regional dynasties began to emerge across northern India. The most well known of these were the Candellas, Kalacuris, Paramāras and Kacchapaghātas, whose histories have been discussed in Chapter 1. These dynasties fostered temple building on an unprecedented scale. To accompany the new building projects long inscriptions were prepared and these throw considerable light on patronage after the disintegration of the Pratīhāra kingdom. While there are no abrupt changes, there is a clarification of the ties between ruling kings and the temples they supported. The inscriptions and monuments at Khajurāho are perhaps the most dramatic illustration of this. The inscription associated with the Lakṣmaṇa temple can be taken as symptomatic of building activities under the Candellas and their contemporaries.[75] This record follows the established manner, with an invocation and a long eulogy of the Candella house. The inscription then enters into some unusual detail by describing how Yaśovarman forced the Pratīhāra king Devapāla to surrender an ancient and celebrated metal image of Vaikuṇṭha. This image was set up in the Lakṣmaṇa temple, a building expressly constructed by Yaśovarman for the purpose.[76] At the close is a reference to Vināyakapāla, the Pratīhāra monarch. While this passing nod maintains the fiction that the Candellas were somehow tributaries of the Pratīhāras, they soon set aside their token homage. The Viśvanātha temple inscription of VS 1059/AD 1002–3 omits any mention of an overlord.

In an effort to protect the remains at Khajurāho, the Archaeological Survey of India has moved some of the inscriptions with the result that the records do not necessarily belong to the temple in which they are now housed. At the Sās Bahū temple on Gwalior Fort, however, the dedicatory inscriptions are still beside the main entrance as originally intended. The slabs, surrounded by carved frames in the temple porch, are carefully incised with over one hundred verses giving a history of the Kacchapaghāta dynasty. The record states that the temple was founded by Padmapāla and completed by his successor Mahīpāla.[77] As at Khajurāho, direct links are made between the temple and the dynasty, in this case reinforced by the building's dedication to Padmanātha (Viṣṇu) in honour of Padmapāla.

One of the most fascinating inscriptions of this period comes from the ruined Śiva temple on a hill called Harsha or Uchāpahar, not far from Sikar in Rājasthān. The superlative quality of the sculptures from the site is matched by the historical importance of the inscription.[78] The record describes how additions and endowments were made to the temple by a line of Cāhamāna princes and their tributaries. In the course of detailing these activities, many references are made to the temple complex. Verse 12, for example, describes the main shrine:

[eta]t svarṇṇāṇḍakāṁtipravaratamamahāmaṇḍapābhogabhadraṁ
prāṁtaprāsādamālāviracitavikaṭāpāṇḍuputrābhirāmam /
meroḥ sṛṁgopamānaṁ sughaṭitavvṛṣasattoraṇadvāraramyaṁ
nānāsadbhogayuktaṁ jayati bhagavato harṣadevasya [harmmyam] //

Glory to this mansion of holy Harṣadeva! It is auspicious for the
expanse of its superlative halls which are radiant like eggs of gold; it is
Pleasing like Paṇḍu's mighty sons for the rows of shrines at its edge;
it is comparable to the pinnacle of Mount Meru, and it is
Pleasant for the skilfully carved bull at the entrance gate, and for
its endowment of manifold objects of enjoyment.

From the perspective of patronage the central point revealed by the inscription is that a Cāhamāna clan had this temple as their family shrine. Construction was initiated in the mid-tenth century by Siṁharāja who provided the necessary funds and who 'set on Śiva's dwelling his own golden form, a body of glory like the full moon'.[79] The custodians of this shrine were a line of Śaiva ascetics who supervised the building of the temple and its surrounding wells, courts and gardens. The ascetic Bhāvarakta Allaṭa began the work and it was finished after his death by Bhāvadyota. These ascetics did not do the actual work, of course, but hired craftsmen with the funds provided by their patrons. The architect's name is given as Caṇḍaśiva, son of Vīrabhadra; the temple was completed in VS 1013/AD 956–7.

The ascetics mentioned in the Harsha inscription introduce an important element of temple life.

While the cults represented by these individuals were quite ancient, it is only in the tenth and eleventh centuries that their history and social position emerges with any degree of clarity. That ascetic orders were well established in northern India by the eighth century is shown by a number of records, a good example being the Indragarh inscription of VS 767/AD 710–11.[80] Two ascetics named Vinītarāśi and Dānarāśi of the Pāśupata sect are its central figures. After an account of the merits of these teachers the record states that Dānarāśi was responsible for making a temple (*mandira*) of Svayambhorlokanātha (Śiva). The inscription does not specify what sort of relationship existed between Dānarāśi and Ṇaṇṇappa, a ruler whose exploits are praised at some length. One would suspect that Ṇaṇṇappa was a patron, but this is not actually stated, a circumstance that is not unusual. However, an inscription from Rannod shows how ascetics might establish a relationship with a prince and subsequently become sponsors of architectural projects.[81] This record explicitly states that a king named Avantivarman was desirous of being instructed in Śaiva doctrine and so resolved to bring Purandara to his country. Purandara belonged to a respected line of teachers known from several sources.[82] The saint eventually initiated Avantivarman and then founded a monastery (*maṭha*) in the king's city. About one hundred years after Purandara's passing, a master named Vyomaśiva took charge of the establishment. He restored the building and constructed a tank and temple. The tank and adjacent monastery are still extant at Rannod (ancient Araṇipadra). The inscription is not dated but probably belongs to the late tenth or early eleventh century.

Inscriptions of related Śaiva ascetics are known from a number of locations in northern India and in many cases the temples and monastic structures have been partially preserved.[83] That Śaiva cults enjoyed wide currency is indicated not only by the preponderance of dedications in favour of Śiva but by incidental depictions of Śaiva ascetics on temples. Several examples are found at Khajurāho, one of the most detailed being on the Lakṣmaṇa temple. This relief shows a master seated in a small pavilion; in front of him is a female attendant and a row of four bearded disciples. To the left is a doorkeeper with a sword who appears to be introducing two individuals.[84]

What emerges from this material is that Śaiva cults had a long history in northern India. Close ties could be established between individual ascetics and princes and this, in turn, could lead to the construction of temples and monasteries. In some cases the temples became closely associated with the dynasty, the ascetics becoming royal intimates and enjoying, albeit indirectly, the revenue belonging to the god. The relationship was beneficial to all concerned. The ascetics established and controlled the temple, but the dedication was made in the royal patron's name. A link between the god and king was thus forged through the application of the *ācārya*'s sacred knowledge. From this the king received legitimacy and the *ācārya* support for his order. The tangible product was a temple that advertised the power of the dynasty and its associations with a particular manifestation of the godhead.[85]

These arrangements were substantially different to the old Vedic scheme of kingship. Up to the fifth century Śrauta rituals propelled the king upward into contact with the divine, from whence he returned infused with power and a mandate to rule. After the abeyance of royal sacrifices, power was seen as flowing down from the divine through whole or partial incarnation (in the case of Viṣṇu) or manifestation (in the case of Śiva). Kings no longer reached up through sacrificial effort but sought to associate themselves with the sacred as it was known and revealed in this world. Those rulers devoted to Viṣṇu saw themselves as participating in the descent of the divine through noble deeds and an august lineage that recapitulated the god's incarnation into the world for the maintenance of universal order. Those rulers devoted to Śiva identified their personalities with the infinite power of the supreme lord that eternally pervades the whole creation. Given that nobles had long built temples and that inscriptions display remarkable continuity in organisation and poetic style, it seems likely that these connections were always inherent, if not openly articulated. They become clear after the mid-tenth century due to the decline of the Pratīhāras and the increasingly unstable condition of northern India. Regional princes made free use of imperial titles and competed vigorously with each other in the arts of peace and war. Yet, however powerful some of these later princes became, no ruler was able to claim paramount status. In the absence of a recognised imperial centre, there was no impetus to return to the detached role once played by the Pratīhāra monarchs. Regional princes, rather than withdrawing from patronage as the Pratīhāras had done, maintained and amplified their programmes of temple construction. In the competitive climate of the period the small temples of earlier days gave way to projects of unprecedented size and elaboration. The passing of the Pratīhāras thus inaugurated an era in which temple building, typically on a vast scale, became one of the central acts of Indian kingship. This pattern of patronage prevailed until the establishment of the Islamic Sultanate in the closing decades of the twelfth century.

Notes

1 A general introduction will be found in my 'XII. Patronage' in *The Dictionary of Art* 15: 737–9. A somewhat truncated version of this chapter appeared in *Gods, Guardians and Lovers: Temple Sculptures from North India* AD *700–1200*, ed. Vishakha Desai and Darielle Mason (New York: Asia Society, 1993), pp. 49–65.

2 The term is also spelt *āgara* and *agrāhāra*, the latter being an early form; see K. V. Ramesh and S. P. Tewari, *A Copper-Plate Hoard of the Gupta Period from Bagh, Madhya Pradesh* (Delhi: Archaeological Survey of India, 1990), p. xi.

3 For example EI 25 (1939–40): 173–83; A. C. Mittal, *The Inscriptions of the Imperial Paramāras* (Ahmedabad: L. D. Institute), p. 322–39.

4 EI 19 (1927–8): 52–65. Ahar is located in District Bulandshahr, Uttar Pradesh; the inscription is now in the State Museum, Lucknow.

5 Günther-Dietz Sontheimer, 'Religious Endowments and the Juristic Personalities of Hindu Deities', *Zeitschrift für vergleichende Rechtswissenschaft einschliessende ethnologische Rechtswissenschaft* 67 (1965).

6 Excavations at Ghazna have uncovered a variety of Indian items, among them Brahmanical stone images which were set up in the palace as souvenirs of the conquest; U. Scerrato, 'The Two First Excavation Campaigns at Ghazni, 1957–58', *East and West* 10 (1959): 39 and fig. 39.

7 Sheldon Pollock, 'The Theory of Practice and the Practice of Theory in Indian Intellectual History', JAOS 105 (1985): 499–519, and Pollock, 'Mīmāṁsā and the Problem of History in Traditional India', JAOS 109 (1989): 603–10.

8 EI 32 (1957–58): 207–12.

9 *Gauḍavaho*, verses 507–8; the construction was said to have been completed in a single day (*surapāsāo pahuṇā ekkeṇa diṇeṇanimmavio*).

10 IA 19 (1888): 310; the inscription dates to the ninth or tenth century.

11 Prabhācandrācārya, *Prabhāvakacarita*, p. 94 (verses 139–40), and Rājaśekharasūri, *Prabandhakośa*, pp. 28–9.

12 IA 19 (1890): 55–62. The record is dated Mālava year 795/AD 738–9.

13 Kanaswa or Kamsuvan = Kanswa, Survey of India map 45 D.16.5. Elaborate synonyms being typical of these epigraphs, the temple is also described as a *mandira* of Dhūrjaṭi.

14 Munshi Debiprasād [and F. Keilhorn], 'Ghaṭayālā Inscription of the Pratihāra Kakkuka of [Vikrama] Saṁvat 918', *Journal of the Royal Asiatic Society* (1895), pp. 513–21.

15 As evidenced by Bāuka, EI 18 (1925–26): 87–99, also discussed below. As regards royal patronage of Jainism, see my 'Architecture in Central India under the Kacchapaghāta Rulers', pp. 11–16.

16 PRASIWC (1906–7): 34–5.

17 EI 12 (1913–14): 10–17. The inscription probably belongs to the

tenth century.

18 EI 3 (1894–5): 263–7. The inscription was found in the ruins of a temple called Nīlakaṇṭha Mahādeva in Pāranagar, south of Rajor; it is dated Vikrama year 1016/AD 960.

19 The Karmdand inscription of Gupta year 117/AD 436–7 records the setting up of a linga by Pṛthivīsena and naming it Pṛthivīśvara. Ram Swaroop Mishra, *Supplement to Fleet's Corpus Inscriptionum Indicarum, Vol. III 1888, Inscriptions of the Early Gupta Kings and their Successors* (Vārānasī: Benares Hindu University, 1971), no. 19.

20 EI 9 (1907–8): 248–56.

21 EI 9 (1907–8): 198–200. M. A. Dhaky, 'The Genesis and Development of Māru-Gurjara Temple Architecture', pls 63–4.

22 IA 10 (1881): 34–6. The inscription is damaged and consequently all the details of this foundation are not clear.

23 EI 36 (1965–6): 32.

24 Illustrated in Donald M. Stadtner, 'The Śaṅkaragaṇa Panel in the Sāgar University Art Museum', in *Indian Epigraphy: Its Bearing on the History of Art*, pp. 165–8, also AA 43 (1981–2), fig. 6.

25 The inscription, datable to the early tenth century and probably critical for late Pratīhāra and early Candella history, has not been published. The slab is illustrated in *Gods, Guardians and Lovers*, p. 55.

26 Sircar, *Select Inscriptions* 1: 345.

27 *Inscriptions of Gopakṣetra*, figs 2–3; J. C. Harle, 'An Early Indian Hero-stone and a Possible Western Source', JRAS (1970), pp. 162–4; Günther-Dietz Sontheimer, 'Some Memorial Monuments of Western India', in *German Scholars on India*, 2 vols (Vārānasī: Chowkhamba Sanskrit Series Office, 1976), 2: 264–75.

28 *Inscriptions of Gopakṣetra*, pp. 1–2.

29 See Salomon and Willis, 'Three Inscribed Hero-stones from Terāhī', forthcoming. The significance of Gwalior as a centre of the Pratīhāras is also explored in the discussion of imperial patronage on p. 96.

30 *Inscriptions of Gopakṣetra*, p. 2.

31 EI 20 (1929–30): 37–46; the temple has not survived. Buddhist foundations were not unusual in the eighth century as shown by an inscription from Shergarh (District Kotah), IA 14 (1885): 45–8.

32 EI 9 (1907–8): 1–10. The two plates are dated Valabhi year 574 and [Vikrama or Śaka] year 956.

33 IA 12 (1883): 190–95.

34 *Inscriptions of Gopakṣetra*, p. 109 (pl. 8).

35 EI 4 (1895–7): 29–32.

36 EI 36 (1965–6): 52–3; EI 10 (1927–8): 52–62; EI 14 (1917–18): 176–88; EI 1 (1889–92): 162–79.

37 EI 1 (1889–92): 162–79.

38 The adjective 'lowest' is undesirably amorphous but is forced upon me by the paucity of information about the humbler levels of Indian society during this period.

39 *Annual Report on the Workings of the Rajputana Museum, Ajmer for the Year ending 31st March 1924* (Simla: Government of India Press, 1924), p. 3; see also EI 19 (1927–8): 54, n. 1.

40 EI 36 (1965–66): 49–52. The inscription is dated Harṣa year 182/AD 788 and comes from Tasai near Alwar.

41 EI 1 (1889–92): 184–90 and 162–79.

42 EI 1 (1889–92): 242–50.

43 Illustrated in Trivedi, *Temples of the Pratīhāra Period*, pls 83–4.

44 EI 4 (1895–7): 309–10.

45 A listing of the records from Sonāgir is given in *Inscriptions of Gopakṣetra*. While the site is ancient, most of the present buildings are little more than a hundred years old.

46 EI 36 (1965–6): 52–3; the inscription is fragmentary.

47 EI 24 (1937–8): 329–36; further comments in EI 36 (1965–6): 52–3.

48 EI 1 (1889–92): 184–90.

49 EI 5 (1898–9): 208–13; EI 19 (1927–8): 15–19; IA 15 (1886): 105–13.

50 IA 15 (1886): 105–13 and 138–41; EI 14 (1917–18): 176–88.

51 EI 14 (1917–18): 176–88. The inscription was found in the platform of a well and is now in Ajmer; it carries two dates, VS 999/AD 942–3 and VS 1003/AD 946–7.

52 EI 17 (1925–6): 99–114; Sircar, *Select Inscriptions* 2: 242–6, pl. XVII.

53 Sircar, *Indian Epigraphical Glossary*, s.v. 'antaḥpura'. In 'Some Notes on the Palaces of the Imperial Gurjara-Pratīhāras', JRAS 5 (1995): 351–60, I have elaborated the discussion given here.

54 EI 1 (1889–92): 184–90. The record is dated Harṣa year 276/AD 882–3.

55 EI 1 (1889–92): 154–62.

56 ASIR 2 (1864–5): 337; J. P. Vogel, 'The Sanskrit *Pratoli* and its New-Indian Derivatives', JRAS (1906), pp. 539–51.

57 Mahdi Husain, *The Reḥla of Ibn Baṭṭūṭa (India, Maladive Islands and Ceylon) Translation and Commentary* (Baroda, 1953), pp. 45 and 163. Pilasters illustrated in my 'Some Notes on the Palaces', figs 4–6.

58 Keith, *Preservation of National Monuments; Gwalior Fortress*, p. 75, records that the capital was found at Trikonia Tāl, Gwalior. Illustrated in Department of Archaeology, Gwalior State, *A Guide to the Archaeological Museum at Gwalior* (Gwalior, [193?]), pl. vii; Pramod Chandra, *The Sculpture of India, 3000 BC to 1300 AD* (Washington, 1985), p. 209.

59 Illustrated in my 'Some Notes on the Palaces', fig. 1.

60 EI 17 (1925–6): 87–99. The inscription was recovered from Jodhpur; though belonging to the ninth century, it refers to events and building activities from as early as *c.* AD 600.

61 The reassertion of imperial Pratihāra power in the region is evidenced by the Siwāh plate which records that Bhoja reinstated a grant of Vatsarāja that was in abeyance; EI 5 (1898–9): 208–213. Though called the Daulatpurā plate, it was in fact recovered at the

village of Sewa or Siwāh, Survey of India map 45.I.11.7.

62 EI 19 (1927–8): 287–90.

63 Michael Rabe, 'Royal Portraits and Personified Attributes of Kingship at Mamallapuram', *Journal of the Academy of Art and Architecture, Mysore* 1 (1991): 1–4; more generally Rabe's contribution on Tamilnadu sculpture in the *Dictionary of Art* 15: 506–20.

64 Louis Renou, 'The Vedic Schools and the Epigraphy', in *Siddha Bharati*, 2 vols, ed. Vishva Bandhu (Hoshiarpur: Veshvarananda Vedic Research Institute, 1950), 2: 214–21; but see also IHQ 35 (1959): 259–64 and ABORI (1959): 218–30.

65 EI 36 (1965–6): 47–9; R. Salomon, 'Translation and Interpretation of the Kusumā Inscription', in *Indian Epigraphy*, pp. 111–14; IA 19 (1890): 55–62.

66 EI 14 (1917–18): 176–88; Pramod Chandra, 'The Kaula-Kāpālika Cults at Khajurāho', *Lalit Kalā* 1–2 (1955–6): 98–107; EI 2 (1892–4): 116–30 and V. S. Srivastava, 'The Ancient Śiva Temple at Mt. Harsha, Sikar', *The Researcher* 5–6 (1964–5): 17–32.

67 The temple is dated AD 961; R. C. Agrawala, 'Inscriptions from Jagat, Rajasthan', JOI 14 (1965): 75–8; Agrawala, 'Unpublished Temples of Rajasthan', *Ars Asiatiques* 11 (1965): 53–72.

68 I cannot therefore agree with Inden, *Imagining India*, p. 252, n. 38, where he suggests there was a large imperial temple or temple complex at Kannauj. There is no archaeological or epigraphic evidence for this.

69 ASIR 2 (1864–5): 336–7 describes the location but incorrectly identifies the image as Varāha.

70 Tripathi, *History of Kanauj*, p. 290.

71 V. S. Agrawala, *Matsya Purāṇa – A Study* (Vārāṇasī, 1963), pp. 333–5; Frederick M. Asher, 'Historical and Political Allegory in Gupta Art', in *Essays on Gupta Culture*, ed. Bardwell L. Smith (Delhi: Motilal, 1983), pp. 53–66.

72 EI 7 (1902–3): 43.

73 V. V. Mirashi, 'Three Ancient and Famous Temples of the Sun', *Purāṇa* 8 (1966): 38–51; Sircar, *Studies in the Geography of Ancient and Medieval India*, pp. 301–7.

74 EI 18 (1925–6): 243 (verse 9); EI 6 (1900–1901): 243 (verse 8); IA 11 (1882): 157.

75 EI 1 (1887–92): 122–35.

76 The theme of objects looted by Indian kings was explored by Davis, 'Indian Art Objects as Loot', *Journal of Asian Studies* 52 (1993): 22–48.

77 *Inscriptions of Gopakṣetra*, p. 6 (pl. 10).

78 EI 2 (1892–4): 116–130.

79 *haimamāropitaṁ yena śivasya bhavanopari / pūrṇṇacandropamaṁ svīyaṁ mūrttaṁ ya[śa][piṁ]ḍakaṁ*. The description is somewhat opaque and I am grateful to Siri Gunasinghe for his suggestions. I take *haimam* (golden) with *mūrttam* (form). This apparently refers to the *haimapuruṣa* or *hiraṇyapuruṣa*, the 'golden man' who often holds a temple's crowning flag staff. Surviving examples are of stone, but this description suggests they could be gilt or made completely of metal. The donor is apparently being identified with this figure near the summit of the spire. Epigraphic descriptions of temple buildings (among them EI 39 [1972]: 189–98 and EI 41 [1975–6]: 49–57) merit comprehensive study. An important instance of the use of this material is M. A. Dhaky, *The Indian Temple Forms in Karṇāṭa Inscriptions and Architecture* (Delhi: Abhinav, 1977).

80 EI 32 (1957–8): 112–17. The inscription is in the Central Museum, Indore.

81 *Inscriptions of Gopakṣetra*, p. 119.

82 V. V. Mirashi, 'Gwalior Museum Stone Inscription of Pataṅgaśambhu', JMPIP 4 (1962): 3–12; see also IA 12 (1883): 190–95 (copper-plate grant recording the gift of a village to Śrī Maheśvarācārya of the glorious Āmardaka tradition, *śrīmadāmarddakasantāna*).

83 R. D. Banerji, *Haihayas of Tripuri and Their Monuments* (Memoirs of the Archaeological Survey of India, no. 23) (Calcutta: Government of India Central Publication Branch, 1931); M. B. Garde, *Surwaya: A Short Guide* (Gwalior: Archaeological Department, 1939); for inscriptions, see CII 4.

84 Illustrated in *Gods, Guardians and Lovers*, p. 61. The doctrines and practices of some of the Śaiva cults are summarised by Pramod Chandra, 'The Kaula-Kāpālika Cults at Khajurāho', *Lalit Kalā* 1–2 (1955–6): 98–107.

85 These circumstances neither prevailed in all temples nor applied to all ascetic orders, see PRASINC (1905–6): 14; IA 16 (1887): 173–5.

Select Bibliography

Archaeological Department, Gwalior State. *Annual Report, Saṁvat 1980, Year 1925–26* to *Saṁvat 1997, Year 1940–41. Gwalior, 1937–43.*

Kalyan Kumar Chakravarty. *The Gwalior Fort.* New Delhi: Arnold-Heineman, 1984.

Krishna Deva. 'Extensions of Gupta Art: Art and Archaeology in the Pratihāra Age'. In *Seminar on Indian Art and Archaeology 1962*, pp. 85–106. New Delhi: Lalit Kalā Akademi, 1965.

Krishna Deva. *Temples of North India.* New Delhi: National Book Trust, 1969.

Krishna Deva. 'Telī-kā-Mandir, Gwalior'. In *Indian Epigraphy: Its Bearing on the History of Art*, ed. Fredrick M. Asher and G. S. Gai, pp.161–3. New Delhi, 1985.

S. K. Dikshit. *A Guide to the Central Archaeological Museum, Gwalior.* Bhopal: Department of Archaeology and Museums, Government of Madhya Pradesh, 1962.

Harihar Nivās Dvivedī. 'Gvāliyar rājya meṁ prācīn mūrtikalā'. In *Vikrama Smṛti Grantha*, pp. 667–708. Ujjain: Scindia Oriental Institute, vs 2001.

Harihar Nivās Dvivedī. *Gvāliyar rājya ke abhilekh.* Banāras: Sulemānī Press, vs 2004.

M. B. Garde. *Archaeology in Gwalior.* 2nd edn. Gwalior: Alijah Darbar Press, 1934.

J. B. Keith. *Preservation of National Monuments: Gwalior Fortress.* Calcutta: Superintendent of Government Printing, 1883.

Michael Meister, M. A. Dhaky and Krishna Deva, eds. *Encyclopaedia of Indian Temple Architecture: North India, Foundations of North Indian Style c. 250 B.C. --A.D. 1100.* Princeton and Delhi: Princeton University Press and the American Institute of Indian Studies, 1988.

D. R. Patil. *A Guide to the Archaeological Museum, Gwalior.* Gwalior: Alijah Darbar Press, 1945.

D. R. Patil. *The Descriptive and Classified List of Archaeological Monuments in Madhya Bharat.* Gwalior: Department of Archaeology, Madhya Bharat Government, 1952.

D. R. Patil. *The Cultural Heritage of Madhya Bharat.* Gwalior: Department of Archaeology, Madhya Bharat Government, 1952.

S. R. Thakore. *Catalogue of Sculptures in the Archaeological Museum, Gwalior, M.B.* Lashkar: [Madhya Bharat Government] n.d.

R. D. Trivedi. *Temples of the Pratīhāra Period in Central India.* New Delhi:Archaeological Survey of India, 1990.

Odette Viennot. *Les divinités fluviales Gaṅgā et Yamunā aux portes des sanctuaires de l'Inde.* Paris: Presses universitaires de France, 1964.

Odette Viennot. *Temples de l'Inde centrale et occidentale.* 2 vols. Paris: L'école française d'Extrême-Orient, 1976.

Michael D. Willis. 'Architecture in Central India under the Kacchapaghāta Rulers'. *South Asian Studies* 12 (1996): 13–32.

Michael D. Willis. *Inscriptions of Gopakṣetra: Materials for the History of Central India.* London: British Museum Press, 1996.

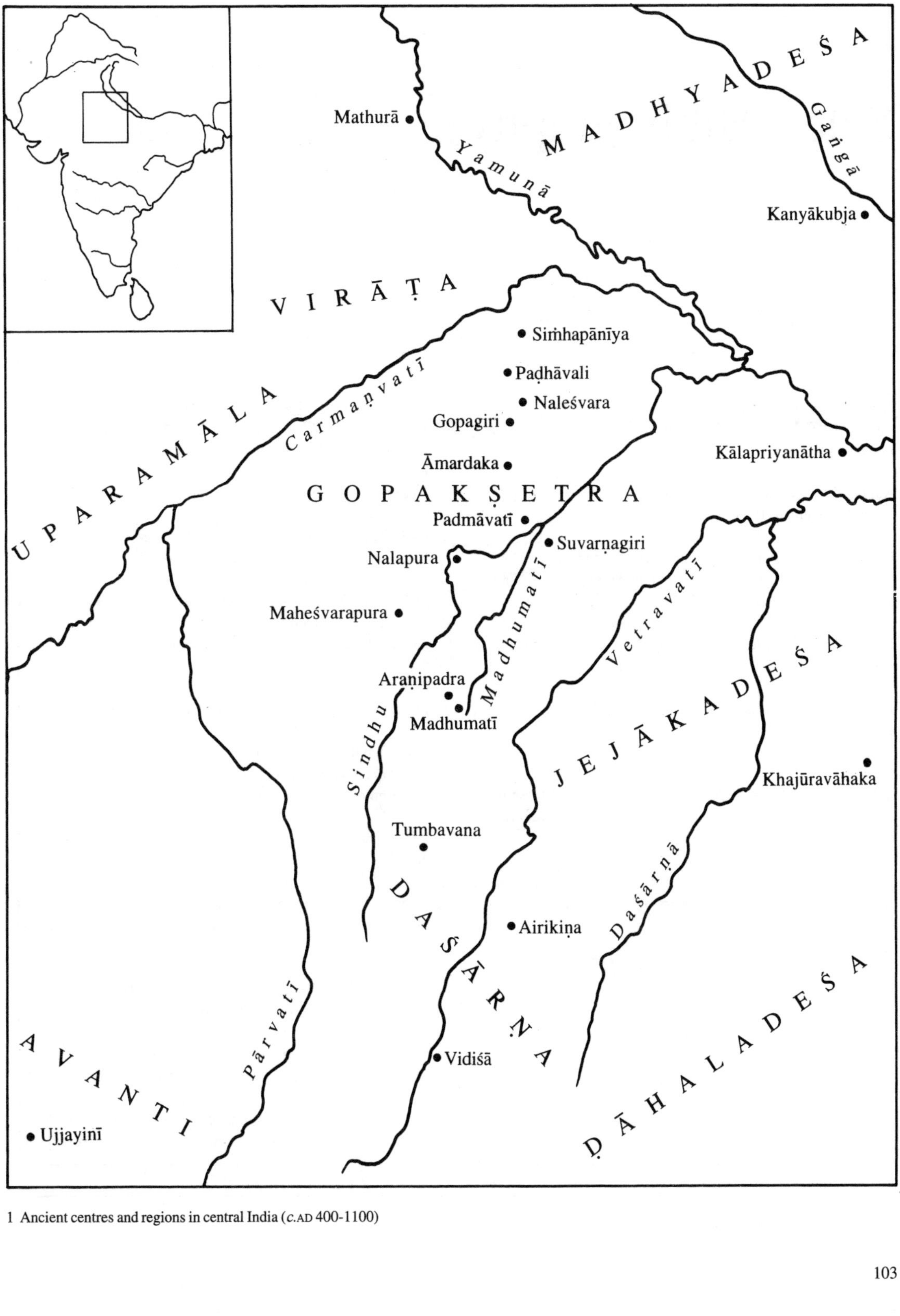

1 Ancient centres and regions in central India (*c.* AD 400-1100)

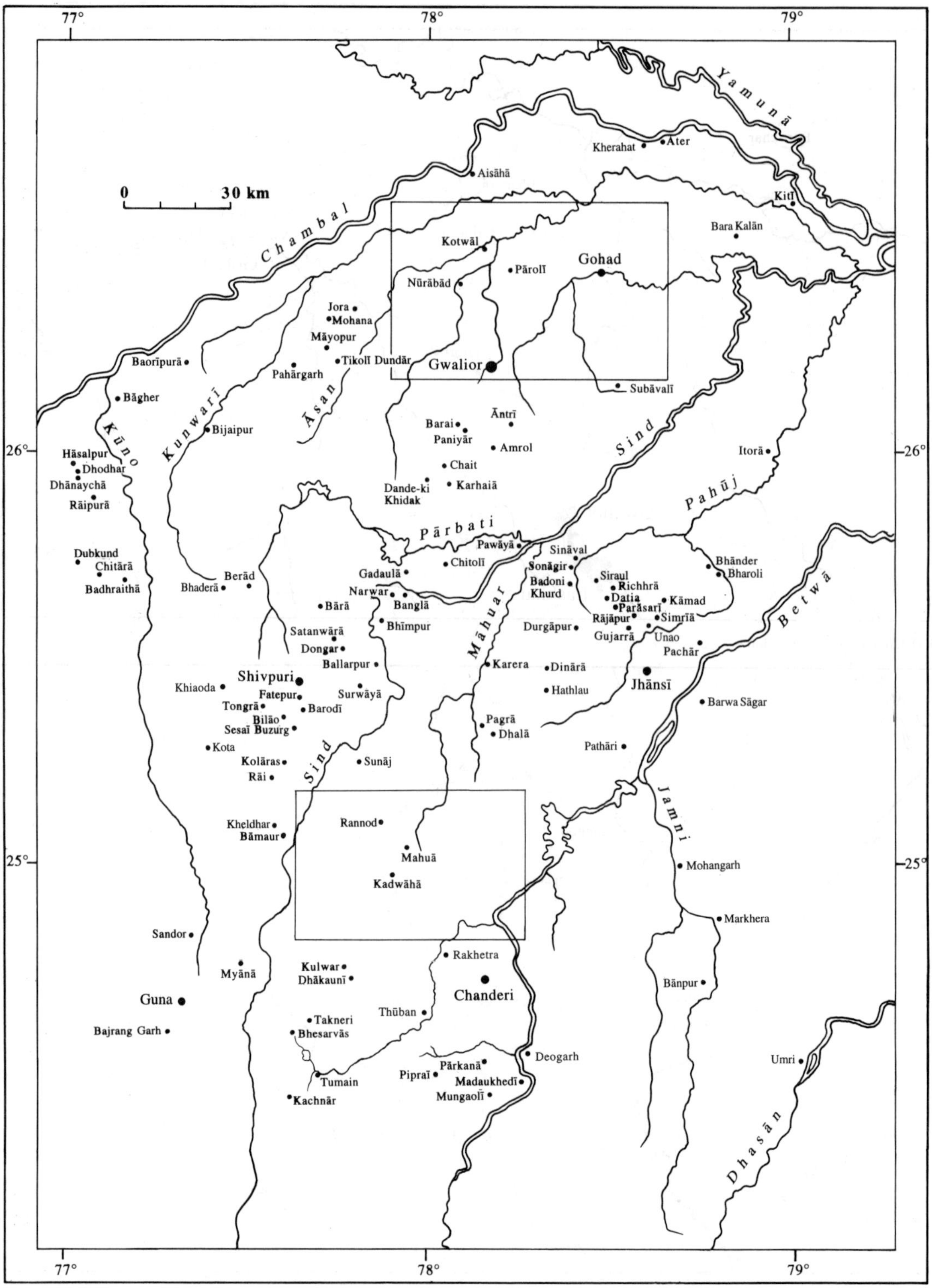

2 Archaeological and historical sites in the Gwalior region

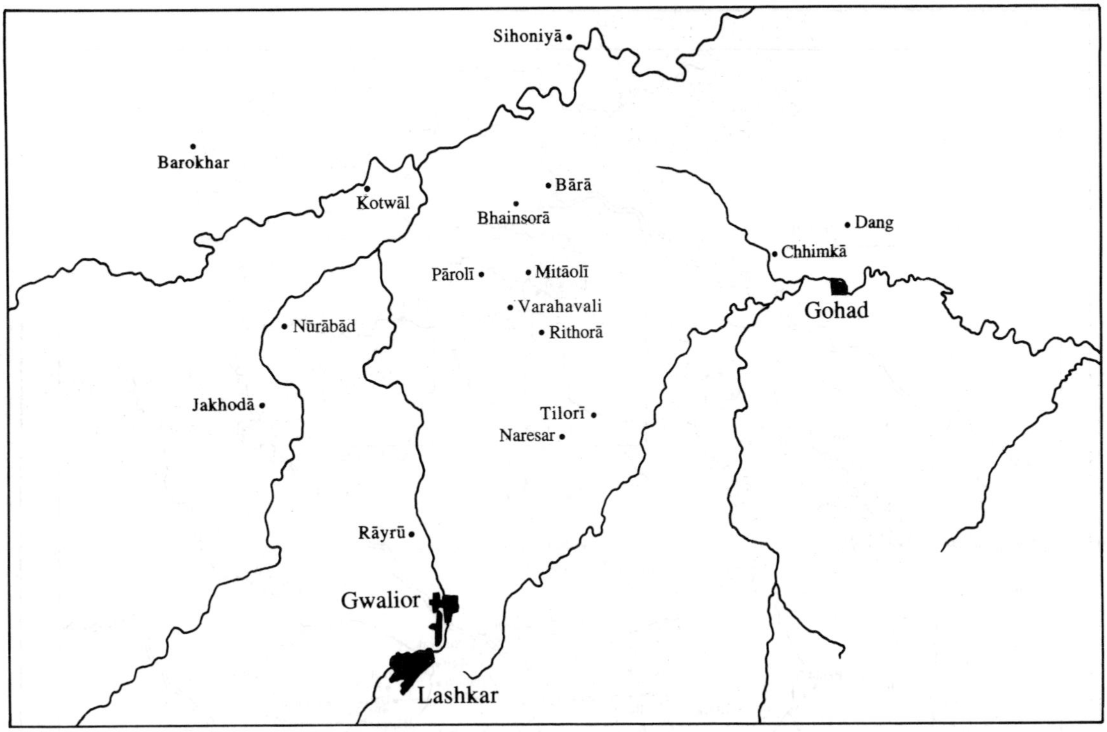

3 Detail of the Gwalior region

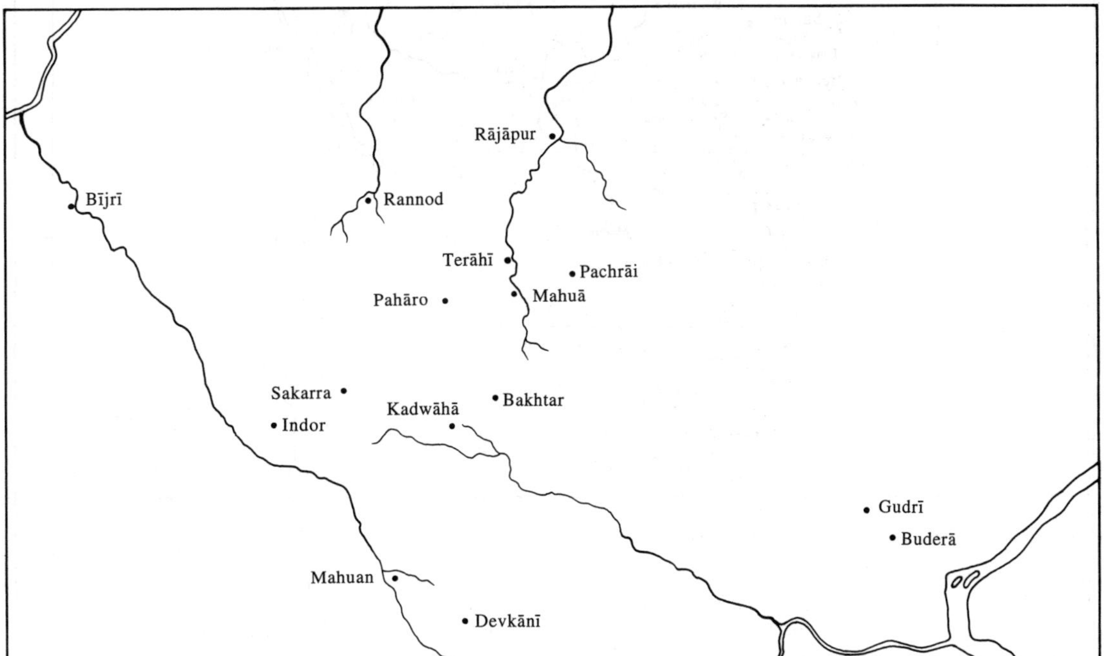

4 Detail of the Mahuā region

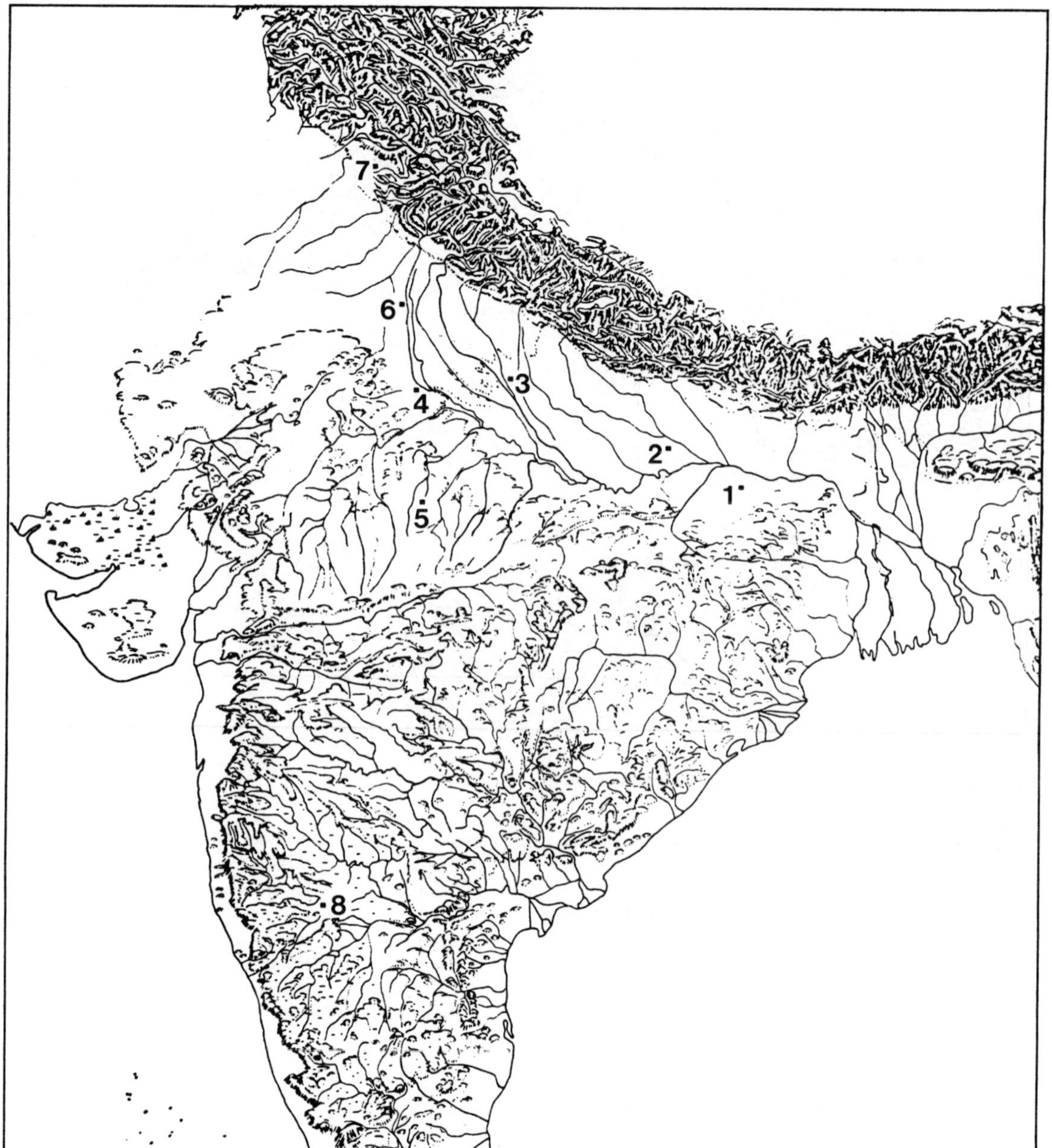

5 Inscription sites of the Vardhanas and their contemporaries

Key

1 Nālanda	Seal of Harṣa (EI 21: 16); inscription of Yaśovarman (EI 20: 2)*
2 Madhuban	Plate of Harṣa (EI 4: 29)
3 Banskhera	[=Banskhera Khūrd] Plate of Harṣa (EI 7: 22)
4 Mathurā	Fragmentary Maurya inscription (EI 32: 25)
5 Mahuā	Inscription of Vatsarāja (EI 37: 11)
6 Sonepat	Seal of Harṣa (CII 3: 52)
7 Nermand	Plate of Samudrasena (CII 3: 80)
8 Aivalli	[= Aihole] Inscription of Pulakeśin (EI 6: 1)

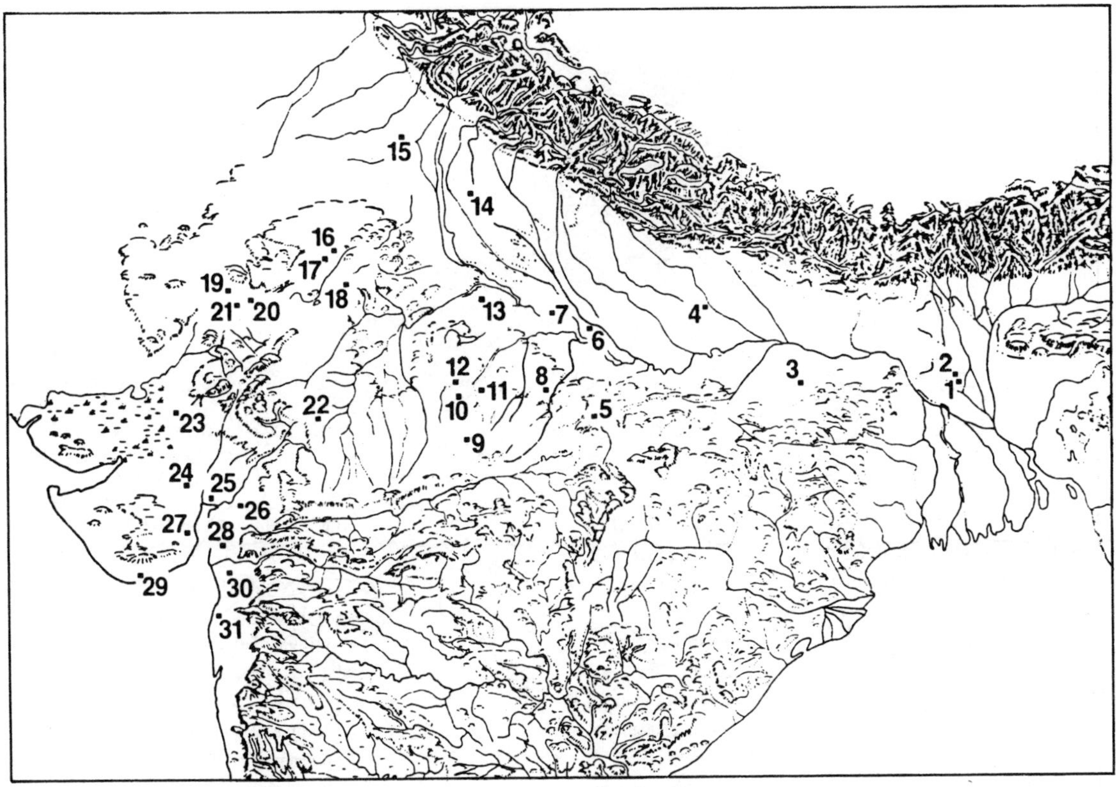

6 Inscription sites of the Gurjara Pratīhāras and their contemporaries

Key

1	Paharpoor	(= Pāhārpur) Inscription of Mahendrapāla (ASIAR[1925-26]: 14)*
2	Badal Kutcherry	Pillar inscription of Devapāla (EI 2: 10)
3	Gaya	Image inscription of Mahendrapāla (MASB 5 [1915], p. 64)
4	Kahla	Plate of Soḍhadeva (EI 7: 74)
5	Jura	Praśasti of Kṛṣṇa III (EI 19: 51)
6	Asni	Inscription of Mahīpāla (IA 16: 174)
7	Barah	Plate of Bhoja (EI 19: 2)
8	Khajurāho	Inscription of Harṣadeva (EI 1: 19)
9	Badoh	Inscription of Parabala (EI 9: 34)
10	Rakhetra	[= Bithlā] Inscription of Mahīpāla (EI 19-23 [appendix]: 2110)
11	Sīron	Inscription of Mahendrapāla (EI 1: 21)
12	Terai	[= Terāhī] Hero-stone of [V]S 960 (IA 17: 201)
13	Gwalior	Inscription of Bhoja (EI 18: 13); Caturbhuj temple inscriptions (EI 1: 20)
14	Ahār	Inscription of Bhoja (EI 19: 7)
15	Pehowa	[= Pehoa] Inscription of Bhoja (EI 1: 23); inscription of Mahendrapāla (EI 1: 30)
16	Harasnāth	Inscription of Vigraharāja (EI 2: 8)
17	Siwāh	[= Sewa] Grant of Bhoja (EI 5: 24)
18	Chātsu	[= Chaksu] Inscription of Bālāditya (EI 12: 4)
19	Osiān	Inscription mentioning Vatsarāja (JRAS [1907]: 1010)
20	Buchkala	Inscription of Nāgabhaṭṭa (EI 9: 27)
21	Jodhpur	Inscription of Bāuka (EI 18: 12)
22	Partābgarh	Inscription of Mahendrapāla (EI 14: 13)
23	Radhanpur	Grant of Govinda III (EI 6: 23)
24	Hadāla	Grant of Dharaṇivarāha (IA 12: 193)
25	Cambay	Plates of Govinda IV (EI 7: 6)
26	Baroda	Grant of Karkarāja (IA 12: 156)
27	Bhaunagar	[= Bhāvanagar] Barton Museum impression (EI 19: 27)
28	Hānsot	Grant of Nāgāvaloka (EI 12: 23)
29	Una	Grants of Mahendrapāla (EI 9: 1)
30	Bagumra	Plates of Indra III (ARE [1959-60]: B, 19)
31	Sanjān	Plates of Amoghavarṣa I (EI 18: 26)

*References in maps 5 and 6 are to volume and inscription number unless otherwise stated; spelling of place names follows Survey of India maps and *Corpus Topographicum Indiae Antiquae* (*Part I, Epigraphical Find Spots*) by R. Stroobandt (Gent, 1974).

Index

Page numbers in *italics* indicate figures in the text ; numbers in **bold** refer to the numbers of the plates, located after the index.

–A–

Ābhira 88
Ādityavarman 19
Ādityasena 21
aedicules (*bālapañjara*)
  Deogarh 74
  elimination of 57, 65, 66, 68
  Mahuā 40
Ahar 86, 91
Aihole 19
Ānarta 24
Alla 70, 90
Allabhaṭṭa 90
Allajiyapa 90
Āma 22, 88
Amrol, Dhane Bāba temple 55; **83**
  ground plan *55*
Amrol, Kumāra 78; **128**
Amrol, Rāmeśvar Mahādev temple 51; **46–50**
  compared to Dhane Bābā, Amrol 55
  compared to Dāng 51
  ground plan *51*
  sculpture compared to Naresar 51
Āparājita 91
appliqué niches 67, 70, 71, 72, 76
Araṇipadra 17, 98
Āryarāja 21
Asīrgarh 19
Aulikara, 19
Avanivarman 90
Avanti 17
Avantivarman 19, 98
awning (*chādya*)
  Gwalior 70
  introduction of 66
  Khiaoda 72
  Sakarra 74
  Sihoniya 70
  Terāhī 68
Ayodhyā 88

–B–

Bachhofer, L. 29
Badoh
  Bhīmgaja 75; **121**
  Gadarmal 70
  Sola Khambi 94
Bagumra 25
Bālāditya 89, 90
bālapañjara see aedicules
Balavarman 90
Bamora, Śiva temple 77
Banskhera 19
Bapuka 89
Barah 25
Bārāhet 44; **18–20**
  ruined temple hall 80; **134**
  sculpture compared to Amrol 51
Batesar, Batesar Mahādev temple 54; **60–64**
  compared to Gwalior 56
  compared to Terāhī 68
  ground plan *54*
Batesar, subsidary shrines and temples **65–82**
  compared to Gwalior 71
  patronage of 92
  9th century, early 65–6
  9th century, middle 74
Bathurst, Charles 10
Bāuka 24, 94
Bhainsora, Śiva temple 80; **133**
Bhānugupta 19
Bhartṛvaḍḍha 22
Bhavabhūti 17
Bhāvadyota 97
Bhāvanagar 25
Bhāvarakta Allaṭa 97
Bhoja II 25
Bhṛgukaccha 22
Bhumara 38
Bose, N. K. 28
Broach 22
Buchkala 89
Buddharāja 19, 20
Bundelkhand 17
Burgess, J. 29

–C–

Cāhamāna 97
Cakrāyudha 22

Cāḷukya 90
Caṇḍaśiva 97
Candella 26, 97
Candragupta 21
Carmaṇvati 16
chādya see awning
Chandra, Pramod 28, 29
Chapāra 37
Chātsu 25, 89
Chhimkā 80; **136**
Chittaur 21, 90
Citrakūṭa 20, 26
Coomaraswamy, A. 28, 29, 30
Cousens, H. 29
Cunningham, A. 27

–D–

Dānarāśi 98
Dāng, Śiva temple 45–7; **23–7**
  compared to Amrol 55
  compared to Naresar 49
  ground plan *45*
  style of sculpture 46
  superstructure 46
Daśārṇa 17
Deogarh 38
  dated pillar 75, 91
  Jaina goddess 53; **59**
  temple (no. 12) 74–5; **120**
  Varāha 42; **13**
Devagupta 19, 20, 21
Devapāla 26, 97
Devarāja 22
Devaṭa 88
Dhaky, M. A. 28, 29
Dharasena IV 21
Dharmapāla 21, 22–3
Dhavalappa 21
Dhavalātman 21
Dhruva II 25
Dirks, N. 23
Durgadāman 89
Durgarāja 22
Durggagaṇa 21

–E–

Eran 90

–F–

Fergusson, J. 29

–G–

Garde, M. B. 27
Ghatiyālā 88
Ghazna 86
Ghosrāwa 88
Gopādri 16
Gopagiri 16, 22
Gopakṣetra
  historical geography 16
  regional history 18–26
  regional styles in 47, 78
  see also regional and sub-regional styles
Gopāla 20
goṣṭhī 92
Govinda III 23, 25
Govinda IV 25
Grahavarman 19
Guhila 25, 89, 91
Gujarrā 18
Gurjara Pratīhāra 22–6, 92–6
Gwalior
  historical geography 16, 88, 93–4
  importance to Pratīhāras 25, 90, 93
Gwalior, architectural fragments
  8th century, early 45; **21–2**
  8th century, middle 52; **51–2**
  9th century, early 69; **99**, **104–5**
  9th century, middle 73
Gwalior, Caturbhuj temple 70–71; **108–11**
  compared to Batesar 74
  compared to Deogarh 74
  compared to Khiaoda 72–3
  compared to Sakarra 73–4
  compared to Terāhī 71
  ground plan *70*
  inscriptions 90, 93–4
Gwalior, Gajāsuravadha 96
Gwalior, palaces
  fort 94
  Sāgar Tāl 93
Gwalior, Sās Bahū temple 79, 97
Gwalior, sculpture
  8th century, early 44, 52; **17**
  8th century, late 61; **97**
  9th century, late 78, 96; **125–7**
  9th century, middle 73; **114–16**
Gwalior, Telī kā Mandir 55–8; **85–92**
  date and style 59
  dedication 58
  iconography 56
Gwalior, Urwāhī caves 73, 78
Gyāraspur
  Ambikā 42; **14**
  Cār Kambhā 77; **122–3**
  Hindola Toraṇ 77–8; **124**
  Mālā Devī temple 70

–H–

Haddala 91
Hariścandra 21
Harivarman 19
Harṣadeva Candella 26
Harṣarāja Guhila 25
Harṣa Sīyaka 26
Harṣa Vardhana 19–20, 87
Harshagiri 97
Hathlau, Varāha 78; **129**
hero-stones 90
  Pāroli 39, 61; **6**
  Terāhī 25, 79; **130**
Huṇa 18

–I–

Inden, R. 23, 101 (n. 68)
Indian polity 23–4, 89
  and Śaiva orders 98–9
  and Śrauta ritual 94–5
  and temple building 96, 99
Indor, Gargaj Mahādev temple 59–60; **93–6**
  date and style 61
  ground plan *60*
  sculpture compared to Batesar 61–2
  sculpture compared to Gwalior 61
Indra III 25, 96
Indragarh 42, 47
  Gajalakṣmī **15**
Īśāna Bhaṭṭa 36
Īśānavarman 19
Īśvaravarman 19

–J–

Jajjaka 89
Jayāvalī 89
Jura 26, 94

–K–

Kacchapaghāta 17, 26, 97
Kadambaguhā 17
Kadwāhā 17
  Morāyat temple 80; **137**
Kakkuka 88
Kakustha 22
Kālapriyanātha 18, 96
Kāliñjara 25, 26, 90
Kālpī 18, 25, 96
Kamaladeva 92
Kāmān 89, 91, 92
Kannauj 17, 27, 36, 93, 96
Kanswa 42, 47, 88
Kaṇvāśrama 88
Kānyakubja 17, 20, 36, 93
Karka Diṇḍirāja 20, 21
Karkarāja 24
Khaḍga 21
Khajurāho, Lakṣmaṇa temple 80
  inscription 97
  phāṁsanā roof 71
  sculpture 80, 98; **139**
  shrines (*devakulikā*) 81; **138**
Kharagraha I 20
Kheldhar, Śiva temple 69
  ground plan *69*
Khiaoda, Sun temple 72; **112–13**
Khoṭṭiga 26
Kirāta 24
Kota
  Brāhmī 44, 47; **16**
  Gajāntaka 53; **56**
  Mātṛkās 53; **53–4**
  Śiva 53; **55, 57**
Kramrisch, S. 30
Krishna Deva 28
Kṛṣṇa II 25
Kṛṣṇa III 25–6, 94
Kṛṣṇalīlā scenes 46, 71, 79; **27**
Kṛṣṇarāja 20, 21
Kubler, G. 30
Kuchdon, Maṛhiā Dhār, 74
Kumāragupta 19

–L–

Lacchukā 89
Lakṣmaṇa Kacchapaghāta 26
lotus moulding (*padma*)
  introduction of 70

–M–

Maḍḍodara 21, 88
Madhuban 19
Madhumatī 17, 36
Madhyadeśa 17, 27
Mahendrapāla I 25, 90
Mahendrapāla II 26, 93
Maheśvarapura 17
Mahīpāla 25
Mahīpāla Kacchapaghāta 97
Mahuā 17
Mahuā, larger Śiva temple 39–41; **8–12**
  compared to Mahuā, smaller Śiva temple 41
  compared to Naresar 50
  compared to Sirpur 41
  date 41–2
  ground plan *39*
  style of sculpture 41
  veṇukośa, double 40
Mahuā, smaller Śiva temple (*maṇḍapikā*) 36–9; **1–5**
  date 36–7
  ground plan *36*
  iconography 38
  stylisitic significance 39
Malada 90
Mālava 24
Mānabhaṅga 21
Maṇḍapadurga 25
maṇḍapikā *see* shrine, *maṇḍapikā*-type
Māṇḍavyapura 21
Mandor 21, 24, 94
Māndū 25
Manorathavarman 21
Mānyakheṭa 24, 26
Markhera, Sun temple 76
Mathanadeva 89
Mathurā 20, 86, 87
Matsya 24
Maukhari 18–19
Maurya 21
Mihira Bhoja 25, 70, 88, 90, 93, 96
Mihirakula 19
models, political 23–4
  see also Indian polity
Mohangarh 89
mouldings *13, 37*
  Amrol 51
  Badoh 75
  Indor 60
  Khiaoda 72
  Naresar 47–8, 49
  Terāhī 68
  7th and 8th century compared 37, 40
  8th and 9th century compared 67, 68, 70

–N–

Nāga 17
Nāgabhaṭṭa I 22
Nāgabhaṭṭa II 23, 24, 25, 89, 92
Nāgāvaloka 24
Nāgavarman 19
Nālanda 19, 22, 90
Nalapura 17
Naleśvara 17, 47
Ṇaṇṇaka 88
Ṇaṇṇappa 21, 98
Nārāyaṇapāla 22
Naresar 17; **28–45**
  site plan *48*
Naresar, Bhītupreneśvaradeva temple 47–8; **29–31**
  compared to Dāng 47–8
  ground plan *48*
Naresar, Durgā temple 49–50; **38–41**
  compared to Batesar 54
  compared to Gwalior 57
  compared to Mahuā 50
  ground plan *49*
  sculpture compared to Amrol 51
  sculpture compared to Gwalior 57
Naresar, Krakoṭakeśvaradeva temple 48; **32–3**
  ground plan *49*
Naresar, Mātā kā Mandir 50; **43–5**
  compared to Gwalior 55
  ground plan *50*

sculpture compared to Gwalior 57, 58
Naresar, Sītaleśvaradevī temple 49; **35–6**
Naresar, Śiva temple 48–9; **34**
ground plan *49*
Narwar 17
navagraha see 'nine planets'
Nermand 20
'nine planets' (*navagraha*)
introduction of 66

–O–

Osiān, Mahāvīra temple 62

–P–

Paḍhāvali 17
see also Pāroli
padma see lotus moulding
Padmapāla 97
Padmāvatī 17
Pāhārpur 25
Parabala 24, 75, 89
Paramāra 26
Parivrājaka 19
Pāroli 17, 54
hall (*raṅgamaṇḍapa*) 79; **131–2**
hero-stones 39, 61; **6**
Kubera 67; **98**
platform 80
see also Batesar
Partābgarh 25, 91, 93
Pāśupata 98
Pawāyā 17, 36
pediment, tall (*udgama*)
Gwalior 57, 71
introduction of 54
Indor 60
Terāhī 68
Pehoa 25, 91, 92
political models 23–4
see also Indian polity
Prabhākara Vardhana 19
Pṛthūdaka 25, 91
Pulakeśin 19
Purandara 98

–R–

Ram Raz 28
Rannod 17, 98
Rājāpur 39; **7**
Rajor 89
Rāmabhadra 24, 90, 94
Rāṣṭrakūṭa 23, 24, 26, 90, 96
Raṭṭavā 89
regional and sub-regional styles
Amrol and Naresar 51
Batesar 66, 67, 74, 78
Dāng 47
decline 63, 65, 70, 74, 78–9
definition of 47, 52–3
Deogarh 75
Gwalior 52–3
Indor 60
Ṛjjūkā 91
Rohinsakūpa 88
Rudra 91

–S–

Sāgar, Śaṅkaragaṇa stele 53, 89
Sakarra 73; **118–19**
Saṁkuka 88
Samudrasena 20
Sānchī 37, 38, 78
Śaṅkaragaṇa 20, 53, 89
Sarasvatīpaṭṭana 17
Sarvavarman 19
Satanwāra 69
Sesai, Sūrya temple 76
compared to Kadwāhā 80
ground plan *76*
Shivpuri 17
shrine, *maṇḍapikā*-type
characteristics 37
coalesces with *latina* type 74
epigraphic mention 36
Sihoniyā
historical geography 16
maṇḍapikā shrine 80; **135**
ruined temple hall 69–70; **106**
Viśvarūpa 73; **117**
Śiluka 21
Siṁhapānīya 17
Siṁharāja 97
Siron 91
Sirpur, Lakṣmaṇa temple 41
Śivagaṇa 88
Siwāh 25
Sīyaḍoṇī 91
Somanātha 86
Sonāgir 92
Sonepat 19
Śrauta ritual 94–5, 98
Śrī Deva 92
Stein, Burton 23
Strzygowski, J. 30
stūpa 39
Sūrasena 89
Surwāyā 17
Surwāya, Śiva temple 81; **140**
compared to Pāroli 81

–T–

T-shaped door
discarded 46–7, 66
Terambi 17
Terāhī
hero-stones 25, 79; **130**
historical geography 17
Mohañjmātā temple 81; **141–2**
Terāhī, Śiva temple 68; **100–103**
compared to Badoh 75
compared to Batesar 68–9
compared to Gwalior 71
compared to Sesai 76
ground plan *68*
Tughluq 87
Tumain
Mātṛkās 53; **58**
Śiva 53
Tumbavana 17
Turuṣka 24

–U–

Uccakalpa 19
udgama see pediment, tall
Una 90
Undabhaṭa 91

–V–

Vacchikā 89
Vairisiṁha Paramāra 26
Vajradāman 26
Vākpati Muñja 26
Varāhasiṁha 91

Vardhana 19–20
Vatsa 17, 24
Vatsarāja 20, 36
Vatsarāja Pratīhāra, 23, 25
vedībandha see mouldings
Vedic ritual, *see* Śrauta ritual
veṇukośa, double *13*
  elimination of 52, 55, 71, 72
  Gwalior 57
  Mahuā 40
Vetravatī 17
Vidiśā 18, 20
Viennot, O. 30
Vinītarāśi 98
Vīrabhadra 97
Virāṭa 24
Voppaka 21
Vyomaśiva 98

–W–

Wölfflin, H. 28

–X–

Xuan Zang 17, 20

–Y–

Yajvapāla 17
Yaśodharman 20
Yaśomatī 91
Yaśovarman 22, 87, 90
Yaśovarman Candella 26, 97

1 Mahuā (Shivpuri) *maṇḍapikā*-shrine dedicated to Śiva, south side, first half of the seventh century

2 Mahuā, *maṇḍapikā*-shrine, over-door (*uttarāṅga*)

3 Mahuā, *maṇḍapikā*-shrine, south side, niche (*rathikā*) with image of Gaṇeśa

4 Mahuā, *maṇḍapikā*-shrine, west side, niche (*rathikā*) with image of Māhiṣāuramardinī

5 *above* Mahuā, *maṇḍapikā*-shrine, door-jambs (*śākhā*) with pilaster flanking the door

6 *above right* Pāroli (Morena), hero-stones, first half of the seventh century (left) and late eighth century (right)

7 *right* Rājāpur (Shivpuri), stone *stūpa*, *c.* sixth or seventh century

8 Mahuā (Shivpuri), Śiva temple, north side, late seventh century

9 Mahuā, Śiva temple, south-west corner (*karṇa*), showing podium mouldings (*vedībandha*) and wall (*jaṅghā*)

10 Mahuā, Śiva temple, west side, subsidiary offset (*pratiratha*) and dentils (*nīvrapaṭṭikā*) in podium mouldings (*vedībandha*)

11 Mahuā, Śiva temple, east side, entrance door

12 Mahuā, Śiva temple, east side, entrance door, river goddess and attendants

13 Deogarh Fort (Lalitpur), Varāha temple, main image of Vāraha, late seventh century

15 Indragarh (Mandasaur), seated Gajalakṣmī, datable VS 767/AD 710–11

14 Gyāraspur (Vidisha), Ambikā, late seventh century

16 Kota (Shivpuri), standing goddess, early eighth century

17 Gwalior Fort (Gwalior), seated Gaṇeśa, early eighth century

18 Bārāhet (Bhind), Gaṇeśa image on a linga, early eighth century

19 Bārāhet, Viṣṇu image on a linga

20 Bārāhet, architectural fragment, early eighth century

21 *above* Gwalior Fort (Gwalior), fragment of a niche (*rathikā*), early eighth century

22 *right* Gwalior (Gwalior), pillar, early eighth century

23 Dāng (Bhind), Śiva temple, north-west side, early eighth century

24 Dāng, Śiva temple, south side, wall of porch (*prāggrīva*)

25 Dāng, Śiva temple, east side, door

26 Dāng, Śiva temple, south side, central niche (*rathikā*) with image of Gaṇeśa

27 Dāng, Śiva temple, east side, base of superstructure, niches (*rathikā*) containing images of Kṛṣṇalīlā and Kārttikeya

28 Naresar (Morena), general view of temples in the lower section of the complex

29 Naresar, temple dedicated to Śiva as 'Śrī Bhītupreneśvaradeva', north-east side, mid-eighth century

30 Naresar, Bhītupreneśvara temple, north-west side

31 Naresar, Bhītupreneśvara temple, entrance door

32 Naresar, temple dedicated to Śiva as 'Śrī Krakoṭakeśvaradeva', east side, mid-eighth century

33 Naresar, Krakoṭakeśvara temple, entrance door

34 Naresar, Śiva temple, west side, mid-eighth century

35 Naresar, Sitaleśvaradevī temple, entrance door, mid-eighth century

36 Naresar, Sitaleśvaradevī temple, inscription recording a land grant, *c.* ninth century

37 Naresar, Durgā temple, south-west side, mid-eighth century

38 Naresar, Durgā temple, entrance door

39 Naresar, Durgā temple, entrance door, damaged river goddess and attendant figures

40 Naresar, Durgā temple, dancing figure in corner niche

41 Naresar, Durgā temple, east side, central spire offset (*madhyalatā*)

42 Naresar, screens and seat adjacent to Durgā temple, mid-eighth century

43 Naresar, Mātā kā Mandir, south-west side, mid-eighth century

44 Naresar, Mātā kā Mandir, entrance door

45 Naresar, Mātā kā Mandir, entrance door, damaged river goddess and attendant figures

46 Amrol (Gwalior), Rāmeśvar Mahādev temple, south side, mid-eighth century

47 Amrol, Rāmeśvar Mahādev temple, south side, central offset with image of Gaṇeśa

49 *above* Amrol, Rāmeśvar Mahādev temple, north side, dancing figure in corner niche

50 *above* Amrol, Rāmeśvar Mahādev temple, north side, Īśāna figure in porch (*prāggrīva*) niche

48 *left* Amrol, Rāmeśvar Mahādev temple, east side, entrance door

51 Gwalior Fort (Gwalior), miniature dormer (*candraśālā*) with head of Śiva, mid-eighth century

52 Gwalior Fort, part of a shrine wall, mid-eighth century

53 Kota (Shivpuri), Indrāṇī, mid-eighth century

54 Kota, Kaumārī, mid-eighth century

56 Kota, Gajāntaka, mid-eighth century

55 Kota, Śiva, mid-eighth century

57 Kota (?), Śiva, mid-eighth century

58 Tumain (Guna), Mātṛkā fragment, mid-eighth century

59 Deogarh Fort (Lalitpur), Jaina goddess built into wall surrounding temple 12, mid-eighth century

60 Batesar (Morena), general view of main temple complex from the west

61 Batesar Mahādev temple, east side, detail of arched antefix (*śukanāsā*), late eighth century

62 Batesar Mahādev temple, north side, superstructure

63 Batesar Mahādev temple, north side, mouldings and niches of porch (*prāggrīva*) and corner section (*karṇa*)

64 Batesar Mahādev temple, east side, detail of door jambs

65 *above* Batesar, Śiva temple immediately west of the Batesar Mahādev temple, east side, superstructure, early ninth century

66 *right* Batesar, Śiva temple immediately east of the Batesar Mahādev temple, south side, early ninth century

67 *above* Batesar, Śiva temple immediately north of the Batesar Mahādev temple, east side, early ninth century

68 *above right* Batesar, Śiva temple immediately north of the Batesar Mahādev temple, west side

69 *right* Batesar, superstructure of a shrine buried in rubble beside the Batesar Mahādev temple, early ninth century

70 *above* Batesar, row of three Śaiva shrines to the north of the Batesar Mahādev temple, early ninth century

71 *left* Batesar, Śaiva shrine to the north of the Batesar Mahādev temple, north-west side, early ninth century

72 Batesar, Vaiṣṇava shrine to the north of the Batesar Mahādev temple, east side, mid-ninth century

73 Batesar, Vaiṣṇava shrine, entrance door

74 Batesar, *maṇḍapikā*-shrine to the north-east of the Batesar Mahādev temple, west side, early ninth century

76 Batesar, ruined shrine to the south-east of the Batesar Mahādev temple, open porch (*mukhacatuṣkī*), early ninth century

75 Batesar, *maṇḍapikā*-shrine (as pl.74), entrance door

77 Batesar, ruined shrine to the south-east of the Batesar Mahādev temple, ceiling panel

78 *left* Batesar, partially ruined and rebuilt shrine beside tank, entrance door, early ninth century

80 *right* Batesar, ruined temple to the south-east of the Batesar Mahādev temple, entrance door

79 *below* Batesar, ruined temple to the south-east of the Batesar Mahādev temple, detail of south side showing central offset (*bhadra*), subsidiary offset (*pratiratha*) and corner section (*karṇa*), early ninth century

81 *above* Batesar, carved panel in rebuilt shrine beside tank, Kalyāṇasundara, late eighth century

82 *above* Batesar, fragmentary set of Mātṛkā figures, early ninth century

83 *right* Amrol (Gwalior), Dhane Bābā temple, east side, late eighth century

85 *above* Gwalior Fort, Telī kā Mandir, north side, depressed barrel vault (*skandhavedī*) and barrel-vaulted crown (*valabhī*)

84 *left* Gwalior Fort (Gwalior), Telī kā Mandir, west side, long back wall (*pṛṣṭhabhadra*), mid- to late eighth century

86 *above* Gwalior Fort, Telī kā Mandir, west side, long back wall (*pṛṣṭhabhadra*), central niche in the form of a door

89 above Gwalior Fort, Telī kā Mandir, east side, entrance door with later infill

87 *above* Gwalior Fort, Telī kā Mandir, west side, long back wall (*pṛṣṭhabhadra*), subsidiary offset (*pratiratha*) and corner section (*karṇa*)

88 right Gwalior Fort, Telī kā Mandir, south side, wall of porch (*prāggrīva*) with niche in the form of a temple

90 Gwalior Fort, Telī kā Mandir, east side, river goddess on entrance door

91 Gwalior Fort, Telī kā Mandir, north side, river goddess on niche of porch (*prāggrīva*)

92 Gwalior Fort, Telī kā Mandir, south-east corner section (*karṇa*), detail of recess (*antarapatra*) in *vedībandha*

93 Indor (Guna), Gargaj Mahādev temple, south side, late eighth century

94 Indor, Gargaj Mahādev temple, entrance door

95 Indor, Gargaj Mahādev temple, south side, wall of porch (*prāggrīva*)

96 Indor, Gargaj Mahādev temple, north side, wall of porch (*prāggrīva*), image of Īśāna

97 Gwalior Fort (Gwalior), bust of Parśvanātha, late eighth century

98 Pāroli (Morena), Kubera and Ṛddhi, early ninth century

99 Gwalior (Gwalior), Jaina stele, early ninth century

100 Terāhī (Shivpuri), Śiva temple, south-west side, early ninth century

101 Terāhī, Śiva temple, south wall (*jaṅghā*)

102 Terāhī, Śiva temple, entrance door

103 Terāhī, Śiva temple, pilaster in open porch (*mukhacatuṣkī*)

104 *left* Gwalior Fort (Gwalior), miniature temple, early ninth century

105 *right* Gwalior Fort, temple model, possibly a miniature spire (*kūṭa*) from a temple hall (*maṇḍapa*), early ninth century

106 *below* Sihoniyā (Morena), ruined hall of the closed type (*gūḍhamaṇḍapa*), early ninth century

108 *above* Gwalior Fort, Caturbhuj temple, south side, mouldings, wall and entablature (*maṇḍovara*)

109 *above* Gwalior Fort, Caturbhuj temple, north side of superstructure

107 *left* Gwalior Fort (Gwalior), Caturbhuj temple, south-east side, dated by inscription VS 932/AD 875–6

110 Gwalior Fort, Caturbhuj temple, north side, Viṣṇu Trivikrama in central niche (*rathikā*)

111 Gwalior Fort, Caturbhuj temple, entrance door

112 Khiaoda (Shivpuri), Sūrya temple, east side, mid-ninth century

113 Khiaoda, Sūrya temple, south side

114 Gwalior (Gwalior), seated Jina, mid-ninth century

115 Gwalior Fort (Gwalior), standing Tīrthaṁkara in cave near Urwāhī Gate, mid-ninth century

116 Gwalior Fort, strut from a temple hall, mid-ninth century

117 Sihoniyā (Morena), Viṣṇu Viśvarūpa, mid-ninth century

118 Sakarra (Guna), Śiva temple 1, north side, mid-ninth century

119 Sakarra, Śiva temple 2, east side, Ardhanarīśvara in central niche, mid-ninth century

120 Deogarh Fort (Lalitpur), Jaina temple 12, west side, screen wall with niche flanking entrance, datable before AD 862

121 Badoh (Vidisha), monumental pillar (*dhvajastambha*) known as Bhīmgaja, detail of platform mouldings, dated VS 917/AD 861

122 Gyāraspur (Vidisha), Cār Khambā, fragment of a temple spire (*kūṭa*), datable MS 936/AD 879–80

123 Gyāraspur , Cār Khambā, detail of pillar, datable MS 936/AD 879–80

124 Gyāraspur , Hindola Toran, datable MS 936/AD 879–80

125 Gwalior (Gwalior), fragmentary female figure, probably a Jaina goddess, late ninth century

126 *above* Gwalior Fort (Gwalior), cave near Urwāhī Gate with Jaina divinities, late ninth century

127 *left* Gwalior Fort, cave near Urwāhī Gate with Tīrthaṁkara, late ninth century

128 *above* Amrol (Gwalior), Kumāra, late ninth century

129 *above* Hathlau (Datia), Varāha temple, main image, late ninth century

130 *left* Terāhī (Shivpuri), hero-stone, detail showing battle scene, dated by inscription VS 960/AD 904

131 *above* Pāroli (Morena), open hall (*raṅgamaṇḍapa*), interior, early tenth century

132 *above* Pāroli, open hall (*raṅgamaṇḍapa*), interior

133 *right* Bhainsora (Morena), Śiva temple, central offset (*bhadra*) with opening for spout (*praṇāla*), early tenth century

134 Bārāhet (Bhind), ruin of an open hall (*raṅgamaṇḍapa*) with fragment of fence-like parapet (*vedikā*), early tenth century

135 Sihoniyā (Morena), Dubalia, ruined shrine, south-east side, early tenth century

136 Chhimkā (Bhind), Śiva temple, east side, early tenth century

137 Kadwāhā (Guna), temple in the Morāyat group, early tenth century

139 *above* Khajurāho, Lakṣmaṇa temple, detail of sculpture on the wall section (*jaṅghā*), dated VS 1011/AD 954–5

138 *above* Khajurāho (Chhatarpur), Lakṣmaṇa temple, south-east subsidiary shrine (*devakulikā*), datable after AD 955

140 *right* Surwāyā (Shivpuri), Śiva temple 1, entrance door, mid-tenth century

SRW-41/74

141 Terāhī (Shivpuri), Mohañjmātā temple, south-east side, mid-tenth century

142 Terāhī, Mohañjmātā temple, freestanding gate, mid-tenth century